UNVEILED

UNVEILED

THE HIDDEN LIVES OF NUNS

Cheryl L. Reed

BERKLEY BOOKS, NEW YORK

B

A Berkley Book
Published by The Berkley Publishing Group
A division of Penguin Group (USA) Inc.
375 Hudson Street
New York, New York 10014

This book is an original publication of The Berkley Publishing Group.

First edition: March 2004

Library of Congress Cataloging-in-Publication Data

Reed, Cheryl L.
    Unveiled / Cheryl L. Reed.—1st ed.
        p.   cm.
    ISBN 0-425-19511-2
    1. Monasticism and religious orders for women—United States.   2. Monastic and religious life
of women—United States.   3. Nuns—United States.   I. Title.

BX4220.U6R44 2004
271'.90073—dc22

2003062914

PRINTED IN THE UNITED STATES OF AMERICA

10   9   8   7   6   5   4   3   2   1

For Greg,
who always believed

The nuns in the photographs throughout this book are all nuns the author encountered. All of the photographs, with the one exception, were taken by the author.

CONTENTS

ACKNOWLEDGMENTS

Working on a book for five years will make any writer beholden to a long list of people who either encouraged or excused such obsessive behavior. My list, while long, is nowhere near as inclusive as I wish it could be, and I apologize for any names I have overlooked.

First, I must thank all the nuns I encountered on this journey. They risked much by letting me observe their private lives, by trusting me with their stories. I am deeply indebted to their honesty and generosity.

The first financial contributor to this unusual and controversial mission was the Alicia Patterson Foundation and its director, Margaret Engel, who funded the initial research. Without such generosity, this book would have never been written.

Other groups made significant contributions: the Minnesota Arts Board, the Jerome Foundation, the Loft, and SASE. I am also grateful to the artist colonies who gave me space and time to work: Hedgebrook, the Vermont Studio, Norcroft, New York Mills, and Ragdale, which remains my favorite. Living among other artists and writers in temporary communities allowed me to experience a version of the nuns' communal lifestyle.

Editors at various publications along the way gave me a venue for my articles about nuns: the *Minneapolis City Pages, Philadelphia Inquirer Magazine, Natural Health, Extension Magazine,* the *Minneapolis Star Tribune, Poets & Writers,* and especially *Catholic Digest,* whose managing editor, Kathleen Stauffer, has been my tireless promoter.

During the writing, friends and colleagues read version after version and offered encouragement and insight. Chief among them was Margaret Nelson, who often overlooked her own writing to offer crucial feedback. Elaine Beale and Diane Wilson pointed out gaping holes and offered words to fill them. Members of several writing groups suggested profound questions. My writing students offered me their adulation. And then there were good people like Kim and Raju Narisetti, who provided a bed and conversation on my many trips to New York. Others, like Chris Ledbetter, celebrated my achievements and encouraged me when I hit obstacles. Dr. Catherine Cory, a theologian at the University of St. Thomas, where I taught for two years, checked the theology in the book. My transcriber, Sheila Jessen, listened intently to the sisters' stories, becoming equally committed to my effort of preserving their voices. During the publishing phase, my editors at the *Chicago Sun-Times*, especially Don Hayner, were understanding when I needed time off for the book.

The calm and soothing voice of my agent, Laura Langlie, assured me through each arduous step. I often thought of her as God's angel sent to inspire me when it felt foolish to keep believing when others warned that readers wouldn't care about the lives of aging and forgotten nuns. For us, it became a mission to both showcase the complexities of the sisters' lives and at the same time shatter old stereotypes. My book editor, Denise Silvestro, a young, modern Catholic herself, intrinsically understood the book. Courageously, Denise didn't try to romanticize the end of an era or weaken strong women's words, including my own, in order to sell books. Instead, she valued exploring whether nunhood was still a viable option for modern women.

The unknown stars of this book are my family. My children, Nick and Ali, never complained about my frequent trips to monasteries or that they had to share my attentions with hundreds of nuns. Instead, they shared my fascination. They thought it was "cool" that they could tell their friends that their mother had gone off to a convent—again. Meanwhile, my husband, Greg Stricharchuk, was my first and last reader. He critiqued version after version, spending nights and weekends, even holidays and vacations, going over revisions and offering suggestions. A journalist himself, he understood the quest, the search. He never questioned my obsession nor did he ask me to stop—even after years of visiting monasteries and making the rounds at artist colonies. He remains my biggest fan, my confidant, my best friend.

LIFE BEFORE THE NUNS

I had always been afraid of nuns. They seemed so spooky in their long black cloaks and starched wimples that pulled their skin unnaturally from their faces. I had grown up believing that nuns, like the Catholic Church, were evil. My immersion into their mysterious world was a circuitous path, one that began with a young girl's fascination and fear and grew into a journalist's pursuit of an enigmatic subculture.

I had been raised fundamentalist Protestant and taught that Catholics worshipped statues, believed Mary was equal to God, and went to church on Saturday evenings so they could get drunk afterward and sleep in on Sunday mornings. Catholics, we were told, were going straight to hell because they thought they could sin as much as they wanted just as long as they confessed to a priest before they died.

Strangely enough, the church I attended as an adult was Catholic. Perhaps I was drawn to the forbidden. More likely, I was enticed by the beauty of cathedrals, the tranquility that ornate chapels offered. I always felt a sense of peace sitting among the cold stone pillars, gazing up at the stained-glass windows, inhaling the incense, listening to the choir. Yet, I couldn't convert because I disagreed with the Church's assertion that the Pope was infallible and birth control was wrong—the same sentiments I would later hear expressed by many modern nuns.

Instead, I converted to the Orthodox Church, which doesn't take a stand on birth control and doesn't have the papal hierarchy. Orthodoxy gave me entrée into the ritualistic world of ancient Eastern Catholicism with its icons, incense, somber litanies, and monastic traditions of fasting and praying that were so enticing to me. It was the part of Catholicism that I adored, that I longed for. Yet, even then I tried to overlook the fact that it offers few roles for women.

Then, at a Sunday liturgy, I met my first nun. She wore a traditional black habit, with a tight white wimple and a boxy headdress. As a child, I would have been terrified to have come so close to such a woman. Although I was nervous, I introduced myself and began asking questions about her life. She patiently listened to my queries, gazing at me with sympathetic blue eyes and nodding her head, her cheeks soft and pale. When she spoke, her voice was graceful and melodic. Those few minutes hinted at a profound way of life, one that would absorb my interest for years to come.

Not long after the nun's visit, I attended a lecture given by my Orthodox priest in which he explained the option of religious life, showing a video of the nun's monastery. The nuns run a small farm for food, plow the fields in their habits, and pray every day in a chapel filled with burning candles and incense. Their life seemed so idyllic, so romantic, so focused, and, yet, so powerfully purposeful.

I felt an immediate attraction. Suddenly I understood that as an Orthodox, I could become a nun. As a fundamentalist Protestant, that was never an option. The realization both startled and thrilled me: Imagine, me a nun! At the time, though, I was engaged to be married and about to become the adoptive mother of my fiancé's two young children. How could I also feel the allure of religious life?

Within weeks, I wrote the nun asking for prayers and blessings on my impending marriage. My letter brimmed with more questions: Was she happy? Was she at peace? What was her life really like? I wondered if she ever grew bored praying the long Orthodox liturgy day after day, when I had trouble praying it once a week. I questioned whether she was lonely.

I coveted her seclusion, her remoteness from modern problems. I viewed her as a possible mentor, a woman who could provide a map to the spiritual world.

Months passed. Then a letter arrived a week before my wedding. I rushed to my bedroom and in the dim light tore open the envelope, quickly reading the careful cursive letters. To my disappointment, the nun only vaguely remembered meeting me. She was quite busy, she said, and didn't have time to answer my many questions. Instead she enclosed a brochure for a retreat week at her monastery in upstate New York. I was heartbroken. The secret world she inhabited would remain cloaked in mystery.

My curiosity didn't go away, though. Less than two years after I met that first nun, I began traveling around the country interviewing and living with Catholic nuns for a series of magazine articles that grew into this book. Initially I was pursuing a journalistic quest to understand nun spirituality, how these women are so fulfilled and happy while giving up everything the world says is valuable, like sex, money, and men—aspects that, frankly, are important to me and most women I know. I wanted to know why young women are still entering religious orders, particularly strict, habited ones. I was especially interested in the growing trend of older women in their forties and fifties and even sixties who are joining religious life. I approached the nuns as a journalist chronicling a shrinking subculture. But deep down I suspected there was more than a professional interest.

For four years, I crisscrossed the country, meeting more than three hundred nuns from fifty different orders, living and praying with them, observing their daily lives, eating their food, rising in the middle of the night for silent worship, celebrating their saints' days, mourning their deaths, witnessing their vow ceremonies. I drank beer with them; I shared the communion of Christ's body with them. Through it all, I felt privileged to hear their stories, their most private musings about love and life and loss.

Through these experiences, I discovered a secret society where women are powerful and in control, and sometimes *too* controlling. In my mind, these women are living the ultimate feminist lives—almost totally devoid of men. Despite sisters' frequent challenges to Church hierarchy and male authority, conservative and liberal Catholics alike revere nuns as consummate spiritual and religious women. Unlike my experience in the Protestant church, where "religious women" are typically quiet, pious, and married with children, exalted women in the Catholic Church are most often celibate nuns who are ambitious and outspoken.

Most sisters I met in my travels were tired of living on a pedestal and welcomed questions that "good Catholics" would never ask nuns. They entrusted me with the intimacies they had rarely shared with anyone. With so few women becoming nuns these days—the number of sisters in this country has dwindled to nearly a third of what it was thirty-five years ago and the average age is now older than sixty-nine years—the sisters could see their way of life was threatened, and they were willing to break their "cult of secrecy." Though their life of prayer and contemplation is called "the hidden life," they were willing to unveil its mysteries for me. Some sisters died before I finished writing their stories. Others left religious life altogether. I felt lucky to have known them, if only briefly.

Although the sisters I met are all vowed nuns, their beliefs and lifestyles are as diverse as orchid species. Some orders embrace traditional habits while others abhor them. While one group supports abortion rights, another runs antiabortion counseling clinics. Some rise in the middle of the night to pray and spend hours in the chapel throughout their day; others work so ceaselessly they hardly pray at all. A few orders encourage their members to discuss their sexuality, while others stifle such talk and restrict "particular friendships." Some sisters never venture beyond their monastery walls, talking to family and visitors through steel bars, while others live alone in apartments far from the convent grounds. Some orders focus on prayer as their labor, depending entirely on charity, while others insist that their jobs support their convents. Their ministries are as varied as secular careers. There are traditional nun nurses and teachers, but there also are lawyers, massage therapists, social workers, political activists, computer programmers, stock analysts, marketing gurus, and prison chaplains, to name a few.

As a journalist, I was thrilled to vicariously experience their lives, to adopt the ritual of being a nun, if only for a few days. Initially I told myself this story was just like all the others in my life as a journalist, that writing about nuns was fueled by the same curiosity that had challenged me to spend months hanging out with girl gangs or prostitutes. This was simply the pursuit to uncover another subculture. But truly it was much more.

I saw how difficult it is for a woman to choose an order. The process seems like a dating ritual, with women expressing interest and the community courting the ones they feel are the most promising. I wondered which order I might join if I were a single woman or a widow. I began to see myself as more than a journalist, but as a surrogate for modern women who can't take off months or years to explore multiple orders as I was doing.

It became a mad pursuit, trying out this monastery and that one. Sometimes I felt like some strange version of a restaurant critic, sampling each monastery, evaluating its lifestyle and traditions. Other times, I felt as though I were putting myself through a religious boot camp, testing the rigors of my religious willpower, trying on the vows one by one, all the while questioning whether religious life is still a relevant choice for modern women. Looking back, I can see I was asserting a personal challenge to determine whether I, as a modern woman, could live like a nun, whether I could give up my relationships along with the material and physical things in my life that are so precious. Ultimately, I wanted to know whether I had what it takes to join the spiritual elite.

Indeed, my immersion into the nun world—and this book—follows the same path that virtually all women take when they decide to become a nun: First, they choose a community that reflects their lifestyle and beliefs; then, they learn how to live each of the vows; finally, they transcend those vows to develop their own commitments to God and their communities.

Like the nun's path to maturity, I, too, struggled with what religious life required. I tried to walk away from each order, each experience, with some facet that I could apply to my everyday world. Through it all, I discovered a deepening spirituality, one that expanded my belief system beyond anything I had ever experienced. Though I had sought out the nuns to understand their subculture, these celibate women, in turn, taught me more about myself, motherhood, and feminism than I ever before gleaned from the world in which I live.

The following is a first-person journalistic account. All names are real and their stories and observations, in most cases, are taken directly from tape-recorded interviews. Many sisters allowed me to photograph them; some of those photos are included here. My hope is that through this book you'll come to see the nuns, as I did, not as icons of perfection but rather as spiritual sisters, guides to the interior world.

PART ONE

COMMUNITY

THE FIRST STEP IN BECOMING A nun is choosing a community. Finding a religious order that fits a woman's personality is much like finding a mate. It is a courtship between the woman and the community, with each charming and trying to impress the other, all the while discovering whether they are compatible, whether their beliefs and lifestyles fit each other's expectations.

The prospective nun visits as many orders as she can before selecting the community of women she wants to spend the rest of her life with. Often it is the intense personal relationships between sisters that draw women to religious life. It is the one aspect that seems to appeal even to those, like myself, who aren't overtly religious. In most cases, a community will attract women who reflect the values and personality of its current membership. Yet, the larger the community, the more possibilities for a diverse population.

Regardless of whether a sister joins one of the biggest communities, like the Benedictines in St. Joseph, Minnesota, or one of the smallest, like the Visitation Sisters in Minneapolis, the women have to learn to get along, even if it means forming communities within a community or relying on personality tests in order to understand each other.

BEYOND STEREOTYPE

BENEDICTINE SISTERS IN ST. JOSEPH, MINNESOTA

"We didn't know we were all supposed to be alike."
—SISTER COLMAN O'CONNELL

The weekend of St. Patrick's Day, I was looking forward to a rowdy party. But when a nun offered me a last-minute invitation to a "live-in experience" at her monastery, I opted to pray with the sisters instead. I'd never been to a monastery, but that was part of the lure. I wanted to know what was behind the mysterious image of nuns instilled by my Protestant upbringing and reinforced by Hollywood movies and friends' tales of stern women smacking students with rulers.

Of course, I didn't know accepting that first invite would only cultivate my curiosity and propel me on a four-year journey, taking me from that monastery near my home in Minnesota to the border of Mexico where I'd help deliver a baby at a nun-operated birthing center. Before it was over, I would pray with nuns from coast to coast, teach school with nuns on Arizona's Indian reservations, sleep among homeless women in a shelter run by feisty Chicago nuns, enter cloisters where nuns shave their heads and beat their bare bottoms, and witness protests where sisters were arrested for civil disobedience. I even encountered dour mother superiors who tried to order me around like a naughty child: one sending me to the chapel to pray after I'd listened to a nun detail her romantic encounters, another kicking me out because she said her sisters didn't want to eat holiday meals with a stranger.

That wintry day I pulled into St. Joseph, Minnesota, though, I didn't know what to expect. The Sisters of St. Benedict, once the largest order of its kind in the world, would not only dispel the stereotypes, but introduce me to an array of sisters who neither looked alike nor thought alike, including some who didn't even like each other. To my delight, I would meet avowed feminists who abhor the Church's male hierarchy and others who proudly cling to medieval traditions. One of the most diverse monasteries, St. Benedict's provided an ideal springboard into the larger world of nuns, an aging and rapidly vanishing subculture.

At first glance, the dreary town offered only rows of saltbox houses and cracked sidewalks. Then I noticed a small sign directing me off the main road and away from Sal's Bar and Grill, its neon beer signs flashing as if to tempt young women—or me—with a last call before entering the convent. Turning the corner, I was confronted by an enormous cathedral dome towering over a campus of blond and redbrick buildings flanked by evergreens dusted with snow.

As I stepped into the retreat house, a gray-haired woman flung her arms around me, introducing herself as the sister leading the "live-in experience." I'd expected nuns in long habits and tight wimples but this nun was casually dressed in navy blue slacks and a polyester blouse.

The retreat had drawn a dozen women, most of them married and a few, like me, who weren't even Catholic. They represented the public's growing fascination with monastic life. Monasteries like St. Benedict's, which no longer staff schools and hospitals, have seized on this new interest by offering retreats where they teach women how to apply monastic attributes to their busy, chaotic lives. Besides, there was the slight chance that one of us would want to join them.

Studying my fellow retreatants, that seemed highly unlikely; we were a disparate bunch, from college students to women in their late sixties, including one who was a former missionary nun. Our reasons for coming were just as dissimilar. Some said they needed a break; others sought to nourish their souls. My Lutheran roommate, married and in her early thirties—my age at the time—wasn't sure why she had come but had read meditative books by a Benedictine nun and felt pulled to the monastery. Common among the group was a need to live meaningful and balanced lives and to connect with other spiritual women. It didn't strike us as odd that we were seeking answers from celibate women who had separated themselves from men, children, and, for many, even balancing a checkbook.

THE NUN IN THE RED SLIP

The Benedictines tried their best to demystify our dated images of nuns. Appearing in a red dress accented by a trendy haircut and bright lipstick, Sister Pat Reuther represents the new nun icon; a progressive, highly educated woman who isn't afraid to express her opinions or emphasize her individuality. She wasn't always like that, I would discover.

Like many progressive sisters, Pat became a nun in the turbulent 1960s when sisters were leaving in droves. Society in general was undergoing tumultuous changes. Opportunities for women suddenly were opening in education, business, and industry. But the Church mandated the biggest change in sisters' lives.

In an effort to modernize the Church, Catholic bishops from around the world met at the Vati-

Sister Patricia Reuther

can from 1962 to 1965—a meeting that became known as "Vatican II"—
and pushed into the modern age an institution that hadn't changed sig-
nificantly since medieval times. Called "the greatest religious event of the
twentieth century" by theologians, Vatican II inaugurated the most dis-
ruptive era of modern Catholic history. Bishops ordered that the traditional Latin mass be translated into common languages so everyone could
understand and participate. The church altar was turned so that the priest
now faced parishioners. Whereas the mass for centuries had been a
somber affair, Catholics were now asked to greet their neighbors with a
"sign of peace." It was the beginning of a democratic revolution in the
Catholic Church, a time when old customs and rituals were abandoned,
when the Church made an attempt to lessen the hierarchical structures
and tried to include more laity in church councils. Vatican II theology
emphasized the importance of individual conscience and taught that the
Church was the people, not the hierarchy.

In the midst of this restructuring, religious orders were told to modernize, to update their lifestyles and habits. The Vatican II Council wanted
nuns treated as adults rather than as "children," which many communities
tended to do through archaic systems of punishment. Bishops told superiors to abandon customs that made their members feel infantile or inferior.
Sisters were to learn current culture—manners and social customs—so
that their missions would be relevant. The bishops encouraged sisters to
initiate "fresh forms of religious life."

Some orders quickly took up the challenge, changing attire, ministries, and lifestyles. Progressive-thinking nuns heralded the changes.
Other sisters resisted. For some, religious life was changing too quickly
and for others, not quickly enough. An exodus ensued. Dozens of orders
closed; others merged in an attempt to hang on. Now many await the in-
evitable as few women take the places of those who have left or died.
Though there were 180,000 nuns in 1965—the year Pat joined—nearly
four decades later there are just 73,000 sisters living in some 730 different
orders. Ironically, monasteries attracting the youngest women today are

those that have, for the most part, maintained their mysterious rituals and medieval garbs.

Despite the chaos that swirled around the monastery, Pat decided to remain a nun. She was like many sisters whose struggle for a modern identity made them more committed. Pat, who joined St. Benedict's as a twenty-one-year-old college senior, experienced the peeling away of the old habit, the single piece of clothing that so defined nuns. Although some orders still maintain a religious dress, most nuns today wear secular clothes.

Like most young nuns, Pat initially adored the habit. The romance of ritual waned quickly, though. For Pat, wearing black day after day was psychologically detrimental. The traditional habit was hot and damp when she took it off on summer nights and still wet when she put it on again the next morning. Although in 1965 the sisters no longer wore habits made of serge wool, polyester proved to be just as sweltering. Sisters were allowed to wash their habits once a month. Pat perspired so much that she received special permission to wash hers every week. She longed to wear something different to make a distinction between normal days and the more festive religious holidays and Sundays.

"I needed color in my life," she said. "So I made a red slip! My signature color is red," she added, looking down at her scarlet dress.

On regular days Pat wore traditional gray and white slips. But when she wanted to feel "dressed up" she wore her long red chemise. The spring Pat graduated from the College of St. Benedict she stepped lightly up the stage stairs to receive her diploma, smiling as she slightly lifted the hem of her black habit; beneath the folds of polyester was her silky red slip.

Her novice director was horrified. She thought Pat's crimson undergarments would cause a scandal. But Pat didn't care. It was important to Pat to wear a special garment that distinguished one day from the next, which set her apart from other sisters, even if she was the only one who knew. It was the beginning of Pat's struggle to assert her own identity.

In the early 1970s, as Pat was about to make her final vows, she began to comprehend what she'd sacrificed to become a nun. As she watched her younger sister wed, Pat suddenly grasped that she was never going to marry or have children. She had intense migraines. Sensing her distress, her superiors asked Pat to postpone her formal vows for a year and to seek therapy.

"I always wanted to be this ideal sister," Pat said. "I had never admitted that I had losses, that I wanted my own house, my own apartment, my own pots and pans, my own children. I thought a good sister doesn't get angry. I stuffed everything."

Gradually she learned to let out her anger, which meant yelling, if need be, something she thought a good nun would never dare to do. She had fewer and fewer migraines and eventually none at all. Though Pat had worked through her commitment to remain a nun, most of the sisters in her entrance class didn't: only five of the twenty-two who joined with Pat are still at the monastery.

Like those who stayed, Pat reconciled her differences. She discovered that she could be part of the Catholic Church but disagree with its leaders.

"I am a feminist," she said, "but not in the radical sense. I think that's one of the lessons I've learned in life: to be honest and up-front in a gentle manner. I don't want to bulldoze. But I need to express how I feel. It doesn't mean I'm going to start a rebel church. As religious women we can support each other and try to have a voice a little bit louder."

Recently she, a priest, and a deacon were giving a talk to grade school children when a student asked if they thought women would ever be priests. The two men answered by quoting statements from Rome. Despite the men's furrowed brows, Pat said she believed that one day women would be priests and deacons, although it might not be during her lifetime.

THE HABITED NUN

Before evening prayers, we were escorted to the oratory, an underground auditorium where the sisters gather three times a day to chant psalms. As an active order, the Benedictines don't pray together as much as contemplative orders whose main ministry is praying day and night.

Since Vatican II, the Benedictines, like many other orders, have adopted new terms to explain their life. They no longer refer to their home as a convent. Instead they use the language of monks and call their community home a monastery. Likewise, the terms "nun" and "sister," which once differentiated between a cloistered and an active religious woman, are used interchangeably by many.

As the sisters showed us how to follow along in leather-bound books, my eyes scrutinized the collection of women. Most were older and gray-haired. Those under seventy tended to wear simple, drab clothing while those over seventy wore a "modified habit," a black skirt with a short black veil and a white blouse.

To my amazement there was even one fully habited nun who resembled Sister Bertrille, actress Sally Field's character in the old television show *The Flying Nun*. She sat in the front row in a flowing black habit with a crisp starched wimple that outlined her youthful-looking face.

Her image brought back terrifying memories. As a child, I viewed habited nuns as mysterious, evil, and even ghoulish. Throughout my life, I'd had nightmares of sinister nuns in medieval garb chasing me down long corridors. Still, I felt compelled to meet this nun, to dispel my irrational fear and to find out what nuns were really like behind all that billowing black cloth and starch.

After prayers ended, I asked one of the retreat sisters to introduce me to the habited nun. A few minutes later she arrived, bowing and smiling. Her hands were folded over one another inside large sleeves, just like in the movies. Only her face was visible, framed by a wimple that stretched into a square from the top of her eyebrows to the bottom of her chin and cut across her cheeks. The exposed pale pink skin belied her real age. Her thick glasses made her blue eyes look much larger, like someone peering out from a blanket. The smile on her face did not change, even when she spoke.

She introduced herself as Sister Verenice, then led me through a maze of tunnels below the monastery, directing me to chairs near the Blessed

Sacrament Chapel. The Blessed Sacrament are communion hosts that Catholics believe become the body of Christ during mass. Hosts not consumed during mass are stored in an ornate tabernacle, a vessel usually no larger than a tabletop urn. At the time, I didn't understand the significance of sitting near the tabernacle. Later, I realized Verenice wanted to be near Christ.

At first I was edgy, unable to look directly into her face. But Sister Verenice spoke with such tenderness that I couldn't imagine her raising her voice to anyone. Before she entered the convent, she had been Eileen Barbara Ramler, eldest of twelve children from a poor family in a nearby German farming village. She had gone to work after the eighth grade, helping women who had just given birth.

Sister Verenice Ramler

The self-admitted "fashion freak," who loved jewelry and makeup, entered St. Benedict's when she was only eighteen—common at the time. As important as her fashionable clothes once were, the habit, likewise, has become a profound garment, her public statement that she has railed against change as much as other nuns, like Pat, have embraced it. For Verenice, putting on the habit is akin to a daily baptism, a reminder that she is a vowed religious woman, dedicated to God.

The ritual begins around 4:45 A.M. She stands in front of her bureau mirror wearing only her underwear, stockings, and a T-shirt. Verenice pulls her black dress over her head until its hem reaches her ankles. "Clothe me a new person with justice and holiness of truth," she begins her morning prayer.

She wraps a cloth belt around her waist. "Gird me, O Lord, with the girdle of chastity," she prays.

She places a round white skullcap on her head. Sometimes, she remembers brushing her long, thick black hair as a teenager, a time when people told her she looked like Princess Grace of Monaco. Today her graying hair is kept in a crewcut.

Makeup is applied lightly. In her early sixties, she hardly looks over forty-five. She opens a bureau drawer and pulls out her pleated and starched coif, a tight elastic headdress that wraps around her head like a sock, framing her face and jutting out beneath her chin like a bib. She attaches a large, hard headband.

"Pour into my heart the Spirit of St. Benedict and take away the levity of mind and vanity of dress," she says, having uttered the same prayer for forty-five years.

Atop the headband and coif, she attaches a short veil, which can't be seen, and then an outward veil. Looking in the mirror, she adjusts her headdress and pins the pieces together.

"Place upon my head, the helmet of salvation," she says.

Finally, she pulls on a black scapular, a long vest that reaches past her knees. Her daily baptism is complete. "For my yoke is sweet and my burden is light," she says, looking in the mirror. Now, fully dressed, she is The Nun.

When Verenice entered St. Benedict's, remnants of class distinction between sisters still existed. For hundreds of years, many convents maintained two tracts: the educated, called the "choir sisters," and the domestics, called "lay sisters." Lay sisters received little formal education, were relegated to manual labor, were taught only the simpler prayers, and couldn't vote in convent decisions. The practice arose from medieval times when aristocratic women entered the monastery bringing servants. Although St. Benedict's formally ended its class distinctions in 1894, the monastery still groomed sisters to be either teachers or homemakers when Verenice joined in 1954.

Despite her pleas to attend the order's high school, the sisters rebuked Verenice, telling her she was too old for that and would be a homemaker.

She tried to befriend the more educated "school sisters," but Verenice was bluntly informed that she was too dumb to understand their conversations. Her requests to obtain her high school diploma were repeatedly denied, until at age thirty-eight she finally was allowed to take the high school equivalency test and passed.

"Education was the priority here," Verenice said. "The ones who did domestic work were always on another level than the ones in academia. In a sense, we were treated like second-class citizens."

Maybe her lack of prestige contributed to Verenice's decision to retain the full regalia when nearly the entire order discarded it long ago. Now the habit is her shroud of honor, a dig at fellow sisters with advanced academic degrees.

AVOIDING CONFLICT

Because St. Benedict's is home to sisters whose political and religious beliefs are vastly different, most sisters avoid conflict by living with those who hold similar views. In an old monastery building next to the chapel, Verenice lives with fourteen women, the majority of whom still wear veils and are known as the "conservative sisters." On the other side of the monastery campus live the most progressive group, mostly historians, writers, photographers, and artists. Many have doctorate degrees and have taught at the monastery's college. One is a former prioress.

The benefits of such living arrangements became apparent one evening when the retreatants were dispatched to different groups for dinner. My hosts turned out to be the radical group, whose home operates like a small commune. The smell of fresh-baked bread permeated the dining room, which was decorated much like one in any middle-class home. As we sat around a long table, passing bowls of spinach casserole and beans, our discussions moved from books to complaints about papal edicts to a recent mass where the priest overslept and never arrived.

"We just sat there—a hundred women waiting for one man to show up so we could have the Eucharist," one nun complained. "You know if it had been a woman priest, she never would have made a whole church wait for her. But that's the way these guys are."

Stunned by the women's open distrust of male clerics and by their profession of feminist values, I asked how they abide by the Church's patriarchy. Everyone laughed. They view their lives as part of a women's community, not as part of a parish run by male priests. Besides, they said, their order has a long history of fighting against men of the Church.

Shortly after their monastery was founded in 1857—only the second in the country—an abbot dubbed the sisters "the disorderly convent of runaway nuns," claiming their mother superior had disobeyed his orders and snatched six of the most talented nuns from a Pennsylvania convent to start the new one. Only after the superior's death did Rome acknowledge the convent's existence.

"I feel more Benedictine than I do Catholic," said Sister Linda Kulzer, a writer, historian, and former professor. "There were Benedictines in the world before there were people called Catholics," she said, referring to the Benedictine order's sixth-century beginning. "I don't know if I would be in the Church if I weren't a Benedictine. I just knew I needed to stay with this faith."

THE EDUCATED NUN

One afternoon I caught up with Sister Linda as she was editing a manuscript at her computer. I had been struck by Linda's intelligence and her fierce feminism. As someone who'd entered almost two decades before Vatican II but had embraced and pushed for change, Linda's story of radical transformation was one I'd continue to hear throughout my journey.

Like most sisters at St. Benedict's, Linda grew up in a large Catholic family on a farm in central Minnesota. She attended a one-room schoolhouse. In high school, she came to the sisters' boarding school, which was called an "aspirancy" program for girls considering sisterhood. At first, Linda didn't want to be a nun. She simply wanted an education, a life beyond the farm.

"I'm sure for a lot of us, we came here subconsciously looking for advancement," she said.

When Linda entered in 1947, the St. Joseph convent was the largest Benedictine monastery in the world, with 1,278 sisters. Sisters slept twelve in a room, with only curtains around their single beds for privacy.

"The hardest part was finding a private place to cry," Linda remembered.

Other American convents also were burgeoning with young women who had few options besides marriage and child rearing. Some orders had waiting lists. Most orders were semicloistered, habited, and maintained a rigorous prayer and work schedule.

Linda tried to overlook the habit and what she considered absurd medieval practices. She dreaded monthly "Chapter of Faults" meetings in which sisters had to publicly accuse each other from a standard list of wrongdoings.

"You didn't keep your eyes cast down, you didn't walk in a stately way, you didn't keep your hands under your scapula," recounted Linda in her high-pitched, squeaky voice. At age seventy-one, Linda is a tall woman with soft, full jowls and squinty eyes.

Yet, this was the way older sisters had lived their entire religious lives. She wondered if it was the lack of solitude and proper training, coupled with the monastery's hardness of life, that drove a few sisters to become those cruel, ruler-wielding nuns who gave all sisters severe reputations.

During Lent, the sisters were given a choice of penances that included kneeling at the refectory door and asking for the prayers of sisters as they were leaving. The second option was eating meals off the dining room floor. Though Linda found eating off the floor humiliating, it wasn't as degrading as having to kneel and kiss the shoes of the other sisters.

As she mindlessly carried out the rituals, Linda kept wondering how long educated, intelligent women could tolerate being treated as children.

She tired of having to ask permission for such things as staying up beyond 9 P.M. for school meetings. She never considered leaving, however, because she adored most of her sisters and observing their stamina inspired her strength.

Within ten years of entering, Linda was teaching at the sisters' college. While she was working on her doctorate, her father asked her why she was still in school and the other nuns were working.

"My family did not have an appreciation for the educated life," she said.

While Linda and I walked to evening prayers, I asked what she thought would have happened if she hadn't become a nun.

"I probably would have married right after high school. He probably would have been a farmer, since those were the boys who were in that area, and I would have had a house full of kids. I never would have gone to college."

The trade-off was never bearing children. "There is something unnatural about being a celibate," she said sadly, "of not finding a life partner and not having children, which you always think in the back of your mind you could do someday."

THE FIRST NUNS

Since the time of Christ, women have consecrated themselves as virgins and chaste widows. For the first three centuries, such religious virgins lived either with their parents or in small house communities where they devoted their lives to prayer and works of charity. These women didn't take permanent vows and their professed virginity wasn't necessarily a permanent state; occasionally such women married.

The biggest attraction to religious celibacy appears to have been the freedom such a life offered from marriage and childbearing. Some women escaped from their husbands and joined houses along with their daughters. As the Church increasingly forced priests to remain celibate, their wives often went to live in such houses.

By the fifth century, Roman cities were collapsing and devout Christians sought an ascetic life in the desert where solitary hermits and colonies of spiritual adventurers were creating their own religious communities. Among such hermits was Benedict of Nursia, who left Rome early in the sixth century to find solace in the countryside. Eventually men flocked to Benedict and asked him to lead them in living reclusive lives. According to legend, the first group of monks he led didn't like his ideas and tried to poison him. He escaped and went on to lead another monastery and write his seventy-three–chapter rule book that outlined how his followers were to live—including everything from who was in charge (the abbot) to how monks were to spend the day (in a combination of work and prayer).

Various communities sprang up throughout Europe. Female communities were often founded by wealthy women, usually with ties to royalty, whose inheritance could support dozens. Still Church leaders imposed various rules on the way these women lived. Increasingly, bishops pressured houses of virgins and widows to take lifetime vows and imposed laws against marrying. Eventually religious life centered on three fundamental vows of chastity, poverty, and obedience. Their daily lives were ordered by a Rule, usually that of Benedict, Basil, or Augustine.

By the tenth century, a religious woman was consecrated to God in an elaborate ceremony resembling a wedding. She was married to Christ with a ring and a crown. Her veil and habit were blessed. She proceeded to the altar carrying a lighted candle much like the biblical wise virgins.

Despite numerous early communities, most have not survived into modern times. The Order of St. Benedict, though, is considered the oldest continuous religious order, dating back fifteen hundred years.

BECOMING A MODERN NUN

Despite the lack of entrants, becoming a nun these days is more restrictive than ever. Women with Sister Linda's or Sister Verenice's background, for example, wouldn't even be accepted today, explained Sister Marlene Meierhofer, the order's recruiter. Marlene discourages women who don't have at least a bachelor's degree because she feels they wouldn't fit in at St. Benedict's. Marlene herself probably wouldn't make the cut either, having been diagnosed with multiple sclerosis two decades earlier. While people might think all monasteries are desperate for women, Marlene spends most of her time turning people down. If a woman is over fifty, disabled, or has had health problems, Marlene tells them up front that they won't be accepted.

Marlene defended the order's discriminative screening, saying the monastery can't afford to take on any more elderly and frail women, especially since more than a third of its 390 sisters already live in the order's nursing home and many more are retired. The community's median age is seventy-two, three years above the national nun median age.

Like most orders, St. Benedict's screening includes an autobiography, reference letters, and questionnaires. Candidates take a standardized psychological test and submit to a five-hour behavior assessment.

"I'm looking to see how the woman has grown and whether she is carrying around a lot of baggage," Marlene explained. "We're not expecting the women to be virgins. We suspect that they've experimented. But if a woman has been with five different men, then we'd really have to look at her carefully."

Candidates are asked about their sexuality, relationships, and family background as well as their faith, church connection, and education, among other things. Sometimes Marlene visits a candidate's parents. Then a committee of nuns votes and the candidate compiles more documents and submits to a battery of medical examinations.

Once accepted as a postulant, the woman lives at the monastery for six months to a year, where she works and learns about Benedictine spirituality. The second year she is called a novice and spends most of her time studying theology. She is not allowed to go home. During the third year, the sister makes temporary vows for the next three years and is called a "temporary professed sister." She has up to six years to make her final life-long vows, after which she is considered a "fully professed nun."

Just that week, two postulants had requested to become novices. One was Denese Rigby, a thirty-six-year-old college professor who's illustrative of modern candidates: women who haven't attended Catholic schools, where most nuns were recruited in the past.

THE SOUTHERN BAPTIST NUN

Denese has a delicate, small face, narrow-set eyes, and short black hair. But her most endearing feature is her Southern drawl. Denese grew up in Bacliff, a tiny Texas town between Houston and Galveston, the Bible Belt.

When she reached her teens, Denese began to question the church her family attended. In particular she didn't understand the Southern Baptist Church's puritanical stand against dancing, drinking, and co-ed swimming. She also didn't like the fire-and-brimstone sermons. Finally, she joined a Catholic church, stunning members of her former church and her parents.

"My mom thought that Catholics went to mass on Saturday night so they could go out and get drunk and wouldn't have to get up for church the next morning," Denese said. "When I started going to the Catholic church, [the Baptists] thought I was going straight to hell and were banging on my door trying to get me to come back."

After college, Denese joined a Franciscan order but left before taking permanent vows. She didn't feel she fit in. She picked St. Benedict's because it is one of the few Benedictine communities left that still runs a college where she can teach.

She found the monastery's application process grueling. "I really wouldn't care to go through it again," she said. "They'd have questions clearly designed to see if you are obsessive-compulsive. I remember the ones I thought were stupid, like: 'I feel there is a tight band around my head,' or 'I have never told a lie,' or 'When I am angry, I have wanted to hurt myself and others,'" she said, laughing.

Ultimately, the analysis and personal disclosure felt better than confession to Denese. It was like an absolution of all the mistakes she had made in her life. "This is a much deeper sharing," she said. "And it spans your whole life, not just since your last confession."

Talking about her sexual experiences to a nun was excruciating, Denese admitted, chuckling. "I think I have a lot more experience with men than they do—at least I hope I have a lot more experience than the ones who entered at fifteen."

LESBIANS

Between 1963 and 1988, 216 women left St. Benedict's, just as nuns fled orders across the country. In recent years, though, the Benedictines have held reunions to try to reconnect with former sisters. The Benedictine Sisters have sponsored research and published a book detailing reasons former sisters departed. Most accounts involve a woman's desire to marry and have children, her realization that she was not cut out to be a nun, or her visceral reaction to the rules and rigidity that characterized much of the sisterhood before Vatican II. A few stories, though, deal with a subject nuns rarely speak of: lesbianism.

Marlene believes the order would accept a self-acknowledged lesbian candidate today, but she doesn't think such a woman would feel comfortable at St. Benedict's. "I think it would be very difficult for her. It would be like putting a chocoholic in a chocolate factory."

Although she suspects some candidates are lesbian, Marlene has never had a woman admit such. Some women, she said, aren't even aware of their sexual preferences until after they have entered.

"There are many sisters who are always together," she continued. "We call them 'pairs.' I don't think they are lesbians."

Nearly every community I would visit has "pairs," women couples who are best friends and often live and work together. Pairs tend to be more common in large orders. Pairing seems a natural adaptation for women who can't marry but want a partner, a friend, to accompany them through life. Nuns are supposed to avoid developing close friendships so that they can be equally present to all sisters, but that simply isn't realistic.

Sister Jeannine Grammick, who ministers to Catholic gays and lesbians in Baltimore, told me there are probably as many lesbians in religious orders as there are in the general population, about 10 percent. But not all of these women are in touch with their sexuality. Many older sisters are asexual; they entered in an era when sexuality was not discussed, and they were too young to have explored their sexual identity before they entered—often as teenagers, she said. Many joined directly from the sisters' female boarding schools and had never dated.

THE HERMIT NUN

There are also those nuns who, after living in a monastery for years, prefer to live alone so they can foster a more intense relationship with God. Such is the case with Sister Jeremy Hall, the community's hermit, who has lived alone for twenty years in a yellow-and-brown-paneled trailer next to a barn on the outskirts of the monastery property. She shares her space with a large, bristly dog who challenges anyone who shows up uninvited on her front stoop.

Sister Jeremy appeared at the scuffed trailer door wearing a navy blue skirt and black veil. Inside, the eighty-two-year-old nun settled into a worn reading chair that looked as if it had become a close friend; I chose a sagging brown couch.

"I want a bigger life than this," she said, looking around at the fake wood-paneled walls decorated with icons and crosses. "I want to pray for the world's needs."

Sister Jeremy is the order's first sister to ask to live alone—permanently. That was in 1981, years before such petitions became more common. Back then a monastic nun living alone seemed nonsensical, heretical, even though St. Benedict himself had been a hermit and outlined how they were to be treated.

Sister Jeremy chaired the college theology department for years and is a spirited extrovert who has degrees in sociology, philosophy, and theology. She entered in 1939, at age twenty-one, when sisters labored from the time they got up until they went to bed.

"This was supposed to be a life of prayer and work. And it would become a life in which I would work and somehow got my prayers in," she said.

In 1980, at age sixty-two, she retired and took a year-long sabbatical at a monk-operated hermitage in New Mexico, aptly named Christ in the Desert. Nearing the end of her year, she realized how much she loved solitude. She felt she was finding God in the silence.

She wrote the newly elected prioress, one of her former students, and told her that she didn't want to leave the community but wanted to live alone. The prioress seemed amenable to her request and when Sister Jeremy returned, she spent a frigid winter at the community's noninsulated cabin.

"There I had my one and only experience of real solitude," Sister Jeremy said, longingly, looking out the grimy windows of her trailer. "I've never had it since."

All she wanted was something small, poor, and simple. But the Sisters of St. Benedict never think small. The community installed the long modular home, big enough for a family of four, next to a cornfield. The college grew up around her, and now she is just a block from campus.

As we spoke, her kitchen phone rang. She ignored it. Though she has an unlisted number, strangers are always calling, inquiring about how to attain the spirituality of solitude.

I didn't understand how a hermit could be so busy, her life so full of people. Because so many people are clamoring to learn about the solitary life, Sister Jeremy said she would feel selfish turning them away. As a result, she has become a much-in-demand spiritual director, a kind of mentor who helps people sort out where their spiritual life is headed. Among her clients are priests and monks from St. John's Theological Seminary, a few miles down the road.

Every day, Sister Jeremy attends mass at the monastery. At home, she reads the Bible and other spiritual texts and often researches topics for speeches. She reads the newspaper quickly every day and watches half an hour of news at night. She tries to maintain a meditative atmosphere, praying while she works. Rarely does she get lonely or crave conversation. And when she does, she recognizes those feelings as diversions.

Lately, she has been talking about perhaps returning to live at the monastery as her health becomes more precarious. She has had heart trouble and increasing problems with Crohn's disease.

The phone rang again, and I urged her to answer it.

"This life is a call to solitude," she said, "and yet there are disruptions."

THE MOTHER NUN

Having sacrificed the normal pleasures and passions of life—a husband, children—many nuns today grapple with accepting formerly married candidates who have grown children. The number of mother nuns is increasing nationally, especially as orders have difficulty attracting young women. At some orders, divorced or widowed mothers make up as much as a third of new members.

St. Benedict's has accepted several women whose marriages have been annulled or whose husbands have died. It's a dicey issue, however. A divorced woman recently professed her first vows, then left two months later after her first grandchild was born.

"The vocation to motherhood is a lifetime commitment," Marlene, the recruiter, said. "You can't divorce yourself very much from your children."

The sisters have had some success accepting older widows like Sister Arlene Hines. A mother of ten children, Arlene entered St. Benedict's in 1980 at age sixty-four—before the monastery set the age limit for entrants at fifty years old. That year Arlene was joined by another widow, a seventy-four-year-old mother of thirteen grown children, including a monk at St. John's Seminary.

Sister Arlene had been making annual retreats to the monastery since her husband died in 1971. She didn't know the community accepted widows her age until the prioress pointed out a nun who had two grown children. By then, Arlene's children were out of college; she was ready to start a new life.

Were other sisters jealous of her being a sister and a mother?

"Ah, some, of course," Arlene responded. "You know, it's very human. A lot of these women would have longed to have been mothers. You see them eagerly reach out to children. You know it was a great hardship that they gave up children. And so, what most people said was: 'You have the best of both worlds.' "

The strongest backlash to her lifestyle choice came from her own family. Arlene's two daughters told her they hated nuns. They thought religious life was a narrow life. They wanted their mother to enjoy life in Washington, D.C., where she was just beginning to afford to go to the theater and concerts.

Now, at eighty-four years old, Sister Arlene has twenty grandchildren and two great-grandchildren whom she sees fairly often. One week each year she takes off to be with her children and grandchildren. After twenty years, her sisterhood has faded as a family issue.

A MICROCOSM OF THE NUN UNIVERSE

I hadn't anticipated that St. Benedict's sisters would be so animated or quizzical or *human*. Nor had I expected them to be so happy, so at peace. I didn't realize that their community would boast such a rich dichotomy, that although they take the same vows, they each approach their journey to God differently. These are deeply fulfilled women who possess a sense of belonging, having realized their calling. And despite outward differences, they appear connected to each other.

St. Benedict's, I would come to appreciate after visiting dozens of other monasteries, is a microcosm of the diverse American Catholic nun universe. While most religious communities tend to attract women who hold similar views and life experiences, St. Benedict's tolerates, and perhaps encourages, diversity. While there are Vatican II–era sisters like Pat in her red dress trying to work out the meaning of modern nunhood, there's still room for traditional nuns like Verenice in her old-style garb. There are converts like Denese Rigby who, against her family's wishes and fundamentalist roots, followed her spiritual yearnings to the monastery. There are staunch feminists like Linda Kulzer and formerly married mothers like Arlene Hines and even hermits like Jeremy Hall.

In some ways, I felt like an explorer who'd discovered a secret land of historically important females. Nuns at St. Benedict's have lived in Japan, Taiwan, and Africa and speak exotic languages. With their nun-taught educations, they have run the order's hospital and college. They are well read and can converse knowledgeably about art, politics, and theater.

St. Benedict's sisters helped me understand that being a nun—and a feminist—is about questioning rules and sometimes breaking them. That's how many female monasteries were formed in the first place: by women who refused to marry and went off to live in collective communities. Since the first female hermitages, being a nun has been viewed as a radical way of life, a rebellion to societal constraints and demands.

Some historians believe that nuns were the world's first feminists. St. Benedict's opened my eyes to the connection between the modern sister and the modern woman. Before visiting the monastery I didn't even realize how similar nuns are to feminists, how both groups have experienced the same kinds of discrimination, the same kinds of retribution, the same kinds of stereotyping.

Before St. Benedict's, I had opposed using the word "feminist" to describe my politics. Many women my age see feminism as a tainted label that describes a dated, militant attitude. But after hearing the nuns use the title so casually, so proudly, I found myself sprinkling my own conversations with the word, not as a label, but as an acknowledgment that I supported equality, that I supported women's long battles against male

dominance and efforts to control them. It was simply a word that connoted solidarity with many social justice issues.

Little did I realize when I traded a St. Patrick's Day party for a St.
Benedict's retreat that the nuns would inspire me to begin a four-year
quest that would cause me to immerse myself in their fascinating and
little-understood subculture. Here it was vanishing before my eyes. I
would frequently thank the Sisters of St. Benedict's for helping me discover the real sisterhood—the world beyond stereotype.

2

SISTERS IN THE 'HOOD

VISITATION SISTERS IN MINNEAPOLIS, MINNESOTA

"We're not living in Utopia here. We do have our struggles. Sometimes you fly off the handle and then you go back and say you're sorry."

—SISTER FRANCES REIS

Sun streamed through lofty maple and oak trees, highlighting the signs of decay along the uneven sidewalk: broken beer bottles, junk car parts, a used condom. Beyond the huffing city buses and belching cars, I could hear the sounds of early morning chanting drifting through an open window. The hypnotic voices led me to a three-story clapboard home that towers over a busy intersection, an unlikely setting for a monastery.

When I pushed the doorbell, a woman with fading strawberry-blond hair greeted me eagerly. The nuns had just begun morning prayers, she told me as she led me inside. A stained-glass panel in the front room chapel cast yellow and purple hues on the sisters, who were dressed in jean skirts and white blouses. Thick chains with palm-sized silver crosses hung from their necks.

The monastery, among the smallest I would visit, housed just five sisters at the time. Prioress Sister Frances Reis beckoned me to sit next to her on the chapel's only pew. Seated behind the organ, Frances's callused fingers picked over music scores. Perched on stools around the chapel, the sisters continued their chanting—one side singing a verse and the other side responding. When they stopped, noise invaded—cars screeching, radios blaring, neighbors yelling, and police sirens wailing.

In 1989, after ten years of praying that God would lead them to a ministry for the poor, four Visitation nuns, who had rarely left the security of their spacious suburban monasteries, moved to a crime-infested neighborhood, among the worst in Minneapolis. Their goal was to offer "a ministry of presence, an island of gentleness in the midst of violence, an oasis of peacefulness."

Instead, they brought disharmony. They had never really worked together—three came from a monastery in St. Louis and another from St. Paul—and didn't know each other well. For the most part, these contemplative women had lived their lives inside their heads. In addition to the constant noise of the inner city, there was the stress of living in close quarters. Most came without knowing how to cook, pay bills, cut grass, shovel snow, or own a home. They had rarely encountered drug addicts, prostitutes, welfare moms, or deadbeat dads, much less befriended such people. And their personalities clashed so often that they took personality tests to understand each other better; to this day, they refer to each sister's numbers on one such test, an open confirmation of their individual strengths, weaknesses, and idiosyncrasies.

Despite their lofty goal of establishing a "monastery in the slums," gaining acceptance from their neighbors turned out to be more difficult than they had anticipated. Initially, some shunned the sisters, thinking they were a group of lesbians. Calling the white sisters' mission elitist and naïve, some black leaders rebuffed them. It would take a drug-related shooting to initiate the sisters. Then it was the people they had set out to serve who helped transform their house into the oasis they had intended.

A RAGGEDY NUN

The leader of this curious group is an unlikely nun herself. The daughter of a professional baseball player turned salesman and an alcoholic mother, Frances did not grow up in a pious household. Yet, it is those rips and tears in her personality that allow her to confront neighbors about their drinking or drug abuse.

"I let people know I come from an alcoholic family pretty freely," she said. "It gets me out of a role. I want people to see me as human. If they think you're just a holy nun, and you don't have any issues, they're not going to relate to you."

When friends call her "raggedy," Frances takes it as a compliment. Indeed, Frances has a workman quality about her; she is the kind of fastidious laborer who drinks volumes of coffee and carries little pieces of paper jotted with lists and phone numbers.

While her family troubles might have distanced her from nuns at her former monastery, they provide her an instant connection to the neighborhood that the other sisters don't have. Frances uses her childhood wounds to make introductions. She believes people sense her compassion has roots in her own experiences.

As a child, Frances often sat up with her mother, who drank when her husband traveled, first as a baseball player for the Brooklyn Dodgers, then the Boston Braves, and later as a salesman. The family was also poor. Baseball players weren't bringing home the six- and seven-figure salaries they are today, and the heat was often turned off in her family's St. Paul home.

During those years, Frances retreated to her bedroom, praying to God when there was no one else to listen. She told no one about her mother's drinking—not even friends whose parents had similar problems. Yet, as an older teenager, Frances succumbed to drinking and smoking, too.

During a Catholic high school retreat, Frances felt her first desire to become a nun induced by the meditative atmosphere. A priest told her to wait forty-eight hours; she did and her religious interest waned. A year later, she and a priest friend spent the afternoon in a cloud of cigarette smoke sorting out her issues. Three months later Frances entered the Visitation Monastery in suburban St. Paul. She was only nineteen.

The same Visitation nuns who had once been her high school teachers became her peers. Though she'd been a mediocre student, they sent her off to college to become a teacher. But once she got her own classroom, Frances resented teaching "rich kids." She made it her goal to teach her students that there was another world outside their large, comfortable homes and luxury cars.

"I identified for sure with blue-collar and simple people," she said. "I was much closer to the janitors and the cooks than I was to the faculty."

Now, Frances is perhaps the best friend a recovering junkie could ever have. She manages to befriend many of the neighborhood's drug addicts, helping them get homes, furniture, and recurring chances. She begs monastery donors to make mortgage down payments, repair roofs, pay rents, raise bail money, and offer legal representation. And though her calendar is rarely empty, Frances drops everything when recovering addicts say they need her.

THE ENNEAGRAM

When Frances volunteered to join the inner-city monastery she hadn't considered how difficult it would be to bond with three nuns she barely knew. Karen, now fifty-five; Virginia, seventy-one; and Margaret, seventy-two, had lived together for decades at the St. Louis Visitation Monastery. Frances often felt left out.

The sisters latched on to personality tests to help them relate, including the Myers-Briggs and the Enneagram. They refer to the Enneagram nearly as much as the Bible. To them, it is a bible of personality traits and foibles that they rely on to help guide their relationships.

Frances confided that she was a Number Three on the Enneagram scale. As she detailed the characteristics of her number, I wasn't surprised.

Threes, she said, are difficult to live with because they are too efficient and organized, too focused on projects and completing tasks. By concentrating on work, she avoids relationships.

The sister she argues with the most is Karen, she admitted. Although they are both extroverts, Karen doesn't like to address pain while Frances prefers to air her feelings. Frances struggles with all three sisters, she said, because as P's on the Myers-Briggs scale, they like to explore all options before making a decision. Whereas she, a J on the Myers-Briggs, just wants to get the job done.

"Margaret calls herself a recovering perfectionist. She thinks I am a perfectionist. On the other hand, I would never spend as much time as she is spending on restoring that door down there," Frances said, referring to the dining room door that had been laid out like a coffin on the front porch for weeks as Margaret carefully sanded and painted it.

Frances said the nuns hash out problems in sit-down talks. "I've said we ought to have our fights on the front lawn so people will see how we deal with our differences. We're not living in Utopia here. We do have our struggles, but it doesn't mean we have to split up or resort to violence."

A VOLATILE MIX

Yet, it was through violence that the sisters were inducted into the neighborhood. Not long after they moved into the house, the sisters realized they were living in the middle of a drug battleground: More than twenty people were killed the first year the monastery was open. It was a shooting two years later that galvanized the neighborhood around the sisters.

On the afternoon of October 4, 1992—the Feast of St. Frances of Assisi—Karen and Frances were alone on the house's second floor debating whether they should pack swimsuits for their separate yearly retreats when they heard an explosion. Frances thought the furnace had blown up. Karen ran down to the staircase landing, looked out the window, and saw a man wearing a red starter jacket run into the alley behind their house.

"Oh, my God!" Karen yelled. "I think someone has been shot."

The women ran to their screened porch and spotted a man facedown in the street near the steps leading to their house. Frances dialed 911. Then they rushed outside and knelt beside the man; his arms were out-stretched, one hand clutching a wad of money. Blood coursed through his hair and the black net he wore over his head. His sneakers were on the other side of the street. Shot in the head, the man had literally run out of his shoes.

Frances held one of his hands, Karen placed her hand on his back, and they began saying prayers for the dead, just as they had prayed with their own sisters in their final hours. They recited prayers they thought the man might know: the Lord's Prayer, the Lord Is My Shepherd. The man began moaning, so the sisters believed he could hear them. Police allowed the sisters to continue praying as paramedics strapped the man onto a gurney.

Sister Karen Mohan

That night, the man they came to know as Lulu, known to police as a neighborhood drug dealer, died.

Karen, called to testify before the grand jury investigating the shooting, told police she couldn't identify the killer. But the suspect didn't know that. When he learned that a nun was a witness, he confessed.

Several weeks after the shooting, some of Lulu's friends stopped by the monastery and asked: "Are you the ones that did the last rites on him? That was cool, man, really cool." The men asked that the sisters pray for them so that they might get off drugs. Later, Lulu's girlfriend and relatives came to the monastery to pray with the sisters.

Because the nuns had treated Lulu as a human being, a man who had a family and was loved, despite his flaws, the sisters themselves gained respect and became an integral part of the neighborhood. In turn, their relationships with their neighbors helped the sisters overcome their own problems in getting along; seeing people without a home or struggling to overcome addictions gave the sisters a new perspective on their own trivial disagreements.

"That experience made me realize that people who have been touched by violence seem to understand the violence done to Christ," Frances said.

The sisters roll from crisis to crisis, each time learning a little more about the depths of the neighborhood's problems. Just that weekend when I visited, a fight between a girl and a mentally ill boy at what was billed by the sisters as a "back-to-summer party" led the sisters to the boy's troubled mom.

"We're on the brink, Sister," the woman told Frances as they sat in Frances's car.

"Are you addicted to drugs or alcohol?" Frances asked.

The mother sat silently with her eyes closed and her lips pursed.

"If you care about your kids, you first need to get your act together," Frances told her.

Such relationships have also forced the sisters to redefine their interpretation of being cloistered. At their previous monasteries, they rarely interacted with anyone outside their monastery grounds. Now they view the city's entire Near North Side as their cloister. They are still contemplative nuns, but these days they are "cloistered" only two days a month. Calling them their "shutdown days," the sisters unplug the phone, lock the door, and put out a sign saying they are unavailable.

Of course, signs mean little to children, who invariably ring the doorbell. The sisters realized that if they were to have any contemplative prayer, they needed to set boundaries. So they established an hour in the afternoon when they hang a colorful wind sock out front, a signal that the children can come play. They stock their garage with toys, skates, basketballs, and hula hoops. They keep boxes of books, dolls, and games in their living room.

Occasionally the wind sock works as intended. But kids still tend to ring the doorbell regardless of whether the sock is flying. Initially the kids didn't even believe the women were nuns because they don't dress in full habits like the comedian Whoopi Goldberg does in the movie *Sister Act*. Now the kids have dubbed them "Sisters in the 'Hood." And the nuns have heard kids bragging: "The sisters is a gang. We is the sisters."

Trust has developed. When an eleven-year-old neighborhood boy died after being stabbed more than thirty-five times, his friends came to the monastery and asked if they could pray for their friend in front of the sisters' sculpture of a crucified Christ. One boy mentioned that his father had been murdered; another said his uncle had been killed.

"I pray that my family will come off drugs," one little boy said. "I pray for my best friend who was killed," another spoke up. "I pray," one boy requested, "that the Lord will not be too soon in coming for me."

A MISSION OF RELATIONSHIPS

Every day after morning prayers, the sisters meet to discuss the day's plans. One Monday morning, Frances was particularly keyed up. From her to-do list, she ticked off the names of sisters who would accompany students from Visitation High School, where she once taught; the students were volunteering in the neighborhood for a week to get a firsthand look at poverty. The other sisters seemed overwhelmed by Frances's intricate details. Someone noted that there would barely be enough time for travel between appointments and planned activities.

"Frances is really happy when every second counts," Sister Virginia told me after the sisters had parted for their assigned duties. "That's the thing about small-group living. We're all so different and living so closely."

Virginia Schmidt is a gentle, retired teacher, a grandmotherly figure who accompanies others on errands and plays chauffeur when neighbors need rides. She's spent years trying to figure out what number she is on the Enneagram, which she said meant she is probably a Number Six: the Questioner, a loyal person motivated by the need for security.

We were sitting in the sisters' spacious living room. Above the fire-place mantel is a painting of two African princesses in brightly colored dresses hugging each other. The picture represents an African version of the Visitation, the encounter between Mary, pregnant with Jesus, and her cousin Elizabeth, who was pregnant with John the Baptist. It is from this Visitation, this friendship and bond between women, that the order took its name and its mission to foster relationships.

Leaving the monastery where she'd lived for more than thirty years was the most painful thing Virginia had ever done. "These people were like my family, people I loved, people who nurtured me, people who were my closest friends. They were feeling a little bit like I was abandoning them. They really couldn't spare us," she said, her voice cracking and her eyes tearing.

Just then the doorbell rang. Virginia wiped her eyes and took a deep breath before standing up and excusing herself. There is a constant stream of people at the door or on the phone. Nearly every prayer service is interrupted. Virginia returned trailed by a middle-aged black man. Slurring his words, the man offered a convoluted reason why he needed to use the phone.

"We're not an agency to take away the hurt," Virginia told me while we waited for the man to finish his call. "We don't have any know-how to do any good stuff in the neighborhood. Our main thing is to be in relationships with these people and to be friends. But just because we're present, things happen, people meet here and get connected. The phone has been a way for us to get to know people."

When the stranger left, Virginia turned to me. "I don't think I understood anything he said."

How did she cope with the barrage of people at the door? I asked.

There are times, she admitted, when people's demands become excessive and intrusive. But each time Virginia hears the doorbell ringing, she tries to approach the visitor as if he or she were Christ in disguise. So now when she hears someone ringing or knocking, it's a reminder that she needs to be available to others.

Virginia insists she is the one who has benefited from their "monastery in the slums." "I don't think I would ever have known anyone who was on drugs or who was on probation from jail. And yet, I've gotten to know these people, and they are my friends."

HANGING OUT AT THE SISTERS'

The sisters eat their meals in what had been the house's formal dining room. Previous occupants left a massive dining room set that dominates the room underneath a glass chandelier. Pictures of the order's two founders, St. Francis de Sales and St. Jane de Chantal, adorn one wall. On another hangs a large wooden crucifix, carved by a prisoner more than 140 years ago.

Each week the sisters take turns cooking. Meals usually are homemade dishes, often based on recipes from neighbors. Dinner conversations typically center on the business of the day—who called, who needs to do what.

Once a month, the sisters invite a guest. During one of my stays, the sisters hosted a former neighbor who had recently moved to her own suburban apartment. Brenda talked loudly in a raspy cigarette voice, often exclaiming: "Praise Jesus!"

Margaret served fried chicken, mashed potatoes, green beans, and rolls. Throughout the meal, Brenda entertained us with stories of the sisters. Her two pubescent daughters listened intently as they generously doused their chicken with hot sauce.

When she moved to the neighborhood more than a decade ago, Brenda recounted, she learned that her children, including an older son now in prison, were hanging out at "the sisters'." Not knowing who "the sisters" were, Brenda marched over to have a word. When she walked in the front door, Brenda's mood suddenly changed.

"These sisters were nuns!" she shouted. "As soon as I came in the door, I could feel the peace."

That first night Brenda poured out her heart to the sisters, who offered to give her furniture when she found a new apartment. When she told her boyfriend, they argued. He wouldn't accept anything from "those white women," he told Brenda.

"I didn't look at them as white women," she told me, "but as nuns and people who cared."

BREAD LADIES

One night, Virginia, Karen, and I volunteered to deliver donated bread to a group of recovering drug addicts and alcoholics. We would then check on the boy who had fought at the sisters' summer party.

We loaded the station wagon and drove to a nearby neighborhood littered with vacant and decaying houses. Karen pulled up in front of an old apartment building where men were hanging out third-story windows. As soon as the sisters got out of the car, several men yelled hellos then rushed to hug them. I was surprised these were the sober men the sisters had described. Tall, with thick necks and intense expressions, the men looked like ex-convicts with their dangling cigarettes, low-riding britches, and soiled undershirts. Theirs seemed an unlikely friendship. After a few minutes of listening to the men's troubles, the sisters hugged them and got back into the car bubbling with excitement, as though they were Avon ladies who had just scored a big sale and were racing to the next.

Not far away, Karen turned down a side street, driving slowly as she tried to recall which of the sad, sinking houses belonged to the fighting boy's family. Two girls recognized the sisters and grabbed their waists and legs as the sisters emerged from the car. When Karen saw the boy on his bicycle, she tried to hug him, but he rode off.

His mother appeared looking as if she had been awakened from a deep sleep. Her hair was matted and her eyes held a faraway look. Virginia gave the woman some bread, and Karen asked what else the sisters could do for her. The mother asked the sisters to pray for her and her family. She said her son had so many mental problems that he had to attend a daytime treatment center instead of a regular school. The sisters listened with patience as the woman detailed her difficult life, never mentioning her own drug problem. Karen stroked the woman's arm as she spoke. When we turned to leave, Karen hugged the children again, including the boy. Inadvertently her large cross poked a girl's eye. Karen rushed to make sure the girl wasn't hurt, then, embarrassed, tucked her cross inside her shirt.

THE NIGHT OWL NUN

Late that same evening, I joined Karen in her attic bedroom. She often stays up late, a bone of contention with some sisters who don't appreciate her creeping around at night. Karen Mohan, who entered the Visitation Monastery in 1964, just before her nineteenth birthday, traces the idea for the inner-city monastery to a 1978 meeting of the American Catholic Bishops.

The bishops encouraged religious orders to launch ministries for the poor and Karen said she began to question what her cloistered, teaching

Clockwise from left:
Sister Margaret McKenzie,
Sister Virgina Schmidt,
Sister Frances Reis

monastery could do for poor people because most of its students were well-heeled Catholics. That's when she approached Margaret, who had just returned from a five-year hiatus running a house of prayer in the inner city. Coincidently, within a few days, Virginia approached Margaret with the same yearning. The three women decided to pray and discuss ideas every Sunday morning from nine-thirty to ten-thirty. And so they did—for ten years.

When they were finally given approval for the inner-city monastery, Karen felt underqualified. After all, she wasn't a social worker. The message she kept hearing while meditating was: You have nothing to give; you're not trained in anything; you are not qualified for this. In angst, she confided to her spiritual director, who told her she was ready precisely because she realized she had nothing to offer; her direction would come from God.

"There's not a lot to show for what we do," Karen explained. "It's not the end of the school year, and I haven't taught five classes like I used to. I'm not preparing a lesson plan. I'm not correcting papers. I'm not going to the parents' club meeting. Anybody can do what I'm doing. I don't feel like I'm setting the world on fire."

Yet, Karen has come to realize that the sisters do make a difference, though often the effects are subtle.

One day, Karen was riding a city bus to a class at the community college when a woman recognized her.

"Aren't you one of the sisters from Fremont?" the woman across the aisle asked.

"Yes," Karen said, sure she'd never met the woman before.

"I'm a relative of Lulu's, and I'll never forget what you sisters did for him," the woman said.

It had been three years since Lulu's death. A neighborhood has a long memory.

"His death affected me profoundly. It is always with me," Karen told me, almost in a whisper. "I mean, he wasn't a nice person. He was dealing drugs and making them available for kids. But he had a family; he had people who loved him. God's there for all. There's a ripple effect. We impact one another. It's not like seeing my students going on to some well-known college, but it's another way of being there with people, and it's every bit as important."

Karen assured me that nuns are no different from families; they argue, they fight, and sometimes they let little things get on their nerves. A Number Seven on the Enneagram, Karen is the Adventurer, motivated by the need to be happy, to contribute to the world, and to avoid pain and suffering—almost the polar opposite of Frances, with whom she shares a mutual discomfort.

"If Frances had a bad day, we would all know about it," said Karen.

The sisters resolve their conflicts through prayer and forgiveness and by trying to understand their sisters' motives. They discover one another's inner struggles through their unusual "faith sharing," the impromptu personal reflections they give during their four daily prayer times. It started as simple musings on how their ancient psalms are relevant to modern times but evolved into intimate testimonials about their deepest sufferings and, ultimately, has become the emotional adhesive that binds these different women together.

No one is sure of their faith sharing's genesis, but these daily revelations struck me as identical to the kinds of testimonials common in black Protestant churches, like those their neighbors attend. I wondered how much spirituality the sisters are imparting to their neighbors and how much their neighbors are imparting to them.

Around midnight, Karen suggested we sneak downstairs for a snack. We tiptoed down the creaking back stairs to the kitchen, where the others had left us a large bowl of popcorn. Karen found two cold Heinekens in the refrigerator. On a sagging couch in the finished basement we munched popcorn, drank beer, and shared confidences like two former college roommates.

THE SAGE

The next morning, I was sitting on the back porch sipping coffee and enjoying the spring breeze when Margaret joined me. At seventy-two years old, Margaret McKenzie is the oldest sister at the house. A tall, striking woman with silvery hair and intense blue eyes, Margaret seems to be absorbing everything. She is the quintessential wise woman, her shoulders often draped with a wool shawl, even in summer.

As a Five on the Enneagram, Margaret explained that she is the Observer. Such personalities are stingy with their thoughts and time and like to be alone, she said. She doesn't like to be rushed and needs time to meditate.

"We'd rather leave a dinner party and go read," she said.

Her intense contemplation was what had attracted Karen and Virginia separately to seek Margaret's advice when they were searching for a ministry. It was also her skills as a keen observer that allowed her to see the connection between the psalms the nuns chant every day and street language.

After several years of praying over this ministry, the three sisters began to spend their two-week summer vacations at an impoverished inner-city parish in St. Louis. They wanted to see if their Visitation lifestyle could be lived outside the monastery. In their apartment above the rectory, the women set aside one room where they could pray and meditate. There the windows opened onto a busy intersection and the street noise poured into their seclusion.

"You could hear the language and conversation of the people on the street, and it would be like the same cry that we would be saying in the psalms," Margaret remembered. "We were saying the psalms in our locked room, and they were living the psalms on the street."

From that moment on, every time Margaret chanted the psalms she could still hear the voices of street people—even back at her cloistered monastery.

Later, while living here, at the Minneapolis house, and singing the psalms against a similar backdrop, Margaret developed a theology she calls "incarnation contemplation." The typical monastery, like the one she entered in St. Louis, provides an environment that is both austere and idyllic, with spacious grounds and verdant gardens. Finding God in those environs is easy, she said. But unless people experience God among the poor, their spirituality is limited.

"In the same way you can find God in the beauty of nature, you can find God in the beauty of the destitute. We're not meant to just admire the trees, we're meant to share life."

THE NEWCOMERS

In recent years, the sisters have hosted a parade of women interested in joining their unique monastery. Unlike the sisters, though, these possible candidates are much older than when the sisters joined and have had vast life experiences.

On All Saints Day 1995, Suzanne Homeyer became the monastery's first postulant. The forty-five-year-old had been a peace activist and politician but was so enticed by the sisters' ministry that she sold her house, quit her job, and gave away her dog.

"Growing up in Chicago, my father was very involved in the neighborhood," she explained. "I had a great sense of how a neighborhood can be a functioning, life-giving place. In a lot of ways, that's why I came here."

Raised Protestant, Suzanne converted to Catholicism in the early 1970s after meeting Daniel Berrigan and Dorothy Day, politically active Catholics. "They were living out their faith at great risk to themselves. It was a more practical, real, down-to-earth faith, even though it had all the incense and everything that people might think was hokey."

Her own political activism has included civil rights marches, protesting the Vietnam conflict, getting arrested at the Pentagon, and chaining herself to a gate protesting the Trident submarine. In the 1980s, Suzanne founded a day center in Ypsilanti, Michigan, for deinstitutionalized people who were wandering the streets. She was elected to city council for two terms, representing a district that had many group homes, and became a strong voice for the mentally ill.

Although Suzanne's life experiences are much different from the other sisters'—she was chaining herself to federal property while the others were still cloaked in black and hidden behind grilles—she looks at the sisters as deeply spiritual and wise mentors.

"Here I feel we're all part of a team," she said. "We're peers. I feel that bond of being sisters very strongly. It's kind of like you're blood sisters."

Suzanne came to depend on that bond when, less than two years after joining, an unrelenting toothache turned out to be a brain tumor the size of a baseball. The night before surgery, Frances gave Suzanne a full-body massage to relax her. The next day, the sisters accompanied her to the hospital, where they prayed for her throughout her long surgery. When she awoke, she said she felt as if she had been in the arms of Jesus. The tumor turned out to be benign and the sisters nursed Suzanne until she recovered. (Remarkably, six years later, Frances also would undergo a similar brain surgery.)

It was an awkward dependence for a woman who had always been so independent. As a Number Two on the Enneagram, Suzanne is the Nurturer, the Earth Mother whose downfall is that she often attends to everyone else's needs instead of her own.

In the summer of 2000, Suzanne was joined by a forty-nine-year-old who had lived as a sister for many years in two separate orders but hardly seemed the nun type. Theresa Miller is a funny, irreverent woman. Like Frances, she quit smoking the day she entered the Visitation community. Most of the time Theresa was quiet around the sisters, but I sensed—and guests commented—that there seemed to be something smoldering beneath Theresa's comical expressions. She isn't the trained, polite sister who habitually walks quietly or stands erect. Theresa slouches; she clomps up and down the stairs. She laughs loudly. Her speech is slurred in a lazy, relaxed way, the words sloshing around in her mouth. Although highly educated, she chooses her words carelessly—using plural verbs with singular subjects. Alone with her, I saw a strong personality who was trying hard to fit in, afraid she would offend someone, fearful she would be asked to leave the third religious order she had joined.

As a college senior, Theresa had become an Ursuline nun and spent nearly eight years teaching in one of the order's boarding schools. Feeling she wasn't getting enough community, Theresa left. Seven years later she joined the Franciscans of the Poor. Within two years, she was asked to leave; she didn't get along with the novice director.

Shocked by her dismissal, Theresa signed up with a dating service; at thirty-nine years old, she felt pressured to find the right mate if she were going to have children. She also sought counseling, trying to get over what she saw as an addiction to religious life.

Then one day, someone sent her a clipping about the Visitation Sisters in Minneapolis.

This is perfect, she thought.

When she visited, she was attracted to the idea of a contemplative group that is also active in serving the poor and has a strong community and prayer life. Acceptance into the community is so important to Theresa that she isn't going to risk rejection this time. Since joining, she has tried to stifle her aggressive personality.

"I'm walking on eggshells when I feel a little conflict," she admitted. "I'm like, whatever Karen says, I'll do so I can make it. You wear yourself out trying to do that."

Typically, Theresa isn't afraid of conflict. She is a Number Eight on the Enneagram, she said, also known as the Aggressor.

"I'm a feisty fighter," she admitted. "Anger is my thing. When I'm out of control, I can really hit you below the belt. Kind of slaughter you. I'm not afraid of saying what I think. And some of these holy nuns think you're not supposed to be that way."

Unlike the other communities Theresa had joined, the Visitation Sisters value relationships above all else. "Look at this house," Theresa said, throwing her arms open to the small room where we were sitting. "Everything is unfinished. You got four different pieces of rug down here. Things are where people left them. In a monastery normally everything would have its place. It would be neat and orderly. Here, they really don't care about that.

"Relationships are what matter," she added. "Not the job, not how well you did it or how well you cleaned the dishes and whether you put them back in the right place. Everything does not have its place here. Relationship is key. Relationship is their ministry."

THE MASSAGE

One afternoon, Frances offered to give me a massage. So, at about 3 P.M., I climbed the winding staircase to the third floor. Frances was on the phone in her bedroom and waved me into the massage room, a small bedroom next to her own. A pebble fountain on a nearby table made delicate pitter-patter sounds. A vanilla-scented candle burned.

The phone receiver clinked into its cradle, and Frances appeared. She told me to undress and get under the sheets. She had another phone call to make, she said. I took off my clothes and crawled under the thin, cream-colored sheet with purple flowers. It seemed strange to have an interview subject—a nun—see me naked. Within a few minutes, Frances lightly rapped on the door.

"Are you ready?"

I said I was.

She began by pushing her thumbs against my temples as she mouthed a little prayer. This was a time of contemplation, she said. She encouraged me to relax and turned on a portable stereo; the sounds of seagulls drifted throughout the room.

"Envision yourself going to a place of peace," she said. "A warm place."

Suddenly I was on the beach, the sun piercing my face and dotting me with brown freckles. I felt the grit of sand in my hair. I heard the seagulls fighting like children. Frances poured oil on her hands and ran them through my hair, pushing at the base of my skull, my eyebrows. She moved her palms down my jaw and my neck. Soon she was working my arms and my hands.

"Relax," she said. "The hand of the writer is tense."

Frances rubbed nearly every part of my body. She massaged my buttocks, my thighs, my feet. She wrapped her hands around my belly, pushing down on my midriff. After about forty minutes, she had finished.

"May our God bless you and keep you," she prayed over me. I could smell coffee on her breath. "May *She* let Her face shine upon you. May *She* look upon you kindly and give you peace, today and the days to come." I was surprised by Frances's use of the feminine pronoun for God but would soon become accustomed to hearing sisters refer to God as the Goddess, Sophia, or just She.

Frances said she hoped the massage had healed whatever ached. Then she placed her hands on my back and said she was breaking the energy. She pulled away gently.

Frances told me to lie there as long as I wanted. Then I could take a bubble bath in her bathroom. I heard her walk to her room. Within seconds, she was laughing on the phone. I lay on the massage table for a long while listening to her talk in her true Minnesotan accent, forming long, nasal *o*'s and *a*'s.

Then I slowly got up, wrapped myself in a robe, and sauntered to the bathroom, where I poured blue Calgon beads into the tub. As I soaked in the bubbles, I felt the sunlight filtering through the window hitting my toes, resting on the faucet as the bubbles dripped down. I thought: How is this possible? I'm taking a bath in the middle of the afternoon. I would never do this on my own. But the sisters gave me permission. I suddenly felt deeply cared for, pampered. It was a momentary joy. And I understood in my skin why Frances had chosen her massage ministry for abused women: She is offering a healing touch to women who are not accustomed to physical kindness.

I soaked for nearly an hour. At dinner that evening, Frances put her arm on my shoulder and pronounced me a new woman. The sisters clapped. They told me I glowed. And I suppose I did radiate a certain delight: After all, I'd spent the afternoon surrounded by warmth. Yet, it was merely dessert to the days that I'd lived beside these thoughtful, nurturing women whose ministry clearly is creating relationships. As I drove home, I realized I had experienced the modern interpretation of the biblical Visitation: when women from different backgrounds come together to share their lives, if only briefly.

PART TWO

OBEDIENCE

Once a sister enters an order, she begins to study the vows of obedience, chastity, and poverty and what they mean to her and the community she has joined. The vow of obedience is interpreted differently from order to order and from sister to sister. Some see obedience as submitting to the will of a mother superior who controls even the most trivial aspects of a nun's life: when she rises, when she retires, what job she will perform, to whom she can speak and when. Other orders—like the Passionist Nuns and the Franciscans of the

Martyrs of St. George near St. Louis, Missouri—include wearing a habit. Most traditional orders add in loyalty to the Pope and strict adherence to the principles of the Church. A few moderate orders try to live practically while following a modern version of their orders' traditions, such as the Carmelites in Hudson, Wisconsin. Many progressive sisters—like those at the Maria Shelter in Chicago—however, interpret obedience simply to mean they follow the rules of their order and the leadership of their superior. That obedience, though, doesn't mean they have to agree with Vatican precepts or give up their own consciences. Modern sisters insist that sometimes obedience to their order's core beliefs and values means they must challenge Church leaders' decisions.

For many modern women who enter religious life, submitting to the vow of obedience or the will of a demanding superior is far more difficult today than in the past when women entered while still in high school or directly after graduating. Then becoming a sister presented a certain amount of freedom from the conventional life of marriage and motherhood. Today, obedience is viewed as a major sacrifice of a woman's freedom. Some welcome the simplicity of not having to make major decisions on their own and others say obedience presents the biggest obstacle to their becoming a nun. Most women who enter religious life today are highly educated and have worked and lived on their own for many years. Giving up that independence—which often includes a house, money, and other personal forms of security—is challenging to those who have prided themselves on having maintained their own autonomy.

I found obedience to be the most daunting vow. It was what made religious life so comparable to the military: Both have an institutional order and a chain of command. Obedience to a superior wasn't to be questioned. Submitting to the capriciousness of a controlling leader often made me feel like a rebellious teenager trying to assert her will in the world. Like most who are entering orders today, I had come of age in a postfeminist era and had had to prove myself time and time again as a competitive woman in a man's world. It seemed unnatural to suddenly dismiss that independence and submit unquestioningly to one woman's whims. Though I was a visitor, a journalist, even a mother with her own charges, some micromanaging superiors tried to extend their authority over me—demanding that I write my stories a certain way, instructing me on who and what I could focus on or even who I could talk to and what I could talk about. It was not uncommon for me to arrive at a monastery and be sent to a room where I would wait hours for instructions from the superior. I had fifty-year-old women shun my harmless chitchat and inform me that I hadn't received permission to speak. And I was abhorred by the stories older nuns told of abusive and malicious superiors who held them back professionally—such as assigning those who wanted to become doctors to become housekeepers—under the guise of instilling humility.

If it hadn't been for a handful of charismatic leaders, I probably would have ended my monastery immersion much earlier, thinking that becoming a nun required a woman to lose her identity, to subjugate her beliefs and passions. Instead, I was directed to leaders who brought out an intense loyalty from their orders—and from me. They were dynamic, smart women who trusted their sisters' instincts, who encouraged discussion not dominance. And they instilled in me a believer's devotion, a desire to follow them anywhere.

3

POLITICS OF THE HABIT

PASSIONIST NUNS, REDEMPTORISTINES, AND FRANCISCAN SISTERS OF THE MARTYRS OF ST. GEORGE NEAR ST. LOUIS, MISSOURI

"Wearing the habit says you agree with the Holy Father one hundred percent."

—SISTER MARIE MICHELLE DZIUBELA

aint voices floated from behind the faded parlor drapes that separated the nuns from their visitors. On the visitors' side, an armchair was stationed in front of the curtains, like a theater set for an audience of one. I wondered what was waiting on the other side. Then I heard a rustling, a cough.

"Are you ready?" a voice asked.

"Yeah," I said, wondering what kind of preparation I needed.

With a quick thrust, Mother Superior opened the curtains to reveal a steel grille. Behind the bars stood several women, swathed in black and looking like a row of Grim Reapers. Bright eyes radiated from shrouded faces. Beneath the folds of their habits, white arms reached through the bars to shake my hand.

These are the strictly cloistered Passionist Nuns, and their garb—a full-length dress that drags to their toes and a veil that cascades down their backs—was among the most dramatic I saw throughout my journey. These foreboding figures live austere lives; they shave their heads, rise at 2 A.M. every day to pray, whip themselves with small leather lashes to share in the pain of Christ's flogging, practice long-term fasting, give up fruit and vegetables during the summer as penance, and only speak one hour a day. Their suffering, they believe, saves lost souls.

I had ventured into the Passionist Nuns' monastery in Ellisville, Missouri, a suburb of St. Louis, to understand the politics of the habit, to learn how the religious costume has become a symbol of obedience to traditional Church teachings and why it is suddenly in vogue with young nuns.

In the last three decades, most orders have phased out the habit. The Catholic Church still requires sisters to wear a habit as a sign or symbol of their religious vows, but most orders in this country interpret a "habit" as simple clothing and a crucifix or a small pin with their order's insignia. Progressive sisters feel that the long dark frock and veil are outdated medieval fashions that draw attention and separate them from the people they are trying to serve. After all these years of trying to get rid of the habit, few thought the antiquated outfit would actually attract women who were raised in a feminist era.

Yet, the habit has taken on new popularity among conservative younger women who are drawn to orders that have retained the holy dress. For them, the habit is their wedding gown, the garment in which they make their permanent vows to God. They treat it with great reverence, kissing it before they dress each day and praying litanies for each piece. That a dress—usually sewn by hand, and sometimes from a Simplicity A-line pattern—is regarded as sacred might seem odd to those in the secular world. But these sisters believe the habit is a sign of their devotion and obedience to the Catholic Church, the Pope, and God.

Conservative orders, like the Passionists, disapprove of their modern counterparts who long ago gave up their serge wool frocks and starched white wimples. Traditional sisters view these liberated sisters in their jean skirts and white blouses as rebels. Even in the religious world, clothes make the nun: A sister's loyalty to church hierarchy is largely measured by how much material covers her body.

I had expected sisters to disagree on a number of issues, including the infallibility of the Pope, birth control, and whether women should become priests. However, from sisters in the strictest cloisters to the most radical nuns jailed for protesting, the issue that often divides spiritual women the most is the eight-hundred-year-old habit and what it represents.

THE HABIT MEANS OBEDIENCE

Sitting on a hill overlooking a busy highway, the Passionists' brick monastery doesn't look much different from the Baptist funeral home next door. The driveway winds through a field of verdant grass. Statues of Mary and Jesus and various saints greet visitors along the way.

In the visitors' parlor, the walls are institutional green and bare except for a few pictures of men in red robes and tall hats—Catholic cardinals. The hum of the window air conditioner drowns out the roar of traffic. Staring at these solemn women behind steel bars, I knew I'd entered another realm.

"Wearing the habit says you agree with the Holy Father [the Pope] one hundred percent," explained Sister Marie Michelle Dziubela. "Whereas a sister who isn't wearing a habit, you have to wonder."

Her mother superior, Mary Veronica Loring, added, "You don't have to say a word, and people have you pegged. It's such a strong witness."

Theirs is only one of five Passionist monasteries in the United States. Founded in 1771 by an Italian mystic named St. Paul of the Cross, the first Passionist monastery was in Italy. Its first mother superior, Mother Mary Crucified, is now being considered for sainthood. In 1872, the sisters branched out to a house in France and eventually cloisters were founded worldwide. Each monastery is ruled autonomously.

Passionist Nuns take five vows. The first is "to promote devotion to and grateful remembrance of the passion and death of Jesus." The second, third, and fourth are the traditional chastity, poverty, and obedience. The fifth vow, of enclosure, is a pledge to maintain cloistered life. The sisters are papally enclosed, which means no bishop can uncloister them to work as teachers or nurses.

The nuns in Ellisville looked pale and gaunt, their eyes ringed with black circles the summer day I visited. Still these highly educated women laughed, told jokes, and poked fun at slow-praying sisters or sisters who fell asleep during vigils. Their favorite targets, though, were sisters who didn't wear habits.

"There was this nun," began thirty-seven-year-old Sister Marie Michelle in her Long Island accent, "who recently came out of the habit. She was wearing this short dress, and she said to the priest: 'I guess you didn't know I had pretty red hair?' And the priest responded: 'No, Sister, I didn't. I also didn't know you had varicose veins.'" Marie Michelle burst out laughing with her sisters.

Obedience for these women is equivalent to self-sacrifice, even suffering. When they were searching for an order, they wanted one where they could give their all, or "go all the way." Part of that quest was finding an order that retained the full regalia.

"I wanted something more austere, something more penitential, something more to sacrifice for Jesus," explained Mother Mary Veronica. "I wanted it to hurt a little bit. I know that sounds masochistic, but that's the only way to express how I felt."

In 1980, Mother Mary Veronica was a thirty-two-year-old American Airlines stewardess when her romance of ten years fizzled; she decided becoming a nun would allow her to spend her life with God.

"I thought: Is this all there is—me flying the rest of my days? For about two weeks, I was kind of in a limbo. I didn't want to fly anymore but didn't know what way the Lord wanted me to go."

One night, unable to sleep, Mother sat up in bed and cried out, "Lord, what do you want me to do?" Suddenly she had a vision of herself dressed as a nun. She liked what she saw and immediately fell asleep.

Mother spent several months praying and visiting different orders.

When she visited the Passionists for the first time and saw their habit—a floor-length tunic with buttons from the neck to the waist, a long veil that covers the head and extends down to the thighs, an elongated strand of rosary beads attached to a handmade leather belt, and sandals—she was smitten. The only turnoff, she conceded, was a black-and-white plastic pin the sisters wear over their hearts that looks like a name tag: "I thought it was very tacky."

The habit Mother saw, though, wasn't even as severe as the order's original dress. As a result of Vatican II's mandate to modernize, the Passionist Nuns chose a lighter wash-and-wear fabric to replace their woolen habits. They also shortened their veils. The original veil dragged to the ground; the extra material was used to cover their faces whenever a workman came to make repairs. The sisters would pull their veils over their foreheads and walk around like blind women, feeling their way around the monastery.

The Passionists have never had the wimple around their heads, as many other cloistered orders do; instead they wear a kind of skullcap. The founders didn't want the sisters wearing wimples because they are quite ornate pieces of fabric that are starched and hard to maintain. Their simple skullcap is intended to imply poverty. One reason the sisters shave their hair is because it's easier to keep the skullcap on a bald head. What's more, a bald head is cooler in the summer, and the sisters only have air-conditioning in their visiting parlor.

Despite modifications, the aspect that especially attracted Mother about the Passionists' outfit was that no hair shows from under the veil. "It indicated the type of lifestyle that the sisters lived here. I think every person in the world, whether they believe it or not, yearns for God and wants to sacrifice for God."

Mother lived with the sisters for ten days, following the sisters' rigid schedule. There were no cushy chairs, no carpeting, no mirrors, no drapes. Sisters shared a bathroom. Her room was a bare cell with a single bed. It was perfect: a place sheltered from the world so she could focus on working her way to God.

Passionist Sisters (back row, left to right: Mother Mary Veronica Loring, Sister Marie Michelle Dziubela; front row, left to right: Sister Mary Elizabeth Brungardt, Sister Teresita Kisko

When Mother received her habit, it was the beginning of an intensely humid summer. "The next day I had to clean up the john in the novitiate, and I'm dressed like this," she said looking down at her flowing black dress. "I was in my wedding dress, and I had to clean the toilets. It was so hot. I felt like I just wanted to take off my coat. It's penitential. There's no doubt about it."

After taking her first vows, her long blond hair was shaved off. "If you think in terms of what the world values, for women it's hair. For us, being countercultural, a sign of contradiction, we get rid of the hair."

Curious about what she looked like, Mother gazed into the closest thing she had to a mirror in her room—a framed religious picture. In the dark part of the glass, she saw a dim reflection that reminded her of a marine; so she started to mimic what she saw: "Har, Har, Har," she growled in her deepest voice.

The seriousness of the event wasn't lost on Mother, though. Having saved her hair shavings in a metal can, she planned to offer them up as a sort of "holocaust." One night she took the can outside, to the base of a religious statue. The wind was blowing, and she couldn't ignite the strands. Frustrated, she took the hair back inside the monastery and threw it into the furnace. "It may not have been too romantic or idealistic," she said, laughing. "But it got burned."

Shaving their hair is akin to a sorority hazing: It demonstrates how much they want to be a part of this family, how much vanity they are willing to sacrifice. The initial shearing is such a dramatic experience that each sister has a vivid memory of seeing her bald head for the first time.

Sister Mary Elizabeth Brungardt, aged thirty and the newest member, actually looked forward to getting her head shaved. She'd been having a hard time wearing her veil in the heat. Elizabeth wore her long red hair in braids. Beneath her veil, her scalp sweated profusely. After her shave, she looked in a small hand mirror and was stunned. *I look like Sinead O'Connor,* she thought, her eyes widening with horror.

When Elizabeth first considered becoming a nun in her early twenties, she envisioned herself looking like her fifth grade teacher, the one with the long black habit and lace-up boots. She visited the Passionists after seeing a picture of the them kneeling in front of the Blessed Sacrament, their hands outstretched, forming crosses with their bodies.

The thought of being cloistered was overwhelming, but Elizabeth loved the sisters' habits. Still, she questioned how as a woman in her twenties she could live life cut off from the world. Her faith that God had lured her to the monastery helped her overcome her doubts. She believed God planted the appeal early, starting with her elementary school teacher.

"God is using the habit as a drawing card," she said. "The selling point is that it's the first visual."

A BLACK WEDDING DRESS

Sister Marie Michelle believes that her first encounter with a habited nun inspired her to enter religious life. Standing on a kneeler in church while her mother prayed beside her, four-year-old Marie Michelle spotted a nun sitting in front of them. She leaned over the pew, grabbed the bottom of the nun's veil, and picked it up to see what was underneath. Horrified, her mother seized her hand.

"Don't touch the nun!" her mother ordered. "She's married to Jesus."

That was all it took.

"I found my vocation at that moment," said Sister Marie Michelle, a tall woman with sparkling blue eyes. Even without makeup and after years of less than five hours of sleep a night, her face glowed. If she had hair, it would have been thick and black.

"In my teens, I liked the idea of being a missionary," Michelle explained. "However, when I came to a moment of truth in my life, I realized if I ever went to Africa, and I fed and healed the suffering, I could only help people with these two hands," she said, holding up her pale palms. "That is a limited number of people. And yet, if I gave up everything to Him, I could touch the whole world."

It wasn't until her late twenties that Marie Michelle sent away for information about various orders and started getting piles of nun mail. She kept it all in a huge shopping bag underneath her bed and would periodically go through the pamphlets.

One day the Passionists Nuns' brochure arrived in the mail. "So I opened it up, and I saw three smiling nuns on a staircase; and they were in full habits. I said, 'Gee, they're in black. That's my favorite color.' I was Gothic before there was such a thing as Gothic. My friends always joked about me, saying I would get married in a black wedding gown. And I did."

At the time, Marie Michelle was most serious about the Carmelites, an order known for its severe lifestyle. When she visited the St. Louis Passionists, though, and saw that they chant the Divine Office, practice penance, maintain silence, and pray matins at two each morning, she knew where she was meant to spend the rest of her life.

She quit nursing school and entered the order in 1992 at the age of thirty-two.

"I know that if I had not become a nun, I would probably be just like my mom and be married with eight kids somewhere," she said. "It was a sacrifice for me to give up having my own family, because I had opportunities. I had a chance to have a nice husband and a nice house in the suburbs, a dog, and a bunch of kids. And I thought hard about that; I think that would have been an obstacle to me. I now see my love for black as a premonition for becoming a sister."

At her profession—the wedding-like ceremony that marks a sister's entrance into the order—Michelle, like the other candidates, wore a crown of thorns and carried a cross on her shoulders. She wore the thorns for three days to mark the time Christ was in the grave, signifying the death of her old life. She was also given two new names; the first one was required to be some form of Mary.

"You're aware that He's chosen you to be His bride," Michelle said of the ceremony. "I am forever different now. When I get up in the morning, there's only one thing on the hook waiting for me to put on. I don't have to decide what I'm going to wear that day. If you don't wear this, then you don't wear nothin'! 'Cause you don't have nothin'!"

Most mornings when Michelle rises, she kisses her veil before she puts it on and prays litanies for each article of clothing.

"This is our wedding ring, our wedding dress," she said holding her black habit. "It reminds us that we're married, why we came, why we stay, why we will probably be laid out in this dress, be buried in it."

Michelle takes the symbolism of marriage to Christ even further. If sisters are dragging to make 2 A.M. prayers before the Blessed Sacrament, she tells them to hurry so they can see their husband. "Jesus is waiting for us," she says. "He's all alone down there, and He wants us. He can't wait until morning to see us."

SAVING SOULS

After Vatican II, most religious orders dispensed with the medieval custom of plenary indulgences, prayers by the devout that are believed to retrieve souls from purgatory. But each day, the Passionist Nuns bow before the Blessed Sacrament, the ornate box where the blessed communion wafers are stored, recite the Creed, and pray the Our Father and the Hail Mary for lost souls.

"They [lost souls] died without making the right choice, and there's still a debt to be paid," explained Sister Marie Michelle. "I call purgatory the spiritual showers. They aren't exactly clean enough to go before God. So, we believe we can gain a plenary indulgence, which is a total remission of the time due in purgatory."

Despite getting only four and half hours of sleep, some sisters said they look forward to the 2 A.M. office. "I kind of consider that my kids need me. Kids being souls," said Elizabeth. Mother Veronica agreed: "We're mothers of souls. Since we can't be physical mothers, all that energy of being a woman is directed at being mothers for everyone."

After the 2 A.M. prayers, the sisters line up in the hall and cover the windows so no light gets in. Then one sister leads prayers by chanting and the rest respond. They pray and meditate on Christ's suffering while lifting up their habits in the back and slapping a leather lash across their bare buttocks. They do not wear underwear when they practice discipline.

"It's not something that's sexual or weird," explained Sister Elizabeth.

"The purpose really is to keep us humble," Mother Mary Veronica said. "You get used to it, but in the beginning it can be humiliating."

The sisters believe that by uniting their suffering with Christ's, not just the discipline, but all the sacrifices in their lives, they can deliver sinners from purgatory. Sacrifice is a part of the sisters' daily lives. They revel in it; they wear their sufferings like a soldier's medals. The more they agonize, the better nuns they are and the more chalk marks on their lists of saved lives.

"We're offering ourselves as penance for those who aren't faithful and don't remember Jesus. Those who have quit the Church," said Sister Marie Michelle. "We offer it with His sufferings, and it is as infinite as Jesus' sufferings. We're sure our sufferings reach out to the entire world."

While the Passionists are among the few orders I found that still practice physical discipline, their self-flagellation isn't supposed to break the skin, which is why the orders' founders insisted the sisters strike their bare buttocks instead of the more delicate shoulders.

"It stings," Mother explained. "Passion means to suffer."

I couldn't help but envision these sisters as some sort of religious superheroes who, draped in black cloth, have mystical powers to move souls into the everlasting. I wasn't diminishing their sacrifices. Yet it seemed such a calculated exchange of good for evil. Was God the Great Accountant adding up the sisters' penances and prayers and applying them to the debt of unworthy souls in purgatory? Most sisters outside the Passionists told me they didn't believe in plenary indulgences. Many are embarrassed by this ancient tradition; Martin Luther had objected to the selling of indulgences.

Though indulgences have fallen out of favor in modern times, Pope

John Paul II revived the practice in 2000. Catholics could gain a plenary indulgence for themselves or others through confession, communion, and prayer as well as doing a specific act of love or penance, such as making pilgrimages to certain churches in Rome or refraining from smoking or drinking for a day.

I'd heard so many nuns say that life is penitential enough without taking on additional suffering. With so much pain in the world, I found it hard to believe that a loving God would want us purposely to suffer. Was that true obedience? And what did it mean for all those who were in agony from disease or poverty? Did their suffering save their own souls or others'? Was the sisters' suffering of a higher caliber simply because they chose it in the name of religion? Despite my doubt about penances and indulgences, I couldn't deny that the Passionists seemed to glean some mysterious strength, even happiness, from their extreme asceticism.

THE HABIT AS POLITICAL SYMBOL

No one really knows exactly how the habit came to be. The first piece of clothing nuns wore in Europe was a veil, in the third century. A veil was required of married women, and since nuns were considered brides of Christ, they were also expected to don a headpiece. By the fifth century, monks and many nuns started wearing black; it was easier to keep clean and indicated both mourning and sobriety.

Medieval historian Jo Ann McNamara, who traced two millennia of nuns in her book *Sisters in Arms,* says that nun outfits were possibly women's first uniforms. In the early days, she explained, many nuns came from nobility and bishops pressured them to give up their fashionable clothes and adopt more humble attire.

"Moralist writers complained a lot about women who have consecrated themselves to God and are running around the city dressed in the latest fashions and going to parties and generally living quite a wonderful life without being bothered by a husband," McNamara told me.

The traditional long black habit that most people associate with nuns didn't come about until the twelfth century—a time when many orders were just forming. The wimple, the tight headpiece that some nuns still wear around their heads, traces to twelfth-century fashion. But when wimples became passé, nuns continued to wear the taut headdress. Eventually, various orders distinguished themselves from one another by the style and colors of their dress. The Benedictines wore black, for example, and the Franciscans wore brown.

The biggest threat to the habit came during the French Revolution. That's when revolutionaries, who believed nuns lived frivolous and idle lives, took over convents and prohibited sisters from wearing habits. The move was an attempt to abolish the aristocracy and the Church's clerics, many of whom were part of the upper classes and devoted to the monarchy. By this time, though, nuns had become attached to their habits, which they considered a symbol of their commitment to God. In the ultimate protest, some wore them to the guillotine.

The most dramatic change to the garment occurred in the late 1960s. Before then, virtually all orders wore some type of distinctive garb, many of them involving great swaths of cloth dragging to the floor—so as not to show the ankles—and tight starched wimples. Some religious institutions had seen their original habits' simplicity replaced over the decades by complicated outfits. The time the sisters had gained by not styling their hair and applying makeup now was used to care for an elaborate dress. For example, the Daughters of Charity, made popular by the television series *The Flying Nun,* wore a simple sunbonnet in the 1600s that by the twentieth century had evolved into a starched monstrosity that made the sisters look like they had sprouted wings from their heads.

Between the late 1960s and the early 1980s, nuns experimented with their dress and customs. Some orders raised hemlines from the ankles to the calves. For others, a simple cross became their habit. Younger nuns—those who had lived under the old regime for only ten or fifteen years—usually pressed for a more modern and simpler attire. These are the same nuns who now are generally appalled that young women today want to wear the medieval garb they pushed to abandon.

Most nuns today feel the attention surrounding the habit emphasizes the exterior trappings of religious life. They believe the habit is a relic, an outrageous costume that draws attention to the person wearing it and not to God. Some call it the "holier than thou" dress and a young girl's romantic fantasy. Feminist sisters are embarrassed and even angry that some sisters still wear "the penguin suit." They believe the continued use of the habit in comic books and movies like *Sister Act* and *The Dangerous Lives of Altar Boys* perpetuates the image of the nun as simpleminded, childlike, and silly.

But young nuns say the habit has its own allure. Research at Georgetown University shows that traditional orders that have retained the habit are attracting on average three times more women than progressive orders whose sisters do not wear the habit. While it's hard to say exactly why someone would choose one order over another, and religious women are hardly preoccupied by fashion and clothes, the habit is often part of the equation.

Some sisters have changed convents and moved across the country to be with women who wear more traditional outfits. Sister Mary Regina, a fifty-one-year-old Redemptoristine, was in her second year as a sister when I visited her order outside St. Louis. Regina's graying black hair was teased into a bouffant over her forehead and covered by a white veil on the top and sides. She wore the red skirt and vest and white shirt of her order that is unique in the field of religious dress. The red symbolizes the love of Christ and the white symbolizes purity. Sister Regina transferred to her order in Lagoria, Missouri, from another Redemptoristine monastery in New York because, she said, in Lagoria all the sisters wear habits and veils and at her old monastery some of them didn't.

"I wouldn't want to be a nun if I couldn't wear it," she said. "It's a sign of your consecration to God. You're a visible sign if someone sees you."

But few people see cloistered sisters like Sister Mary Regina, who venture out only for doctor or dentist appointments. The sisters are even secluded in their chapel. A sign warns visitors not to get too close: *We have an electric alarm system. If you pass beyond the communion rail, it will activate the alarm.*

A GROWING ORDER WEARS THE HABIT

The Franciscan Sisters of the Martyrs of St. George in Alton, Illinois— just across the Mississippi from St. Louis—are illustrative of orders that are growing these days. They retain the habit and all the pomp, circumstance, and romanticism associated with the dress and its traditions. Each year, the sisters hold an elaborate ceremony in which young nuns publicly profess their vows and take on symbols of their commitment, including a new name, a blessed habit, and a wedding ring.

On a humid August day, four hundred people, including forty-three bishops, crammed into St. Mary's Church overlooking the Mississippi. As

Postulant Nicole (Anselma) Belongea marching into the chapel along with other postulants

the organist played "Ave Maria," sunlight filtered through the cathedral's towering stained-glass windows and lighted on the altar's pink marble steps.

Within a few minutes, twenty-year-old Nicole Belongea and six other young postulants marched up the aisle carrying slender white candles. A wide smile spread across Nicole's soap-scrubbed face as she spotted her parents seated along with her brother and five sisters, their spouses, and children. She wondered what her family thought of her hair. Her brown tresses had been shorn the day before, leaving strands of less than a finger-length. Nicole kept a long lock for her mother, a gift she would present with tears. Nicole wasn't nervous really, but excited, eager to get through the event. She privately worried she wouldn't turn the right way or bow at the right time.

When Archbishop Agostino Cacciavillan, the Pope's own U.S. ambassador, called Nicole to the altar, he blessed her habit and veil, placed them in her hands, and said, "The religious habit is the garment of your salvation."

The postulants clutched their veils and habits to their chests and hurried to a back room, where they slipped off their black jumpers and white blouses and put on their habits: calf-length, long-sleeved black dresses with pleats in the front and secret pockets in the petticoats. The young women stared at each other.

"You look so holy!" Nicole told one of the women, then giggled. Their veils felt awkward at first, and they reminded each other not to get "veil neck"—when a sister stiffens and won't turn her head for fear she'll lose her veil.

As the postulants reappeared in their new habits, the crowd craned their necks and murmured to each other. Several women in the audience wiped their eyes with wadded tissues. Others wept openly. It was the last day anyone would call Nicole by her birth name. Dressed in her somber black dress and veil, Nicole was anointed as Sister Mary Anselma, the name of the order's foundress. She had been looking forward to this day since she was sixteen. For the new Sister Mary Anselma, the ceremony was God's way of clothing her and giving her a new identity.

After Nicole and the six other postulants received their garments, four novices made their temporary vows. As a sign of their profession, the novices were given black veils to replace their white ones. Then five junior sisters—also known as temporary professed sisters—made their final and permanent vows—lying prostrate before the altar, their habits fanning out at their sides like angels' wings. They were given large crucifixes and rosaries; then the archbishop held each sister's hand and blessed a gold wedding band before sliding it onto her finger, looking as though he were marrying each of the sisters.

While most habited orders today are cloistered, the Alton Franciscans are an active, apostolic order whose sisters work in ministries from nursing to teaching to managing retirement homes for priests. The majority of apostolic or active orders in this country long ago abandoned wearing the habit because they often work outside the convent and believe the long dresses are impractical, especially for those who actively work with the poor and perform manual labor, such as cleaning and cooking. Others feel the habit separates them from those they are trying to serve and reinforces stereotypes of sisters as special and more religious or devout than lay people.

While most active orders are struggling to attract one or two sisters a year, the Franciscan Martyrs have been attracting up to ten women a year. In the last ten years, they have added more than forty-six sisters. In contrast, another Franciscan order just across the Mississippi in St. Louis gave up the habit long ago and hasn't had a single woman enter and stay in more than fifteen years. The average age of the St. Louis Franciscan order is seventy-four years old, while the average age of the Franciscan Martyrs is forty-three. Forty percent of the Franciscan Martyrs are new recruits, mostly conservative young women, many of whom told me they wouldn't even have considered an order that didn't wear the habit. For them, the habit is the uniform of a growing order.

UNDRESSING THE NUN

The habit, and all its intricacies, seems almost as complex as religious life. The habit is never just a single dress, but a layer of petticoats and slips, one material laid over another. Surprisingly, most nuns I met were more than eager to unravel the mystery behind their dress, peeling down to their underskirts and, in the case of the Passionists, exposing their bald heads.

At the Franciscan Martyrs, Sister Mary Dolorosa Roy, aged twenty-three, happily opened her habit and showed me the various snaps and hidden Velcro pockets where she, like other sisters, keeps treats for kids, rosaries, a cross, and other assorted items. She often amazes teenagers she works with by whipping her hand into an unseen pocket to retrieve a pen.

Dolorosa and other young Franciscan Martyrs insist they are much more comfortable in habits than they were in the jeans and T-shirts they once wore. They claim they can play any sport in a habit: basketball, tennis, volleyball. One sister reportedly jogs in her habit.

The Franciscan Sisters of the Martyrs of St. George wear black habits on feast days and for mass but bluish gray habits when they work. The two-piece dress has a front scapular that attaches at the waist and pleats that hang down the front, hiding a large pocket underneath. The other piece reaches to the midcalves and has a white collar. Under the veil is an invisible crown that gives shape to the top of the veil. The veil, which extends to the midriff in the back, is attached by Velcro. Underneath, the sisters wear slips with large pockets.

"One of the reasons you become a sister is that you want to bring God into the world," said Dolorosa, giggling as she nervously unsnapped her habit. No longer called by her given name of Tina, Sister Dolorosa, from Sudbury, Ontario, in Canada, was in her third nun year, having entered when she was twenty-one years old. She is a chunky-cheeked woman with dark hair and eyes whose enthusiasm could charm an ardent cynic. "When people see you in the habit," she said, "it can also make them think of God in a situation where they usually would not. It opens the door to conversation."

That's certainly true for children and teenage girls who often approach the sisters with a torrent of questions: How do they keep the veils on their heads? Do they sleep with their veils on? Discussing the habit often leads to other questions about religious life.

"It kind of takes away some of the mystery that they have about religious life," explained Dolorosa.

The habit can also push people away.

"People have this image of a sister being on a pedestal and not approachable, not human," Dolorosa said. "Like we're already angels," added another twenty-three-year-old sister.

The young Franciscan Martyrs said it took several years of wearing the habit before they felt like real nuns. Since they don't have full-length mirrors in their rooms, they were often startled when they saw their reflections in a window or sliding glass door: "I still stop and think: I'm a sister," said Sister Dolorosa feeling the weight of her statement. "I belong to Jesus Christ."

I began to think that habited sisters keep secret handbooks in their gigantic pockets. They all seemed to describe their attitudes and attachments to the habit in the same way. They regard their dress as a walking billboard for their beliefs. Wearing it reminds them they have given up everything—even their own clothes.

One of the "older" Franciscan Martyrs, a forty-four-year-old woman, takes the habit icon even further. "We stand out for God, not for ourselves. We are to be exemplars of holiness. We're to show the rest of the Church how to live a holy life. The habit is a reminder: We represent God."

Her comments seemed to conflict with what other sisters—both habited and not—had told me. Many sisters detest the idea that nuns are more pious or holier than lay people. Several sisters I'd met said they need the discipline of religious life to maintain the right thoughts or to make time for prayer. Being a nun, they said, is something they do for their own pursuit of spirituality—not as examples for others.

Listening to progressive and traditional sisters debate the habit left me conflicted. Progressive sisters scoff at their habited colleagues as unenlightened women who maintain devotions and rituals to a medieval costume. Habited nuns, on the other hand, insist that they are the ones who have chosen the more humble and simple attire. I wondered whether some sisters resent or even envy the attention the habit brings their traditional counterparts. It seemed unfair that modern sisters who only wear their order's insignia on little dress pins don't get the same recognition. It is as if they have been cheated out of their portion of public respect by not drawing attention to themselves and the sacrifices they have made.

Sometimes it was hard to comprehend that these sisters have taken virtually the same vows and, for the most part, given up the same things. Yet each side points to the other as though they are somehow lacking in spiritual maturity or obedience. It seemed impious that women who have committed their lives to the spiritual could still place so much emphasis on something so material. In truth it isn't the habit itself but what the dress represents that causes so much commotion: an icon of godliness, a stereotypical image of holiness.

While some elaborate habits are impractical, many are stylish, maybe even glamorous with their long sweeping veils. What woman wouldn't want to wear her wedding dress more than once? And let's face it: If we gave up men, sex, money, and our independence, wouldn't we at least want some kind of special dress? Wouldn't we want that recognition, that status of a consecrated woman? Even married women wear wedding rings and use courtesy titles to proclaim their marital commitment.

Nuns whose orders have given up the habit often adopt their own personal "habit," usually simple clothing in black, navy, or white. It is a matter of practicality. They simply don't want to be troubled keeping up with the latest styles or wasting time trying on this or that outfit. Besides, they reason, habits originally weren't meant to draw attention but to reinforce a simple lifestyle, to dress as the common woman, not the noblesse.

Many sisters had worn the habit for forty or fifty years when they took it off and don't feel confident enough to pick out fashionable clothes. Other sisters insist on wearing only donated clothing.

I could see the value in dressing simply. Though my color of choice for years had been black, after months of living off and on with the nuns, I found myself adopting my own sort of everyday "habit": black jeans and white button-down shirts. It was a simple but casually classic outfit. I didn't have to think every morning about what I would be wearing. My closet was filled with black and white. To me, this was practical.

As I pared down my personal style, I began to wonder if, like Sister Marie Michelle, my growing predilection for black and simple clothing wasn't some sort of premonition. Could it suggest that I had a vocation, that my attraction to nuns was more than curiosity? And if this was so, would I want to join an order that retained a habit?

At times I felt that if I were to become a nun I would want to signify that my devotion as a religious person, my faith, was so determined, so strong, that I had given up everything, including my own clothes. I completely understood sisters like Elizabeth Brungardt, who had given up her profession and sought a community where she could "go all the way." Like her, I wasn't one to make halfhearted commitments. When I married, I took on not only the responsibility of my husband but also his two children. In my own professional life, I didn't question personal sacrifice, long hours, or demanding assignments. Covering a breaking story, I often worked around the clock, sometimes forgoing food, sleep, and friends. Why would it be any different if I were to become a nun? To me, habited nuns represented religious type-A personalities, women who were intently focused on their mission. To them, the habit was simply indicative of a larger commitment.

But to me, it signified total obedience, an aspect of religious life I was having trouble accepting. The orders that retain the habit seemed to require complete devotion to Church practices and theology and there didn't appear to be much room for questioning, for debate. Habited orders often are the most authoritarian, the ones with the strictest hierarchy, the most severe names, like Her Reverend Mother Superior. So it wasn't so much a question of the habit, but of what wearing it required. It was a question that would continue to consume me on my journey.

4

SISTERS WITH ATTITUDE

NOTRE DAME, MERCY, AND FRANCISCAN SISTERS IN
CHICAGO, ILLINOIS

*"I have to be obedient to the superiors of my order, but it doesn't mean
I have to be obedient to the larger orders of the Church."*

—SISTER MARGARET TRAXLER

Low moans came from the formal living room. We rushed through the marble foyer and into the dingy yellow room. Sister Margaret Traxler, a radical feminist who has taken on the Vatican and publicly calls the Pope a misogynist, was sprawled facedown on the floor.

My husband lifted Margaret onto the couch. Her face and hair were drenched with sweat; her blouse was partially unbuttoned, exposing her bra.

"Should we call an ambulance?" I asked the woman who managed Margaret's homeless shelter across the street. She had unlocked the front door when Margaret hadn't answered our knocking.

"No," the manager said, shaking her head and frowning as she bent over Margaret, smoothing her hair and wiping her face. "I think she's all right."

"I could come back another day," I offered.

Embarrassed, Margaret ordered my husband and me into her office down the hall while she composed herself.

For months I had been looking forward to meeting Sister Margaret, a woman progressive sisters refer to with the same reverence as feminists speak of Gloria Steinem or Betty Friedan. Now I worried that I had come too late.

In her midseventies, Margaret is a legend: She marched in civil rights protests, campaigned for the controversial Equal Rights Amendment, founded her own women's organization, and headed a women's prison ministry. For the past eleven years she has run homeless shelters for women and children and been called one of the most significant social workers in Chicago's Catholic Church history. Margaret is most known, though, for signing a pro-choice ad in the *New York Times* that forever branded her, in the eyes of the official Church, as an outspoken and dangerous rebel. The Vatican even threatened to expel her from her order, the School Sisters of Notre Dame. It was only after religious communities stood up for her and other sisters who signed the ad that the Vatican softened its stance.

Drawn to the shelter by Margaret's fascinating story, I wanted to know why feminist nuns like her and those she employs are still part of the Catholic Church. How can they remain part of an institution that they fervently believe subjugates women?

What I would discover in Chicago is how much the feminist movement inside the Church mirrors the larger secular feminist movement. Margaret is the grand dame of feminist nuns who persistently battles the hierarchy, at one point believing that the Church would change in her lifetime. But when that didn't happen, the generations that followed took note and are more prudent in what they challenge publicly. Margaret's successors instead prefer to ignore the Church and its male leaders and privately pursue their own course. Both generations believe that their vows of obedience require them to act on their consciences and not mindlessly follow every Vatican edict. Yet, Margaret's conscience compels her to vehemently speak out, while her successors tailor their religious lives so as not to include aspects of the Church they believe are corrupt and incapable of change.

Margaret's cramped office, overlooking the street and the red peeling shelter doors, reveals her iconoclastic character. Small stacks of papers litter the floor, the gray file cabinets, chairs, and her wooden desk. There is a large Star of David with a cross inside: Golda Meir awarded Margaret the Jewish Medal of Honor in 1972 for starting an interreligious conference on Soviet Jewry. On a shelf behind Margaret's desk is a Russian icon of the Mother of God. Next to it is the *Woman's Bible Commentary* and a book denouncing the death penalty. On the wall over these hangs an old painting of the Jefferson Memorial.

When Margaret finally emerged, she walked slowly, her spindly legs straining to carry her dense torso. She seemed worn down. Yet her strong will exuded from her intense blue eyes, her jutting chin, and the straight thin line of her lips. Her determined expression warns strangers: This is not a nun to mess with.

"I've been a feminist with Betty Friedan since 1963," she announced, seemingly gaining strength as she slid behind her desk. "What young woman today would attach herself to the Church that is so male chauvinistic? She would have to be weak in the head."

She railed against priests and bishops for never getting out from their "marble palaces" to care for the poor. Margaret stared at us wide-eyed, perhaps looking for some sign of shock on our faces, daring us to disagree.

She apologized to my husband for criticizing men but continued brazenly to condemn various Catholic leaders. My husband sat in the corner and smiled; he was as enamored with her as I was. Margaret had insisted I not come alone because the Englewood neighborhood, in which her homeless shelter is located, suffers from one of the highest crime rates in the nation. As it turned out, her unnecessary fear for my safety had proved fortuitous in securing her own welfare.

"A priest has no power, a bishop has no power, a cardinal has no power," Margaret continued. "They might have money, but they can't change that poor group in Rome. They're so old they look down at the ground, and they never look up: the Curia. They could already be embedded in monuments for all the work they're doing."

I was stunned by her accusations but concealed my feelings. At the time, I had never heard a nun so openly critical of the Church's inner circle of power, the men who controlled the Vatican. I reasoned that the Church probably couldn't do much to her at this point. The truth is Margaret has long grown accustomed to speaking her mind: She believes she has a moral obligation to challenge evil wherever she finds it.

"Just because I took a vow of obedience doesn't mean that I can't say what I think," she said. "I'm not a puppet. I have my own free will. I have to be obedient to the superiors of my order, but it doesn't mean I have to be obedient to the larger orders of the Church."

Like many progressive nuns, Margaret believes the modern Catholic Church should be defined by its six billion members, not the few hundred men who rule it. Her prescription for staying in the Church is simple: She keeps an "esthetic distance."

"You don't go and say: 'Father, bless me.' You don't contribute to the institutional Church. I give to the women and the poor."

Indeed, Margaret has taken from the institutional Church to fund her mission. In 1989, Margaret convinced the late Cardinal Joseph Bernardin to let her convert the former St. Carthage parish church, rectory, and school into an overnight shelter for women and children. The shelter offers dormitory-style housing: four former elementary classrooms house ten beds each, plus baby cribs. The staff consists of nine black women plus the sisters and a social worker. The shelter has no maintenance staff, no janitors, no housekeepers. Other than the nurse and the doctor who come once a week, there are few volunteers.

Three years after starting the Maria Shelter, Margaret begged Bernardin for another property, a former convent also on the South Side, to create Casa Notre Dame, a long-term shelter where ten women can live for up to two years while working or attending school.

Now semiretired, Margaret spends most days at her desk, often watching the women coming and going from the shelter. She raises money by writing grant proposals and soliciting donations. She manages the shelters' finances but leaves the day-to-day details to nuns who are more comfortable dealing with the problems of the poor and handicapped than lobbying for women's causes.

At night, the sisters who run the shelter return to their apartments. But Margaret continues to live alone in the former rectory, a massive two-story brick building that has been burglarized three times in recent years. On the most recent occasion, the shelter's staff caught the burglar as he pushed a loot-filled shopping cart down the street.

AN ICON IN DECLINE

A year later, I returned to visit Margaret. Standing in the rectory hallway, she seemed smaller, shriveled. She hugged the walls as she shuffled from the hallway to her office. At her desk, she had a hard time turning her body, and it looked like she might fall. I offered her my hand, but she shooed me away and ordered me to sit down. Even her voice seemed less powerful. Her face was droopy, less defined, her eyes more watery.

Still, her spirit hadn't weakened. She insists on keeping her position as chief executive of the Institute of Women Today, the secular, nonprofit organization of Protestant, Jewish, and Catholic women she founded in 1974. The institute owns both shelters.

Margaret has acquiesced in getting help, though. She depends more on her assistant, Maureen Boyd, a Sister of Mercy who has organized Margaret's office, compiling into computer files the bits of information Margaret once kept in scattered piles, including fundraising materials she "filed" in a laundry basket. In the past Margaret would spend weeks writing contributors thank-you letters by hand. Now Maureen prints out thank-you notes in bulk. Margaret has also accepted another Mercy sister as a roommate; so now two women live in the cavernous rectory.

Although she has fallen several times, Margaret refuses to use a walker. She no longer leaves the rectory to lunch with the shelters' sisters and staff. She also is driving less, ever since a semitrailer sideswiped her on the highway. Yet, she refuses to retire to her order's mother house in Mankato, Minnesota.

"The mother house is when you need an elevator," Margaret explained. "When a sister's health is so deteriorated. That's not where I want to go. I want to be where God wants me to be, where He calls me to be. I don't feel I need anything special. I just see myself as a poor old dame, a cool old potato."

She stays connected with people through the telephone and mail, writing her biological sister in Arizona once a day. By the afternoon, Margaret is exhausted and has to nap. A former English teacher with a master's in Chaucer and Shakespeare, Margaret spends her evenings reading literature and listening to classical music.

"If I died now, all the people who would take my part have been filled," Margaret volunteered. "I'm ready to quit. I'm not going to quit. But I'll know when the time comes."

I was baffled that this strong, independent woman, who is unwilling to let anyone help her walk, was admitting her own mortality. It would become a central focus in our conversations during the next two months while I stayed in the Chicago area observing Margaret and the quietly radical sisters who would become her successors.

BUILDING THEIR OWN CHURCH

The Maria Shelter had only been open two years when Mary Schneider, a School Sister of St. Francis, became its resident counselor in 1991. At first it was difficult, she said, because she was an organizer and the shelter was cluttered and chaotic. Her inclusive management style conflicted with Margaret's, who was known for being temperamental and for leading by intimidation.

Shortly after Mary arrived, Margaret fired two people during a staff meeting, one woman for arguing with her.

"From my perspective, it was very inappropriate," Mary said.

If Margaret had ever dressed her down in front of staff or disrespected her opinion, Mary would have left, she said. But Margaret revered Mary—that was evident.

In 1994, Margaret asked Mary to become shelter director. The shelter had run through a number of directors in a short time and needed stability. An acknowledged introvert who can appear distant and standoffish—especially among the often effusive shelter residents—Mary preferred to remain the psychologist. Yet, she could see that the shelter needed leadership, so she agreed to take on the additional role.

"Margaret backed off from this place after I came in as director," Mary remembered. "As she aged, she turned more and more over to me."

In contrast to Margaret, who ruled more by force, Mary leads by gentle persuasion. Even when she encounters drug dealers hanging around the shelter, she doesn't order them off the property. Mary simply grabs trash bags and begins picking up garbage, silently reminding the men that the property where they are loitering and dealing drugs belongs to someone who isn't afraid to face them.

"Cleaning up is my way of chasing away the drug dealers," Mary said. "They can't stand it."

One day, a staff member informed Mary that several men were leaning on the playground equipment out front.

"There must have been ten to twelve men, not kids, in the street," Mary recounted. "There were three sitting on Margaret's steps. Of course, they see me coming. They don't turn. They just all start moving en masse down the street."

Eventually, a few drug dealers joined her in picking up trash; as soon as she was gone, they could resume their transactions. But Mary didn't stop at the shelter property. She bravely made her way across the street to the rectory and the property next door; then she turned the corner to

Vincennes Avenue, a major thoroughfare for both traffic and drugs. The next day the drug dealers had a message for her: Trash bags were hung along four city blocks designating their turf.

Though Mary and Margaret often disagree about the shelter, the discussions are mostly collegial. One time, while leading visitors on a tour around the shelter, Mary commented that she and Margaret talked through their differences. Afterward, Margaret approached Mary privately and said, "But, Mary, we never disagree."

"She saw us not disagreeing because we didn't get into shouting matches," explained Mary, who wears her flaming red hair cropped close to her thin, pale face.

After thirty years as a sister, Mary remains committed to her order, but she no longer tolerates some aspects of the institutional Church. Around 1980, for example, she stopped going to church regularly. She still attends her order's celebrations, which often include a mass, and if she is with her parents, she attends without complaint.

"I don't come out and say: 'I don't go to church.' We talk about everything around that," she said of her parents. "They're suspicious, but they don't ask me directly. I don't make any bones about how I feel about the Church. But for them, going to mass is a sacred thing. I've just never seen a real need to make an issue of it with them."

However, she doesn't hide her opinions from her religious sisters. Some of them, she said, have reached the same conclusion. Still, the decision to quit going to church was difficult for Mary, especially as a musician and liturgist who loves ritual, making music, and ceremony.

"I find other ways to do it," she said. "Prayer is not just mass. I never thought it was. I just don't get hung up on church. Church is where we are. I think we have church here," she said of the shelter. "We don't do religious things here. The life I see here is a very profound kind of life. It is a birth, people coming alive, pulling themselves together. My whole idea of God is much more feminist now. God is Sophia, not even Jesus."

Like many women, she complains that she needs to make time for herself; she needs to start a regular exercise routine; she needs to "throw pots"—make pottery—which she finds to be centering. Her quiet time, she said, is prayer time. "I can be at peace doing laundry."

So why doesn't she just leave? She could have her job as a psychologist without being a sister. She could run a homeless shelter without being a nun.

"It's a kind of family thing," she said. "I think a lot of it is the support, the commonality that we have. There's a history, a belief system, whether Rome knows about it or not. I think we have a church without being in one."

The marble hallways and oversized windows of Mary's "church" belie the poverty housed within. Residents are mostly single mothers addicted to drugs or incapable of retaining jobs for other reasons. Several appear to have mental problems, requiring the sisters to summon police when they become violent.

The shelter's dining hall is in the dark and dreary school basement, where pipes and wires crisscross dingy cement walls. Its few windows are too high to look out of; most light comes from hanging fluorescent tubes. Residents eat at flimsy tables and sit on ripped chairs. At the far end of the former gymnasium, battered couches and recliners form a makeshift living room, an attempt to make the residents feel at home.

At one of the dining tables, five women were practicing writing cover letters. Their instructor, a white social worker, is not a nun but an ordained minister of the Disciples of Christ Christian Church and is married to an Episcopalian priest.

A few tables away, two women labored over boxes of greens, stripping the tough leaves from their stems. One was a chunky, developmentally disabled woman who talked with a pronounced lisp. She introduced herself as Patricia and said she is twenty-four years old. Her friend, Latoya, is twenty-one and has enormous eyes, enhanced by purple contacts. Both mothers of toddler daughters, they complained about the shelter's innumerable rules. In particular, they griped that a woman who had used drugs was kicked out the previous day along with her children.

"I don't think it's right," Latoya said. "It's cold outside, and they have no place to go. How can they kick out children in the winter?"

The women also were angry that the shelter doesn't give them money for toiletries; they are responsible at a certain point for buying their own. They complained that they don't have bus fare for job interviews—although I have seen Mary routinely dole out bus money. The sisters require them to attend too many meetings, and they can't leave the shelter after 5 P.M.

"They live in their fancy homes and drive their fancy cars," Patricia ranted. "They don't care anything about us."

I held back a laugh. Most staffers are paid less than twenty thousand dollars a year, the sisters a little more. The few who have cars drive decades-old economy models. The Institute's annual report shows that the two shelters together operate on less than $650,000 a year, a paltry amount on which to feed, house, and care for hundreds of homeless women and children. The shelters' main funding comes from Christmas donations.

Because the shelters can't afford housekeepers and janitors, residents are assigned daily chores, such as sweeping, mopping, or cleaning the bathrooms. Even children are given tasks. To some shelter residents, the white sisters are viewed as distant caretakers and their black staff as tyrants.

Latoya and Patricia knew that the white women, except the social worker, are "sisters," but they weren't sure what that meant.

Latoya wrinkled her face. "They don't get married?" she guessed.

"They are married to God," Patricia informed her with an air of authority.

I explained what the sisters' vows of obedience, chastity, and poverty mean.

"So they can't have sex? Man, I don't understand that. I could never do that," Latoya said, laughing.

Patricia shook her head. "For their whole lives?"

That made Patricia wonder: "So what happens to them if they break the rules?"

THE LIFE THAT LED TO REBELLION

Margaret wasn't a rule breaker when she first entered the School Sisters of Notre Dame in Mankato, Minnesota, in 1942. Never desiring a family or a husband, Margaret wanted to be a nun, a teacher. Her transformation into a "latent feminist" and radical nun developed over decades, the result of "incompetent and meddling priests," she said.

During the late 1950s, Margaret taught at a large Catholic school in North Dakota where a priest was accused of molesting high school girls. The priest used keys to gain entry to the girls' dormitory. Though the girls warned each other when he entered the building, the molestation continued. Eventually the assistant priest gathered thirty-five affidavits from those who alleged sexual abuse and sent them to the bishop.

Nothing happened.

In charge of the senior girls, Margaret also reported the allegations to her provincial. Nothing was done. She assumed her superior didn't believe her.

"I had done what I thought I should do. I thought: You go to the provincial and you told it all," she laughed cynically. "Now what I would do is tell the state troopers. Who knows what it did to those young girls? That changed my attitude towards priests and towards men, towards leadership, failure of leadership."

Margaret's career as a rebellious nun solidified when she marched in Selma, Alabama, in March 1965. After a group of African Americans were beaten and clubbed by patrol storm troopers on a protest walk to Alabama's capital, Montgomery, Dr. Martin Luther King asked for priests and nuns to march.

Margaret and seven other nuns flew down the next morning. They were met at the door of a Baptist church by the pastor, who took Margaret's hand and led her inside. The church was packed with church members singing and praying. The pastor walked Margaret to the old-fashioned pulpit.

"Tell them why you've come," he told her.

Margaret mounted the pulpit stairs and stood before the hundreds of black faces. She was wearing her black habit, her starched white bib and veil. Only a few months earlier, she had been teaching literature in Minnesota; her only exposure to blacks had been the few students who had sought her out when her Catholic school integrated. She told the congregation that she and the other sisters believed blacks had a right to the same education as whites. They had the right to vote, which was why they were protesting. She told them that God is colorblind.

Her short speech that day was Margaret's first of many public forays.

Each day, she and the sisters stood in the front row and marched, just six feet from storm troopers brandishing billy clubs. At night the sisters slept in encampments set up by local hospital nuns. But even in the middle of a march, Margaret could see inequality: She was troubled that the black women who made the marchers' sandwiches were relegated to the back of the crowd.

"As I look back at those times, it's like the flicker of a match. Life passes quickly," she said one afternoon as the light was fading through the windows, casting long shadows against her face.

In 1968, Margaret's mistrust of church authority grew when she read *The Church of the Second Sex,* by feminist theologian Mary Daly. The book accused the Catholic Church and its male clerics of oppressing women and keeping them out of positions of power. "That book made me realize that I was in a system that was perpetuating its own oppression," she said. "And that's why I stood up."

The following year, 1969, Margaret founded the National Coalition of American Nuns. Its first proclamation demanded that priests stop meddling in women's religious communities. At the time, Cardinal James McIntyre in Los Angeles was mediating a split in the Immaculate Heart of Mary Sisters. Margaret called McIntyre "Cardinal Awful Guy."

"We told the cardinal that he was transgressing the rights of sisters," she said. "It was unprecedented."

Margaret began speaking about her radical beliefs across the country.

In Cleveland, she told her mostly Catholic audience: "Every member of the Gestapo was a baptized Christian." Her speech made headlines, and a New York rabbi sought her out to say that she was a very rare Catholic to admit such things.

"I knew I was saying things that should be heard," she said. "I don't think I made too many friends, though."

Sister Margaret Traxler

In 1974, Margaret began taking teams of women—lawyers, judges, social workers, and psychologists—into women's prisons, where they educated prisoners about their legal rights and taught welding and other job skills. For fifteen years, Margaret and her teams visited prisons all across the Midwest and the South, advocating better conditions. In a few cases, they were able to get women whose civil rights had been violated released.

Dorothy Day, cofounder of the Catholic Worker movement, accompanied Margaret on a few trips. Once, while signing herself in at a prison, Dorothy turned and asked Margaret: "Shall I say that I am a revolutionary?"

"She was beautiful," Margaret remembered. The biggest difference between the two women, though, was that Day did not publicly challenge Church leaders.

"She wasn't a women's advocate," Margaret said. "I think it was because the women's movement was somewhat after her day. She had such respect for men of the Church."

During the push for the Equal Rights Amendment, Margaret and her National Coalition of American Nuns spoke before twenty-three state legislatures.

"The Church was not in favor of the Equal Rights Amendment. It was so typical: those men speaking their own decisions saying they speak for the Church. Well, they don't speak for me. They don't speak for many other women."

That was why in 1984 Margaret decided to lend her name to an advertisement in the *New York Times* during the presidential campaign. The ad initially was meant to support Democratic vice-presidential candidate Geraldine Ferraro, a Catholic whose support of publicly funded abortions was heavily criticized by Church leaders, including New York's Archbishop John O'Connor. The full-page advertisement stated that not all "committed Catholics" and theologians agreed with the Church's official stand against abortion. Twenty-six of the ninety-seven signatories were Catholic nuns. After the election, the Vatican ordered the nuns and clergy who had signed the ad to recant or be kicked out of their orders. The four priests and brothers recanted immediately, but all the sisters refused. The standoff lasted more than a year, during which Margaret suffered her first serious stroke. She believes it was caused by worry over whether she would be expelled from her order.

Margaret and many of the nuns considered leaving their orders. Margaret felt increasing pressure from leaders of her own community to apologize, but she refused. Eventually the sisters were allowed to meet with their superiors to draw up vaguely written clarifications. Two nuns eventually left their order, saying they felt ostracized. Several sisters were pressured to resign from Catholic committees. Some nuns were not allowed to speak at Church-sponsored retreats. The Los Angeles diocese boycotted a homeless shelter run by a nun who had signed the ad. In Chicago, Margaret was forced to resign from a public board that advocated that federal money should be used to pay for abortions in cases of rape and incest.

"Women must choose for themselves what they will do with their bodies," Margaret explained. "Women should have the right to choose. The men want that right. Isn't that terrible? Aren't they awful? One day that's going to be as obsolete as the chastity belt."

Though she had once feared having to give up her life as a nun, the flap with the Vatican only made Margaret more brazen. Exactly ten years after the *Times* ad appeared, Margaret and ten other National Coalition sisters, including several signers of the ad, flew to Rome, where they handed out fliers and marched with placards in St. Peter's Square, directly under the widows of the Pope's apartment. The women were angry that the Vatican was holding meetings on religious life—of which nuns make up the majority—yet only a few sisters had been invited. The protesting sisters wanted a chance to be heard, but what they got was an hour in Vatican police custody.

"They couldn't get over that we were nuns," Margaret said of the police. "We were not in habit. We had on suits and dresses."

Over the years, Margaret continued to shock Catholics. On Mother's Day one year, she and about sixty others demonstrated outside a downtown Chicago cathedral, protesting the Vatican's "gender abuse"—its refusal to allow women to become priests and its opposition to birth control.

So why didn't she ever disengage herself from an institution whose structure, leadership and spirituality she disagrees with?

"When I entered the convent," she explained, "my father said: 'Go with the will to remain.' And I think I did. There's no sense in starting something that you won't finish. I hope to die in the Church, be buried in the Church."

THE BUDDHIST NUN

A few days later, I visited Margaret's assistant, Maureen Boyd, at her apartment on the campus of Misericordia, a large community of mentally and physically disabled adults on Chicago's North Side. Maureen's order, the Sisters of Mercy, runs the complex of group homes and dormitories that are home to more than five hundred handicapped adults, many with cerebral palsy or Down's syndrome. *Misericordia* is Latin for "heart of mercy." Since 1985, Maureen has lived on the campus either as a chaperon in a group home or as a resident assistant in the apartment complex.

Maureen has taken a far different tack from either Margaret or Mary in dealing with the Church: She adopted another religion, Buddhism. Fifty-eight years old, she wears her hair in a gray shag that shows off her signature yin-and-yang earrings. Often she wears heavy sweatshirts with the emblems of her favorite sports teams. In the summers, she attends Chicago Cub baseball games and brings along disabled adults she lives with. Maureen often laughs and tells jokes and makes fun of herself. She speaks in a rambling way, looking down, deflecting any compliments that Margaret gives her. Margaret said Maureen is so self-effacing because she isn't used to getting attention, having labored for nearly thirty years as a pharmacist in the basement of Mercy Hospital. Maureen still rises early and arrives at the shelter at around 4 A.M. each day, leaving around 10 A.M. to be with the Misericordia residents.

Maureen has known a great deal of anguish in her life. She comes from an Irish Catholic family with six kids. Her father died at forty-four when she and her twin, Maryland, were eleven years old. After high school, she and her twin sister both joined the Mercy Sisters, but her sister was asked to leave just before they took their vows: The nuns could see that she was seriously depressed. Though saddened that her sister had to leave, Maureen became part of the many changes after Vatican II. She was one of the first sisters to move out of the convent to share an apartment with other sisters. She pushed for a decreased work schedule at the hospital and enjoyed the freedom of a modern nun. Then her twin sister committed suicide. Maureen fell into a deep depression herself, and a psychiatrist prescribed Prozac. Eventually, Maureen decided to do something totally different: attend an experimental spirituality program at Mundelein, a nearby Catholic women's college.

"My head was all blown up on the right side with all this science stuff," she said. "I needed to do something a little freaky."

Maureen studied Eastern religions and credits Buddhism with helping her understand Christianity. She likes Buddhism because it isn't focused on one person or thing. Buddha wasn't a god, but a teacher. God isn't a visible being that a person can see or touch or cling to and claim as her own. She likes Buddhism's belief that God is within each person; God is nature and the universe. While studying Eastern religions, Maureen was struck by the similarities in world religions and shocked to learn that other people besides Catholic nuns meditated.

"It just blew my mind. Suddenly you figure out that all religions are the same," Maureen said. "Like we have the Blessed Mother, and we have this big thing that it was a virgin birth and Jesus is so special. But Buddha was a virgin birth too. Buddha came out of his mother's side. They have that same myth. They have the same need to have that same mystical experience of a special person's birth."

While she was studying Buddhism, her brother gave her a large, fat Buddha statue, and Maureen began collecting them. Along a table in her living room there are at least twenty kinds of Buddhas: fat, green, small, large, antique, plastic, brass, gold-plated, carved wood. There is even a skeletal Buddha who had starved himself as an ascetic. Several of the figures have rosaries and crosses hanging around their necks.

"That's just to even it out a bit," she said.

The Buddhas show the various phases of life. When someone is younger, Maureen explained, they pass through an ascetic phase, a religiously devoted phase; they see things in a limited way. As a person ages, they begin to see connections between God and nature and God and people and that there is no way to separate God from the world. Maureen prefers the older, corpulent Buddhas.

"The fat Buddhas are more of a role model to me," she explained. "Christ was thirty-three when he got knocked off. How is he supposed to understand what being fifty-eight and fat is all about?" She lifted up her sweatshirt to show me the white roll of her belly. "The Buddha kept thinking and developing his spirituality. We don't know how Christ would have gone on from there, how he would have treated his mother."

Maureen has always tried to remain free of the Catholic Church's politics. Because she was never a teacher, she wasn't responsible for handing down the Church's tenets to the next generation. That distance allowed her a certain amount of intellectual freedom. Though she has never publicly supported abortion, she said she strongly favors women's right to choose.

"I've never had to defend the Church. And I feel very removed from the whole system," she said. "I mean, the Pope means nothing to me. Rome means nothing to me, especially if your mind is inclusive of Hinduism, Buddhism, Wicca, whatever. Let those guys go over there and stay in Rome and not have abortions. I don't care. I've got my internal wisdom. And I know. You know a woman should have the right to choose."

AN INFAMOUS NUN'S LAST INTERVIEW

After several weeks, Margaret's conversations took a turn I was not prepared for. She began discussing her death, her obituary, and where she wanted to be buried. It was as if Margaret knew I was writing the last chapter of her life. "I hope that the Lord will look upon my life and forgive me of my many offenses," she said, sounding as if she were reciting a prayer.

One day in February she placed certain incidents twenty years earlier or later than they had occurred, a sign that her memory was declining. Though we had met several times a week for nearly two months, that day Margaret mispronounced my name. Later, I learned she couldn't recall the names of her longtime shelter workers or her roommate. Yet, she was anxious to recount details she hadn't divulged earlier.

For starters, there was the matter of her benefactor, Cardinal Joseph Bernardin. While in Rome in 1994, Margaret and her friend Sister Donna Quinn met privately with Bernardin, who was attending a conference that the sisters were protesting.

"He smiled and said, 'I just want you to know that I am for the ordination of women.' He never said that publicly, but now I want to make it known. Later in the conversation, he looked up at the top window and said: 'It won't happen in this administration. But it will happen.' "

Bernardin had risked rebuke in quietly giving Margaret the parish, rectory, and school that became the Maria Shelter.

"He gave us all this—no strings attached," she said. "If the official Church knew that he gave it to us free of charge, I think they would protest."

Bernardin, she said, had called the shelter his "secret church." A frequent visitor, Bernardin would walk through the shelter with kids clinging to him. Mothers waited in long lines to have him bless their non-Catholic children. Every Christmas, Bernardin wrote checks to the shelter from his private account. When he died, his last check, she said, was inside an envelope labeled: *For my secret church.*

Margaret railed against Bernardin's successor, Cardinal Francis George, even refusing to meet with him when he invited Chicago-area sisters to the archdiocese after he was appointed. "He probably led the sisters in prayer," she snarled. She accused him of despising women and treating nuns as if they were his "rosary and sacristy society"—the ones who do the cleaning and raise the money.

But she didn't stop there.

"The Pope," she said, "despite all his talks to the contrary, despises women."

There were other great men she thought treated women badly.

"I didn't admire Martin Luther King," Margaret coyly admitted, detailing King's philandering. At first Margaret said that this was "our secret," but when I told her that King's affairs had been publicized, she took that as an opportunity to say how she really felt.

"He was a philanderer!" she shouted. "What kind of man would set that up as a model for young black men? As women, we should express our dismay that this is such a proven pattern in his life. I resent it when men break every vow they ever made, and they are still heroes."

I urged Margaret to explain how she can separate herself from the Church, though she is still a nun. At first, her reasoning sounded murky. But then I began to understand how much Margaret is a traditional Catholic at heart. She rages against the men but still attends mass. Margaret has always had a great devotion to the Virgin Mary, a rarity among the ardent Catholic feminists I know.

"I am angry, but I won't give up the Church because I belong to it," she said. "It was given to me, and I will stay in and chide the men as often as I have the chance. The Church is mine. I am in the Church. I will die faithful."

That day, I sensed her anticipated exit was drawing near. When we said good-bye, I hugged Margaret and kissed her cheek.

"There's some things I've told you that I've never told anybody else," she said, widening her watery eyes.

She was leaving in two days to see her biological sisters, who were meeting in Scottsdale, Arizona. I was looking forward to getting together with her when she returned in ten days.

But that was not to happen.

AN EMPTY RECTORY

Two days after Margaret left for Arizona, I arrived at the shelter to spend the night. It was mid-February, and Chicago was braced for twelve inches of snow, its worst winter storm that season. I found Mary sitting at her office computer. She seemed glad to see me, eagerly clearing a chair.

"I'm afraid I have some bad news about Margaret," she said. "She's in the hospital in Arizona. The doctors think she's had a stroke."

Upon arrival in Arizona, Margaret had become disoriented and collapsed. Her sisters reported that she couldn't walk and could barely speak. Mary and Maureen suspected it was a progressive stroke that had occurred before Margaret left. That would explain her surprising memory loss shortly before her trip.

Mary, calling board members to decide who could write checks in Margaret's absence, was glad that Margaret was with her family because it would force Margaret to make some decisions about where she would retire. Mary was certain Margaret couldn't return to Chicago; mounting the rectory steps would be impossible for her now.

I left Mary to pick out my bed at the shelter. Recently several women had been kicked out; others had left on their own. The former elementary classroom, now called the Theresa dorm room, was mostly vacant, except for the rows of empty beds, covered in turquoise plastic. I picked an empty bed nearest the door.

Across from me was a young woman named Shanita who had an uncombed Afro that rose above her head like a cone. Shanita had an infant girl and a three-year-old daughter. I stuffed my overnight bag into a locker where schoolchildren had once hung their raincoats and stored their boots. My small bag barely fit.

I sat down on the bed and felt an enormous sense of loss that Margaret wasn't just across the street eager to see me when I popped in, offering me a Frappuccino or a Tab. Because I came from her home state of Minnesota, Margaret treated me like I was someone from back home making a social call, not a journalist who had interviewed many nuns she knows, but someone who has mutual friends. Ultimately, though, I had become the person who tape-recorded her last conversations before a stroke robbed her of her formidable speech.

Lost in my thoughts, I didn't immediately notice several children, including three drippy-nosed toddlers, encircling my bed, checking out the new arrival. An eight-year-old boy introduced himself as Emmanuel. He had shoulder-length braids and big teeth.

"There's a black man who is hurting little girls," he informed me.

I told him that the police had caught the so-called South Side serial killer, who had garnered extensive media coverage. Unfortunately, the killer was only one of four serial killers responsible for at least thirteen murders and three rapes in South Side neighborhoods during the last six years. But Emmanuel said he was talking about yet a different man. Later I learned that indeed a new assailant had been attacking young schoolgirls on their way home. The neighborhood is a magnet for convicted sexual predators; the list of released sexual offenders the police periodically provide to the shelter is more than three pages long.

A little later Emmanuel told me it was time for dinner. I followed him down the dark hallways to the dreary basement dining hall that I had come to abhor. Half the dining hall lights were unlit and the children sat at tables in near darkness. The women were already standing in the food line; I would be the last. Those in line stood motionless, with dazed expressions. Twenty minutes later I reached the kitchen window. Dinner consisted of barbecue chicken, mashed potatoes, rolls, corn, and turquoise-colored Gatorade. Dessert was a thick store-bought cheesecake.

I sat next to a screaming child who refused to eat and directly across the table from an enormous woman who ate with sausage-sized fingers smeared with potatoes. Her hands didn't stop moving from her plate to her face, nor did she stop talking as she ate.

After dinner, I trudged up the green-and-orange marble staircase, overwhelmed with sadness. The shelter, the former rectory, and the church—now a senior center—reeked of the past, a history filled with Irish immigrant families who worked hard to send their children to the parish school, who made its church their spiritual center, who revered the priests so much they built a palace rectory as grand as the church.

I was struck by the similarity between the buildings and their latest champion, Margaret. Her zenith occurred during the most tumultuous time in history for sisters, a time when nuns were part of the dramatic changes in civil rights and women's equality. She had reigned during an era when sisters were revered and feared by young people. All that is behind her now. She has made her mark, and the Church doesn't seem to care anymore what this old woman has to say.

As I passed by the Mary dorm room, I saw Emmanuel kneeling, using the bed as a desk while he tried to master his English homework. His ten-year-old sister, Ashley, was changing the diaper of another resident's child. A one-year-old baby, barely sixteen pounds, her nose flowing, stood crying in her crib.

Upstairs in the Valentine dorm room, a thin woman rocked back and forth as she read the newspaper and talked to herself. Later, the woman stood at the pay phone rocking back and forth as she yelled at various pharmacies about needing medicine.

As I roamed the halls, kids followed as if I were the Pied Piper. Few wore shoes; some were barefoot. Amanda, the guard, asked if the kids were bothering me. I sat down near her post and looked out the front windows facing the rectory, whose two lit-up front windows seemed to be staring back. The rectory looked like a giant mausoleum. Amanda stared out the window at the falling snow. She didn't know Margaret wasn't coming back; Mary hadn't told the staff yet.

I asked Amanda if she was ever afraid to walk through the neighborhood late at night. She patted her right front pocket, indicating she was carrying a gun. Later, when she and some of the residents talked about the recent attacks on schoolgirls, Amanda laughed and patted her pocket again, but this time she brazenly displayed the gun's handle.

At 8 P.M. the dorm lights are supposed to be turned off and mothers are expected to lie down with their children until they are asleep. I walked into my darkened dorm room. Loud techno music was playing on a radio and a young woman danced in the dark with a three-year-old girl. The woman's thin hips gyrated to the music and her hands swayed out in front, her palms spread open. The child, dressed in her long nightgown, mimicked the dancing woman's movements. Streetlights seeped through the school's plastic-coated glass, painting the dancers with a shadowy blue cast. As the music blasted, I noticed another woman sitting on her bed, talking loudly to herself. Surrounded by the swaying images, feeling the pulsating music, and hearing the indecipherable mumblings of a crazy woman, I felt as if I had walked into a surreal dream, an Alice in shelterland.

I returned to the hallway and gazed out the windows. The rectory was empty again: Margaret's housemate was uncomfortable staying at the rectory alone. Several lights were left on to give the impression that someone still lived there. The shelter and its history were changing once more. The woman who had spent her life caring for hundreds now needed someone to care for her.

The next few weeks I felt a void when I visited the shelter. As the twelfth of March neared, I felt pained that Margaret would have to celebrate her seventy-sixth birthday in an Arizona nursing home. Meanwhile, the *New York Times* ran a front-page picture of civil rights leaders commemorating the anniversary of the voting rights march in Selma. The story never mentioned the nuns who had bravely joined that historical protest. Would anyone remember Margaret? Would they remember a habited nun who faced state troopers? Would history books overlook the contributions of these women?

Maureen and I met for lunch at the Misericordia restaurant run by handicapped residents. Over bowls of rice pudding, we traded Margaret stories. Maureen credits Margaret for giving her the courage to publicly support her beliefs. Recently, she signed an advertisement supporting Sister Jeannine Grammick, a friend of Margaret's who was being silenced by the Vatican after thirty years spent ministering to Catholic gays and lesbians.

"It took a lot of nerve on my part," Maureen said. "I think I signed anonymously at first and then my name got on there anyway. I don't care. You'd think those dirty old men in the Church would have something better to do," she said, sounding a lot like her mentor. "They probably think I'm a lesbian now."

Maureen admires Margaret as a pioneer who has championed many women's causes that Maureen feels strongly about, including abortion and birth control. "We're on the same page. She's just more vocal," Maureen said. "Margaret fears nothing. She's not connected to the Church. She runs this interfaith shelter. So they can't shut her down; they can't shut her up."

During their years together, the sisters' working relationship grew into a friendship. Occasionally Margaret confided in Maureen about her frequent falls, asking her not to tell Mary, who seemed to have taken on a motherly role with Margaret. One day last December, shortly before Christmas, Margaret fell in her bedroom; she crawled to a phone and called Maureen. Maureen drove the twenty miles to the shelter and helped Margaret get up. Margaret told Maureen then that she was thinking of retiring. "But not yet," she said. "Maybe around the summertime."

Margaret's decline became more noticeable. Her thinking seemed slower; she remembered less. She made noticeable mistakes in paperwork. She had a harder time walking and fell more often.

"I call it a slow leak," Maureen said.

But even when Margaret couldn't get to church anymore—afraid she would fall—she watched mass for shut-ins on television. Suddenly Maureen stopped herself: "Geez, I'm talking about her like she died or something."

It seemed inconceivable that Margaret couldn't at least say what she wanted, that she couldn't give Church leaders one more verbal lashing. The shelter sisters agreed that it would be hard for Margaret to fit in at the mother house because she had lived her life so independently.

"I hope she goes quickly," Mary said. "She's got to be miserable unable to speak, unable to get around."

Mary wasn't being irreverent or flippant. She had cared for her father for seven years after his stroke, when he was unable to bathe or feed himself. She didn't want to see a visionary fed through tubes and wearing diapers.

On one of the hottest spring days in Chicago history, Mary and I sat in her therapy room, which overlooked a vacant lot strewn with trash. The shelter has no air-conditioning, and I was sweating, but the sunlight seemed to brighten what was a somber conversation.

"I'm ambivalent about her being gone," Mary admitted. "I miss her. I miss her a lot. I'm also aware that there's some pretty critical things we need to focus on. There were some pretty gross errors in the accounting. Margaret was a one-woman show. It's time to do something else."

Mary admitted that she didn't have a warm relationship with Margaret, who, for her part, often bragged about Mary. They aren't friends, Mary said.

"Yet, I have a lot of respect for her. Our values were in some ways similar. Hers were stronger. Whatever she believed in she'd be out there supporting. I'm not that strong. I think she got very focused on abortion and Jewish liberation issues, to the exclusion of other things that I felt were more important."

Unlike Maureen, Mary decided not to sign the petition for Sister Jeannine Grammick. Her reason was pragmatic: It wasn't going to change anyone's mind. Mary could see that the Church's feminist movement has not made much progress. More than three decades have passed since Margaret and her National Coalition of American Nuns demanded that the Church allow women to become priests. The Vatican men haven't budged. Nothing has changed.

In fact, the push for women priests was set back by a 1998 papal edict that prohibited Catholics from even discussing the possibility of women's ordination. Those who challenge such principles risk being accused of blasphemy and being excommunicated. Many feminist nuns today keep their politics private, believing that challenging the current regime is futile and only draws undue attention.

"I think a lot of people are being vocal in a different kind of way," Mary explained. "I think there's so much frustration and hopelessness in the current situation. I mean we've been praying for a happy death [of the Pope] for a long time. Nothing's going to change until the death of the current guy. I think a lot of my generation is more into ignoring rather than standing up and shouting. We're doing our own thing, grounded in what we define as church."

AT THE MOTHER HOUSE

I went to see Margaret a few weeks after she was transferred from a nursing home in Arizona to her order's mother house in Mankato, Minnesota—

two hours from my home. It was early May. Margaret was sitting in a wheelchair in an empty room across from the nurses' station. Her head was slumped, her face flaccid. She stared at me with a puzzled expression. A sister asked Margaret if she remembered me. Margaret shook her head no and closed a nearby suitcase containing adult diapers. The sister suggested I wheel Margaret to her room, where we could talk while she listened to her favorite classical music station.

Her room was large, with a hospital bed, a sofa chair, and a television. Cards covered a bulletin board. Plants and flower arrangements were set around the room. Nearby was a baby monitor; nurses listened in because they were concerned that Margaret would try to walk down the nearby stairs.

Margaret pointed to the recliner and I sat down. Her big blue eyes held no trace of recognition. Her voice was so weak I had to lean in so that my ear nearly touched her mouth.

"How far to blame?" she whispered, barely audible.

Margaret repeated her question like an insistent child.

"How far to blame? How far to blame? How far to blame?" she strung her questions together.

Was this a rhetorical question? Was Margaret's intense intellect still churning deep inside? Was she blaming herself or others for the way she'd ended up? I couldn't tell. But the ironies of her unintelligible remarks seemed less than coincidental.

"I want to go home," she announced.

"Where is 'home,' Margaret?"

She glared at me.

"Is home in Chicago?"

She nodded.

I decided to take Margaret outside. Pushing her wheelchair through the dark hallways, I made our way to the sisters' campus, scattered with flowering crabapple trees. The mother house is an old, redbrick complex set on the town's largest hill. I positioned Margaret's chair under a towering oak tree, and there we sat for a long while, she staring at me, searching for some memory of my face. Occasionally her mouth formed words but she was unable to speak. She sliced her hands through the air to emphasize silent viewpoints.

After a while, words began to come. I bent down to better hear her in the wind. She touched my cheek and brushed back my hair. Each time I bent my face to hear her, she touched me, gently, longingly.

"Do you remember me?" I asked.

She nodded.

"Why don't you like the mother house, Margaret?"

She motioned for me to come near. "Uninteresting," she said in her old terse style.

I laughed. "So who's the new CEO at the Maria Shelter?"

She pointed to herself.

"But who has taken your place?"

"No one," she said flatly.

"Is that because no one could take your place, Margaret?"

She smiled.

Later, back in her room, Margaret announced: "I want to feel different." Then she repeated the line, slowly and carefully.

"How? Margaret, how?" I asked, bending so she could look directly into my eyes.

"I want *you* to make me feel different," she said, challenging me with her sad face.

She fingered the strap that held her into the wheelchair. Nurses had to belt Margaret into her chair or else she tried to walk; she had already fallen several times.

Then she uttered the longest paragraph during our visit: "I want you to write me after June first or second. I'm going to be different. I'm not going to change the way I see things, but I'm going to change. I'm going to change."

"You mean you're going to have a more positive attitude?"

She nodded.

After two hours of questions, Margaret was responding. There was a connection. I could feel it. The doctors had predicted that the more mental stimulation Margaret had the more she would improve.

I hugged Margaret. She kissed my cheek and stroked my hair. Then I wheeled her to the room near the nurses' station, where I imagined she would spend the rest of her day alone.

All the way home, I couldn't shake my enormous sorrow. Occasionally there had been a glimmer of the former fierce character. But there was no denying: The Margaret I had come to admire, that fiery spirit, was gone.

Margaret's life touched me in profound ways. I had always thought that being a Christian—and especially a nun—means a woman has to adhere to Church patriarchy, that she isn't allowed to get angry and certainly can't confront the Church's injustices—at least not loudly and publicly. But Margaret believes that any argument worth having should be waged in the open. Being a nun doesn't mean she has to sign away her conscience. To her, an obedient nun is one whose passions fuel her beliefs, not one who shirks from them.

I didn't always agree with Margaret. And I don't think she always agreed with herself, either. Part of her public persona was that of an instigator, troublemaker, rabble-rouser. She worked in the gray areas where no one wants to deal with morality. She made audacious statements that made people uncomfortable. She was like a crazy, unpredictable aunt who was liable to spout off and make a scene at any moment. In that way, she was entertaining and sometimes larger than life. And yes, she could bully people, and she was known for being dogmatic, opinionated, and stubborn. Yet, that was part of her charm, the reason many nuns adored her, why women like myself admired and cherished her: There aren't many like her. In fact, I've yet to meet another nun as daring.

Margaret showed me that seeking peace sometimes means raising a lot of hell. She was the first sister I'd met who fully embodied a passionate, intellectual resistance. Margaret and her shelter nuns provided impressive arguments that refute popular Christian ideals, such as turning the other cheek and letting people take advantage. Even Jesus got angry and threw the money changers from the temple, they said. Being a good person—or a good nun—doesn't mean getting along at all costs.

And while Mary and Maureen aren't as obstinate and public about their feelings, they also aren't endorsing the traditional Church, either. They prove that being a feminist doesn't necessarily mean a woman has to wear a billboard announcing her beliefs or take a combatant attitude with every challenge. The most important lesson they advocate, though, is that church is not a place: It's how they live their lives, where they place their energies, the communities with whom they connect. It's the work they do, how they treat people, how they remember those who aren't as fortunate. The way Mary and Maureen live their lives is their spiritual practice; it is their church.

I see the sisters' different approaches as the yin and yang of Catholic feminists. While forceful and outspoken nuns like Margaret are the conscience raisers, quiet solicitous nuns like Mary and Maureen are the ones who keep the cause alive in a practical, pervasive way.

Though we were only together for a couple months, I found in Margaret a kindred soul, a muse, a mentor. To me, she was the equivalent of a Catholic Gloria Steinem, a woman who could talk about what feminism means to spiritual women, a woman who found her religion in standing up for all people's rights, including her own. But just when I found her and became mesmerized with her words, she fell silent.

On February 12, 2002—exactly one month shy of her seventy-eighth birthday—Margaret Traxler died. As her casket was lowered into the ground at her order's cemetery, her aging sisters and friends banged tambourines while a trumpet blared out a jazzy rendition of "When the Saints Go Marchin' In." The crowd of mourners danced around Margaret's grave, belting out eight stanzas of the brassy tune in memory of a brassy lady.

5

THE ELASTIC CLOISTER

CARMELITE SISTERS IN HUDSON, WISCONSIN

"You don't have to have walls to keep you in. Our cloister is the cloister of the heart . . . a freer way of looking at life, allowing people to be themselves."

—SISTER GEMMA ANGELO

Sister Gemma Angelo hadn't touched an outsider for six years. Sister Mary O'Neill in four. But on August 19, 1963, they and three other sisters shook hands with hundreds of strangers—townsfolk and neighbors curious to meet the area's first cloistered nuns. Each time the Carmelite sisters made the acquaintance of a local parishioner or dignitary at their new convent in Hudson, Wisconsin, they quickly retracted their hands under their scapulars. The reception line stretched from the front door of the former estate, wound through the sacristy (once the living room), and emerged into the sisters' section of the chapel set off by a grille—iron bars and a screen. This was the first time most of the sisters had even stepped outside monastery gates since entering their Carmelite order in Allentown, Pennsylvania. The sisters appeared dazed and overwhelmed as people touched them, talked with them, and stared at them. They were also moved by the parishioners' gentleness and generosity, a salient memory they'd keep long after an "enclosure" fence was built and the bishop "sealed" them in months later, restricting them within the boundaries of their seven acres on bluffs overlooking a Mississippi tributary.

Walking through their new home that evening after the crowd had left, the sisters were surprised to discover habited images staring back at them. Their old monastery did not have mirrors and they had never seen their own reflections in veils and wimples. Their explorations were interrupted when they heard piercing screams from the basement: A Sister had discovered a legion of bats. Fitting their monastic lifestyle into a home would be more difficult than they had imagined.

The next morning, when the sisters tried to line up two by two outside their living room–chapel, they discovered the hall wasn't long enough. It was more like bunching up in one room to ceremoniously step over the threshold of another. Attempts to preserve the old processional tradition, which involved singing psalms on the way to chapel, proved futile, and they disregarded the custom.

Eventually, other rituals fell by the wayside; by 1971, the sisters would be sporting jeans and driving a Volkswagen. While other monasteries throughout the country were undergoing similar transformations, the Hudson monastery was the only community to update within their order, the Carmelites of Strict Observance. Though the sisters took their mandate straight from Vatican II, their own order accused them of betraying six hundred years of Carmelite traditions. The sisters' desire to open up their monastery and release rigid rules castigated them as disobedient nuns.

WOULD-BE GRANDMOTHERS

The Hudson Carmelites were largely a mystery to me the spring morning I rang the bell to their redbrick home. Most of what I'd read about the austere Carmelite lifestyle led me to expect dour and pious women in long, dragging habits. To my delight, I discovered a collection of aging, would-be grandmothers wearing bandannas and sweatpants who opened up their simple way of life and pampered me with the doting attention adult women rarely receive.

Sister Lucia La Montagne greeted me at the door, wearing an apron and brushing back wiry brown and gray hair. She smiled nervously, and then raised her arms to hug me. Thrown off guard, I met Lucia's gesture with an outstretched hand, which she grasped awkwardly.

Lucia led me through the sisters' visiting parlor, formerly the home's two-car garage. Iron bars once divided the room, but the sisters removed all their grilles in 1969. "Now we're with the people," the sisters would often say, sounding like throwbacks to the hippie era they had missed completely.

I stepped carefully across the brown shag carpet, afraid any sudden movement might dislodge the miniature tea sets displayed around the room. Curio cabinets lining the perimeter were filled with more gifts: gold-rimmed wine goblets, vases, and Mary statuettes. Doilies on the end tables, religious pictures hanging from the dark-paneled walls, and the large glass chandelier hanging over a dining table and chairs made me feel like I'd entered my grandparents' den.

Near the parlor entrance is a vertical wooden cylinder, similar to that on a dumbwaiter, which the nuns call a "turn." Visitors once placed gifts inside the turn and gently pushed the contraption so it opened on the sisters' side. I was enamored with this two-by-three-foot apparatus and fingered its dark interior. I pushed it around, imagining that I had come to the monastery to place a pie or a roast inside for the unseen nuns. It seemed so romantic, this notion of keeping cloistered to remain pure from the world. Sister Lucia looked on and seemed embarrassed by this relic from her past.

"We don't use it anymore," she said, a little annoyed.

The sisters maintain a cloistered life but they aren't as stringent as the other monasteries in their order, Lucia explained. Besides Allentown and Hudson, there are two other Carmelite monasteries within these sisters' particular order: Wahpeton, North Dakota; and San Angelo, Texas. A fifth monastery in Asheville, North Carolina, closed in 1978 because several sisters were old and ill, a predicament that the Hudson sisters fear as well, with five aging sisters, several with health concerns.

The boundaries of the Hudson sisters' enclosure are less rigid now. Refusing to be cut off from people who need them, the sisters keep an "elastic" cloister, one that opens to those who seek them out for prayer and retreats at their hermitage.

"If these accidentals—cultural things like the grille and the habit— are essential to contemplative life, then contemplative life would not be relative to this century," Lucia explained. "The accidentals are not what make this life. The essentials are prayer, Carmelite spirituality, the solitude, and the silence."

Just six years earlier the sisters gave up the last vestige of their grueling medieval schedule by rescinding their midnight vigil prayers because of health issues. They still gather four times a day for prayer, beginning at 6:30 A.M. After that, they work their various jobs. At sixty, Sister Lucia is the monastery's self-taught musician, playing the organ and guitar during prayers and services. Their superior is the treasurer and does most of the bookkeeping. She also publishes a biweekly prayer newsletter that instructs about ninety subscribers on how to meditate. Another sister maintains the sisters' webpage, fielding questions about the monastery and responding to an average of fifteen prayer requests a day. The others garden or keep house. Though handicapped, the youngest sister does what she can, putting away dishes, folding clothes, and like tasks.

For the most part, the sisters do not leave the monastery unless for a specific purpose. They have seen plays and movies, but that is rare. Sometimes they rent movies. Each night at seven, they meet for recreation, an hour in which they talk, knit, and watch prerecorded news together, often fast-forwarding through commercials to learn who needs their prayers the most.

They all pitch in when guests stay at the hermitage, another converted two-car garage just outside the "cloister," marked by the monastery's eight-foot-high fence. Several take turns cooking. This week it was Lucia's turn, she said, as she ushered me toward the aroma of turkey roasting in the kitchen.

The modern kitchen windows overlook an expansive backyard, acres of flowers, trees, and informal gardens. This spring morning, several sisters were wearing white bonnets and kneeling as they dug new flowerbeds. Sister Lucia encouraged me to enjoy a meditative walk before prayers.

I drifted through the gardens, admiring tulips as big as cupped hands and fragrantly scented rosebushes towering over my head. Within a few minutes the community's superior joined me. I had just returned from visiting traditionally cloistered orders in Philadelphia where I had encountered several stern and autocratic superiors. One kept me in a room at the back of the chapel for several hours; finally I befriended a stooped Mexican nun who led me around the monastery, introducing me to other sisters. Later, when the mother superior overheard a sister detailing her former life to me—three failed engagements and a career as a buyer for the risqué boutique Spencer Gifts—the superior ordered me to the chapel to pray. Another mother superior at an ethnic order in suburban Philadelphia where I lived for a week wielded her power like a corporate executive, rushing from one meeting to another, complaining about her stressed life while adamantly dictating how I would portray her monastery.

Though some of the superiors I met in my travels are kind and generous, many are rigid rulers whose obsessive need to control others is, by far, the most distasteful aspect of religious life. Indeed, I found such superiors in every kind of community, from progressively active ones to the highly cloistered. The battle for control inside religious communities is an old, ugly secret. Many sisters speculate that because nuns have had so little control over their own lives they become consumed with controlling others when they are given authority. Other sisters believe that when some sisters deny their sexual feelings, refusing to acknowledge or address such basic desires, it causes them to exert their will in other ways. Some younger nuns feel that the older nuns have denied themselves pleasure for so long that they want the newer recruits to experience the same austere lifestyle, rationalizing that this builds character and spiritual willpower.

I was incensed when these superiors thought their authority extended to me. In my nun travels, I was yelled at by nuns and publicly scolded. I was lectured, harangued, reprimanded—all for trespassing some unknown boundary, touching things without permission, talking to sisters without prior approval. Many treated me with hesitation, as if my independence would remind sisters of what they had given up. Often I felt a power struggle as soon as I arrived. The internal conflict frequently left me feeling rebellious, eager to leave, as if I had had to swallow my own identity.

On the simplest level, the vow of obedience means adhering to an order's internal hierarchy, whether that's a traditional mother superior or a team of leaders. Throughout history, mother superiors have been both despised and adored. They have been charismatic leaders and taskmistresses all rolled into one, chastising each sister according to her needs, humbling the forward or talkative, encouraging the meek or shy, and motivating the slothful. Punishments have ranged from mild admonitions to severe corporal punishment—as many as fifty blows. Until Vatican II, some orders still required sisters to prostrate themselves and kiss the floor in gratitude when their superiors rebuked them.

I could tell much about a community based on its superior. If she is a micromanager, her community tends to be spiritually immature, less honest, less up front about their true feelings. It is as if they all aspire to be cardboard cutouts of their vision of the perfect nun—bland, opinionless creatures. I could see how much easier it is for sisters who give up any responsibility, relying wholly on the superior to make decisions. It also became painfully clear how stronger-willed sisters pay for their independent thinking.

Because cloistered Carmelites are often considered the most pious and devout on the religious hierarchy, I wasn't sure what kind of superior

I'd find at the Hudson monastery. Mother Gemma Angelo turned out to be a soft-spoken, dwarfish woman, with closely set almond eyes that overwhelm her diminutive face. She carries a perpetual smile, and when she laughs, every facial feature quivers. Her soft wrinkles and heavy eyes, along with her gentle spirit, remind me of my deceased grandmother, a memory Gemma would often evoke during the four years I intermittently visited.

At the age of twenty-six, Gemma entered the Carmelites in Allentown as "an older vocation." Previously a lab technician in charge of the hospital blood bank, Gemma garnered a reputation among the nuns as being "too independent." She was prone to ask questions about why sisters did things a certain way, and she was heard grumbling about the kitchen's state of uncleanliness. She broke from the decorum expected of sisters, often letting her hands stray from under her scapular and refusing to wear the layers required underneath her habit because they made her hot.

"I was kind of a rebel. I got into a lot of trouble," Gemma said with a proud grin. "I never did completely buckle into what they wanted of me. I was too different."

Gemma resisted religious life—ever since a nun rebuffed her aspirations of becoming a nurse, citing Gemma's smaller, deformed right hand. Gemma was born with several birth defects: The right side of her body is smaller than her left; her right hand had webbed fingers before doctors crafted four stubby fingers using skin from other parts of her body. As a child, Gemma learned to use her deformed hand as well as her normal hand. But the nun at the Sisters of Mercy Hospital didn't accept Gemma's disability.

"She was very, very crude," Gemma remembered.

Though a priest was convinced Gemma had a religious vocation, Gemma was skeptical. She hadn't attended Catholic school. Besides, she really wanted to marry and have children.

"I didn't want anything to do with religious life," Gemma said, her face briefly turning sour.

When she visited the Allentown Carmelites, though, those desires changed overnight. Lured by the Carmelite spirit of prayer, silence, and solitude, Gemma saw becoming a Carmelite as a life that would allow her to focus on building a lifelong relationship with God. As a cloistered and contemplative nun, she could spend her days praying for many people.

"I wanted to give myself to God. All of that wanting to have a family just went out of my head," she said. "It was very romantic."

The Carmelite Sisters in Allentown wore floor-length habits and long veils. Their hair was clipped short. They flagellated themselves for sins and maintained a strict prayer schedule and dietary regimen: eating meat only on authorized days. The sisters ate in silence and spoke only during their daily one hour of recreation. They rose at midnight to pray. Strictly cloistered, they were unable to see even the priest inside the monastery but worshipped mass in the chapel separated by an imposing steel grille, vertical metal bars similar to those in prisons but with protruding spikes. Family members were allowed to visit for one hour every six weeks, talking through a similar grille in the parlor. If a sister's family lived far away, they could come for a day or two once a year. Sisters were not allowed to leave the monastery, even if a family member died.

Mother Superior
Gemma Angelo knitting baby clothes in
the sisters' visiting parlor

During her sixth year at the monastery and about to make her solemn profession of vows, Gemma was tempted to leave religious life altogether. She despised how the monastery's leaders tried to control her, how they seemed to distrust her.

"I just didn't like the way they handled people. They tried to keep you like little children," she said. "In a sense, you were treated subhumanly. I just believed in the freedom of the individual and I didn't think anyone could take that away from me."

Eventually Gemma decided her love for God was stronger than her contempt for the dominating nuns. If she suffered because of her independent personality, she considered it a sacrifice for God. So she stayed and professed her permanent vows.

Not long afterward, the monastery decided to establish a new monastery in Hudson, Wisconsin. Sisters could not refuse the assignment. Of the handful of sisters picked, Gemma was the oldest. Two women were novices and another was a seventeen-year-old candidate. A couple of the young women had been accepted into the community on the condition that they go to the new monastery.

The night before the group left, Gemma learned she would be the mother superior in Hudson. "They saw a leadership quality in me, but they didn't want that there. So they thought I would be ideal to send out."

Having had no instruction on how to be a superior, Gemma at first imitated the Allentown superior's style—the manner that she had so despised herself. Sisters addressed Gemma as Reverend Mother; they bowed and kissed the hem of her habit before they spoke to her. When she reprimanded a sister, the young woman had to kneel and kiss the floor in gratitude. Gemma maintained strict monastic silence. Sisters walked with their eyes cast downward, avoiding eye contact.

Not long after their arrival, Gemma discovered that two of the sisters had major psychological problems. She called upon a Jungian analyst, a Franciscan sister who lived nearby, to work with the sisters. By their second Christmas in Hudson, the troubled sisters had left and were replaced with two sisters sent from Allentown.

In order to protect their cloister, an elderly woman who had recently quit her Franciscan community was installed as the community's extern sister. She lived in the bedroom off the front parlor, collected the sisters' mail, talked with guests, and accepted deliveries. After nine months, she died of a heart attack, and Gemma decided not to replace her. Instead, the sisters depended for years on a mentally disabled neighbor to bring in their mail, mow the grass, and clean the visitors' side of the parlor—since that was considered outside their cloistered boundary.

Within three years of the sisters' arrival in Hudson, Vatican II gave nuns more freedom and encouraged orders to reconsider their overly authoritarian way of life.

"They gave you more leeway and told you that you could do things more humanely," Gemma said. "I think Vatican II made you realize each human being has feelings. And you worked better by being kinder to each other. As time went on, we assumed a very human stance where we would love and care for each other."

The sisters ended their weekly flagellation—striking their buttocks in remembrance of Christ's flogging before his crucifixion. Then they stopped having readings at meals so they could use the time to talk to each other.

"It was just a natural progression," Gemma said, shrugging her shoulders and deflecting any suggestion that she had been a bold leader in embracing change.

The sisters' bishop supported their changes. The sisters' diocese in Hudson was on the forefront of the Church's changes in the sixties and was the first in the area to replace Latin with English during mass. In addition, the sisters observed that the Catholic Church in the Midwest was much more practical and progressive than the traditional and ethnic churches back East.

In 1968, the sisters eliminated the wimple, the tight white headpiece worn around the face, thus becoming the first within their order to modify the habit. The next year, they shortened the habit from ankle-length to midcalf and gave the garment more shape. Over the years, they would gradually dress more and more casually, first wearing a brown work habit for gardening until they agreed that jeans and sweatshirts were more practical. They still wear their habit for mass and official functions.

The sisters' most radical departure with traditional cloistered life came in 1969 when they took down their grilles in the visiting parlor and chapel. Until then, even the priest had not been allowed to see the sisters. He'd dispensed the Eucharist to them through a window in the screen.

"It used to be walls were the most important. You were cloistered, and you mustn't go beyond a certain point," Gemma said as we walked through a gate in the monastery fence to the hermitage on the other side, a quaint white cottage where I would stay. "Our cloister is the cloister of the heart. It's not necessarily walls. I think it is a freer way of looking at life: allowing people to be themselves and allowing them to express themselves in the clothes they wear."

In another bold move, the sisters bought a green Volkswagen Rabbit in 1971 so they wouldn't have to depend on others to escort them to buy groceries or visit the doctor. Most of the sisters' driver's licenses had long since expired, so the sisters called the high school driving instructor and took turns behind the wheel. This, too, would become an embarrassment to the larger order.

When Gemma attended her order's international meeting in Spain in 1973 to rewrite its constitutions—the rules of their order—she drove from the airport to the monastery. Upon her arrival, the host nuns made her park the rental car inside the monastery gates because they didn't want their neighbors to see that a nun had driven a car. But they couldn't hide her appearance from other sisters.

"I was the liberal nun. I had on a shorter habit. They had on longer habits," she remembered.

Her first confrontation arose when the Spanish sisters suggested that their order of Carmelite nuns simply adopt the new constitutions that the male Carmelites had recently rewritten.

"Well, I didn't like that at all," Gemma said. "We went into a big thing about that. I was very adamant."

One reason Gemma had attended the international meeting was to assure that the sisters adopted more modern laws, especially a looser understanding of what it meant to live as a cloistered nun. At the time, Sister Lucia's father was ill and, as an only child, she wanted to return home to Allentown to see him before he died. Gemma wasn't about to let the sisters rubber-stamp constitutions already written by the Carmelite monks and priests. She wanted a say in how their lives were to be lived and she thought all the nuns present should have a voice.

When only one of the Spanish sisters was appointed to speak for all Spanish-speaking nuns at the meeting, Gemma again spoke up: "I come from a country that has democracy and I think everybody should be able to speak for themselves."

Gemma raised eyebrows at the meeting but she achieved a major victory in securing a new constitution that allowed sisters to leave the cloister to visit their families. Not surprisingly, the Allentown monastery was furious with the Hudson sisters for loosening their enclosure and relinquishing traditions that Carmelites had practiced for centuries.

"They got wind of what we were doing and they sent us nasty letters saying: 'You can't do this. You can't change it.' They were very angry. They thought we were betraying them and betraying who we are as Carmelites. We communicated with them very lovingly and let it go at that."

Though they kept the letters that detail their rift with their former mother house, they consider it disrespectful to dwell on the friction in public. The letters, Gemma said, are part of the sisters' secret archives.

"There it's just like it was in the beginning," Gemma said of the Allentown monastery. "They have not made many changes after Vatican II. They wear the longer habit and have pretty much the same observance."

Gemma and I stopped walking to study the splendor of yellow daffodils covering a hillside. It seemed a tranquil life: singing psalms and tending the garden. I felt an overwhelming sense of peace and beauty. There was no question that one felt closer to God here, that a person could be kinder, more Christlike in this atmosphere.

Had the sisters ever had to justify their lifestyle of prayer to people who thought they should be working outside the monastery? I asked.

"People used to say: Why the contemplative life? Why don't you utilize your resources? You hear it less and less. It just seems that people are realizing there is a need for prayer."

Removing the barriers, though, cost the sisters a great deal. Besides alienating them from other Carmelite houses, their progressive lifestyle has prevented them from attracting younger women to join them. Their modern approach does not meet the vision of women who expect habited sisters and a rigid cloistered lifestyle. During my visits, I would meet several women who lived briefly with the sisters but ultimately decided against joining.

"It seems like the people who want to enter religious life now want more of a strict observance," Gemma told me. "They want to be regulated by rules. They want a very strict lifestyle. They want to be told what to do and how to act. They want the mystique of being a cloistered nun. We've gotten away from all that."

Gemma and I stopped at the sisters' small greenhouse. Sister Mary O'Neill was watering seedlings and pampering young tomato plants. Besides Gemma, Mary is the only other founding sister at the monastery. She was only twenty-one years old when she arrived as Gemma's assistant. Now, at fifty-six years old, she remains one of the youngest sisters.

A robust woman with curly strawberry blond hair and blue eyes, Mary giggles frequently at her own mishaps. Mary's family is from Appalachia, and she has a down-home air about her, habitually telling stories to accentuate her point of view, which frequently revolves around themes of poverty and accepting a person's circumstances—making lemonade out of lemons, as she'd say.

While some sisters offered pious, religious motives for becoming nuns, Mary's reason was refreshingly blunt. She simply thought she would come for a couple years, "get this hankering for prayer and contemplative life out of my system," and then become a psychiatric nurse. Just before she joined the Carmelite order in 1960 at eighteen years old, she bet a boy on her school bus that she'd last at least two weeks. That was her goal. He became a network news producer. Mary has never collected the twenty-dollar bet.

Becoming a sister, though, nearly didn't happen for her because many

orders in those days required women to have dowries. One Carmelite order wrote to Mary saying that if she was serious she needed a three-
thousand-dollar dowry. The principal at her Catholic high school helped
Mary find the Allentown Carmelites, who only required certain clothes,
washing basins, and "nunny shoes."

"My girlfriends and I went to this ladies' shoestore to get these nunny
shoes," Mary said after Gemma introduced us and left us alone. "They
have a little high heel and are long, black, and narrow. Very good shoes.
They're not supposed to make much noise. We made up a story that these
shoes were for my aunt. I didn't want anyone to know I was going into
the monastery. As we were leaving, the lady said, 'What's the name of
your aunt?' And I said, 'Aunt Ruth,' and my friend said, 'Aunt Mary.' So
the lady knew we were lying."

Despite having aunts and an uncle who were religious contemplatives, Mary's knowledge of cloistered life was limited. "I didn't know you
went behind a wall," she said. "My dad cried like a baby. It was like they
were closing the tomb. It was that kind of feeling."

At first, Mary didn't think she'd even last as long as the two weeks
she'd wagered. The sisters went to bed at 9 P.M. and got up at midnight to
pray vigils. Then they returned to bed and rose at 5 A.M. Mary planned to
tell the superior she wanted to leave, but she delayed the meeting so long
that she decided to stay.

"You see the benefits of developing a relationship with God," Mary
explained. "You firmly believe that a life of prayer can be efficacious for
the world. Because if you don't believe that, you're just a bunch of old
maids behind a monastery wall."

The Allentown sisters were required to cover their faces with veils
when an outsider, such as a workman or a doctor, entered the monastery.
When Mary heard that a dentist was coming, she wondered what veil she
was supposed to wear.

"In my mind, I thought there must be a special veil that has a hole in
the middle so that the dentist could only see your teeth and not the rest of
your face," she said and laughed.

Mary continued to discover other mysteries of cloistered life. Unsure how the sisters flagellated themselves during the Friday disciplines, Mary's novice director had to give her specific directions.

"We did our butts in those days—our bummers," she remembered, giggling. "I thought you did it over your habit. But my novice mistress said, 'No, no, you do your bare skin.' I said, 'What do you mean? You pull your pants down?' I was just dumb. I didn't get it."

Mary's family came to visit her once a year; her younger siblings would sit on the other side of the parlor grilles and suck on the spikes like lollipops, longing to hug her. "My sisters said when they used to open those grille doors with the curtains and the screen, it was like they had opened a casket.

"It was very harsh in a sense, it conveyed that the world was bad," she added. "And that's not the purpose of grilles and enclosure. It's not to keep the world out. It's to help you focus. It's not because you are afraid of the world, or because you don't want the world in. Otherwise, you are pampered people."

For the first five years at Hudson, the sisters read no newspapers or magazines and didn't own a television set. When President John F. Kennedy was assassinated in November 1963 the sisters didn't know. They were praying the rosary that night when a local reporter called and informed them.

"I missed the whole John F. Kennedy fascination," Mary said with palpable remorse. "We all had gaps. For me, who entered in 1960, there was a knowledge gap of ten years. Sisters who have updated will often say: 'Well, that was during my gap.'"

By 1968, the enclosure seal was cracking. The sisters got their first television shortly before Bobby Kennedy was shot. They watched his funeral. Then they subscribed to *Newsweek*. The first issue they received carried graphic pictures of fighting in Vietnam.

"I read it and just bawled," Mary remembered. "It just hit me: the horror these men and women were going through over there. I just absorbed that *Newsweek*. I was reading every single thing. Then we started to watch the different riots, the demonstrations, the Republican and Democratic conventions. It was like I woke up in the seventies.

"It was kind of like being Rip Van Winkle. It made you realize that you could say: 'What am I doing here when this is all going on out there?' or 'What can I do to help this?' And that's where I think if you really believe in this life, then you believe that prayer can help, a life of prayer."

Part of that prayer life initially included making plenary indulgences—prayers for those in purgatory. "They used to call it the 'green god syndrome'—like green stamps," Mary explained. "If you said enough, you got this or that, like Betty Crocker coupons. If you said an Our Father, a Hail Mary, and a Glory Be eight times in a certain place, then you would get a soul from purgatory."

Mary no longer believes that anyone is unsaved, regardless whether they believe in God or not. For her, a dedicated life of prayer is about trust. She prays for people who need help and turns their problems over to God. "You just believe that good will go out," she said.

Sister Lucia La Montagne digs up rosebushes in the spring as the monastery's hundred-pound collie, Kieran, plays in the background

With no ministries such as a school or a hospital to bring in money and because they don't sell crosses, cards, rosaries, or cheese, the sisters put their fate in God's hands, depending on modest donations.

"Prayer is our product," Mary insisted. "We are giving something that people of faith can appreciate."

Nearly every day Mary receives about fifteen prayer requests through the Internet, many heart-wrenching stories of people with ravenous diseases and only a few months to live. Email messages come from Australia, England, Ireland, and Japan. Mary responds with what she calls "gentle" counseling. Recently, a gay artist from Eastern Europe wrote about how hard it was for him to be accepted into society. Mary suggested he first accept himself.

Like their outreach on the Internet, the sisters welcome the public to the monastery for mass. Praying with people in their chapel seems more human, "more fitting with what Christ would have done," Mary said. Instead of trying to keep a strict cloister, the sisters feel it is better to consider each opportunity to let someone in.

"You make these pastoral decisions about whom to bring in to the monastery," Mary explained. "If they need help, then you bring them in. That's where your enclosure is a little elastic."

Without younger women to take over, closing the monastery remains a looming threat as the sisters continue to age and suffer increasing physical ailments.

"None of us have died yet," Mary said. "Any of us could drop over. You just never know. Jane's health is not that good. She has a chronic illness. We were really getting nervous for a while. Then we just talked about it and we said we have to place this in God's hands."

Still the sisters dismiss any suggestion that they could merge with a sister monastery to survive. They simply couldn't retreat to their former restricted lifestyle. In fact, the other monasteries no longer allow Hudson sisters inside their cloisters.

Recently two Hudson sisters attended the funeral of a sister they'd known well at the Wahpeton, North Dakota, monastery. Maintaining their strict enclosure, the Wahpeton sisters never invited the Hudson sisters inside their cloister. Instead the Hudson sisters ate their meals alone in the guest parlor and talked to the sisters through a partition.

MASS IN THE LIVING ROOM

A high-pitched clanking interrupted my talk with Sister Mary. We looked across the spacious garden at a sister ringing the outdoor prayer bell. The others hurried into the house. They had just a few minutes to change from jeans into habits.

A few minutes later, the sisters entered the chapel wearing prim brown habits with black veils, looking like sisters from the seventies. Actually, the sisters' habits have remained much the same since that time. The chapel, several rows of padded chairs facing a podium and an altar, is housed in the home's former living room. Near the altar inside a lighted case is the sisters' creative version of the tabernacle: a giant glass Hershey's Kiss.

Though the sisters took down their chapel grille in 1969, they remained separated from visitors in the chapel until 1990. That's when they tore down a waist-high partition and installed ceiling-to-floor windows overlooking the garden. Now sitting in the chapel feels like communing with nature.

Guests were already seated. A middle-aged woman, her husband, and their three small children took up most of the back row. A young priest from a nearby university sat near the altar. He had very dark hair, square glasses that matched his square head, and chunky cheeks that suggested he'd often partaken in the sisters' cooking.

Sister Lucia began playing the organ and the sisters took their seats. Wearing only a bathrobe, one sister made her way down the stairs near the chapel entrance; one side of her body was tangled and limp. Aided by metal leg braces, she hobbled to the closet where the sisters keep their choir robes, camel-colored loose smocks. Awkwardly, the handicapped woman, whom I later learned is Sister Jane, tugged the material over her head and her thick glasses then squirmed each arm into its hole.

While a number of women have joined the Hudson monastery, Jane has the distinction of being the only one who stayed. Yet, her situation seemed the most precarious. At forty-nine, Jane is the monastery's youngest sister and the most frail. With cerebral palsy and multiple sclerosis among a long list of ailments, Jane's main goal every day is to get out of bed and dress herself. Painful muscle spasms often keep her bedridden and that morning was no different. She'd missed morning prayers and was arriving late to mass—without her habit.

As the service began, the chapel's peaceful atmosphere was pierced by screaming, the sound of munching Cheerios, loudly whispered admonitions, then the clatter of cereal hitting chairs and walls. The sisters seemed to ignore the chaos, even when stray cereal struck them. After the service, I felt I'd been through a grueling hour of baby-sitting. I wondered how they could endure such a daily dose of unwieldy children. As we headed down the stairs for lunch in the sisters' formal dining room, one sister leaned over and whispered, "She's really a wonderful woman; she just has too many kids."

As we took our places at the dining room table, set with china and silverware and lighted by a low-hung chandelier, a sister brought out some homemade wine and the sisters poured themselves generous portions. Over vegetables and roasted turkey, we talked about national politics, children shooting classmates, and Sister Rita Steinhagen, the Minneapolis nun serving time in a federal prison for trespassing during a protest at the School of the Americas. The SOA, located in Georgia, is a U.S. government training ground for Latin American paramilitaries; its graduates have been blamed for several heinous murders. I expected the nuns to disapprove of Steinhagen's civil disobedience tactics, but the sisters applauded her efforts. They were well versed in the arguments for and against the SOA's closure and adamant about the need to shut the place down. Living inside these walls, the sisters seemed far more knowledgeable about national and international issues than many people on the outside.

★　★　★

At night I stayed in the sisters' hermitage, a white cottage perched at the edge of a steep bluff at the end of a country lane just beyond their fence. In recent years they had acquired the property and buildings next to their monastery. One small cottage houses a hermit priest who leads mass in the sisters' chapel several times a week. The sisters use the other building as a hermitage for their own personal retreats and rent it out to those seeking solace, yet another break with their order. The hermitage brings even more people to the monastery. Such visitors also pray in the chapel and share their lives with the sisters.

The hermitage is as peaceful as the monastery and gardens. Religious artwork hangs from the walls; the few windows are made of stained glass. I couldn't help but feel pampered. There are scented candles and scented soaps and shampoos, stacks of spiritual books and meditative tapes. Junk food fills the pantry. There are cookies, teas, cocoas, popcorn, puddings, colas, Pringles potato chips, soups, candy, Pop-Tarts, Beenee Weenies. The refrigerator holds containers of the sisters' stew and homemade pie.

That night I drifted off to sleep while staring at the moonlight shining through the skylights and listening to the soft chanting of monks on a tape. In the morning, bright beams of sunlight flooded through the same skylights—God's own wake-up call.

When I knocked on the chapel door a few minutes later, Sister Grace, a Hispanic sister originally from Texas, let me in. She and the monastery's hundred-pound collie, Kieran, led me into the empty chapel, where we stared out the back windows. Prisoners with shaved heads and military greens were congregating in the backyard. Since 1995, prisoners have been coming to the monastery to paint, chop wood, and rake leaves—chores the sisters can no longer perform themselves. The prisoners are detached from a nearby prison boot camp that allows young men with drug offenses to reduce three-year sentences by doing six months of hard labor.

On this cool, crisp morning, they had come to clean up the yard. A man in military fatigues issued orders, and the men saluted, then broke into small work groups. They scraped leaves from the lawn and hauled them in wheelbarrows to the back of the enclosed seven acres.

Suddenly the prayer bell rang, and I took my seat in the chapel's front row. The sisters, wearing sweatshirts and pants, quietly sauntered in, bowing toward the Hershey's Kiss tabernacle. They crossed themselves, then sang their morning office in high-pitched voices, sounding like prepubescent girls. One side of the chapel sang a verse and then the other side responded.

As the sisters' voices rose in a long crescendo, I watched the prisoners encircle the Virgin Mary statue in the yard to rake bits of twigs and dead grass from around her.

"From heaven the Lord gazed upon the earth," the sisters sang.

"To hear the groaning of the prisoner;

"To set free those who were doomed to death. . . ."

How surreal, I thought. Here these lifelong virgins were singing in their soporific voices while the convicts' rakes scraped their sacred ground. It was as if the nuns and former drug dealers and addicts were living the verse.

NEED FOR NURTURING

On my last afternoon, Gemma and I sat talking in the parlor as she knitted a baby jumper. She often knits baby clothes as gifts to new parents.

"When are you going to start your own family?" Gemma asked, as she had several times during my stay. Each time, I reminded her that I already had two adopted children. But she always pressed when I would be having my own "natural" children.

Gemma told me that being a mother is as much a religious vocation as being a cloistered nun. She is the first nun who ever emphasized to me how honorable mothers are, how cherished my role is, how proud I should be. Historically, the Church deemed celibates better Christians, more pious, and I had assumed nuns thought married women were weak, that having coupled with a man made us less devout, impure, or perhaps immoral. After all, our children aren't formed by immaculate conception. We were women who had sex, some more frequently and fervently than others, and not always with a desire to conceive children. But that is clearly not how Gemma feels.

"Do you ever feel you sacrificed by not having your own family?" I asked.

"No. If you have a husband and children, your loyalties are to them," she said. "Whereas this type of life, you can give so much to everyone who comes to you and you don't have to be restricted by anything."

So, while mothers nurture their children, nuns are free to nurture—or mother—everyone.

Gemma would have made a great mother. She is an affectionate, gentle spirit. It is obvious in the way she cares for Kieran, treating the dog as her child, hand-feeding him and brushing his hair every day. I saw how nurturing and patient she is with Jane, too. One night we went to the local parish, and Gemma and Lucia, both older women themselves, practically carried Jane, who is bigger than the two of them, up a long entrance ramp.

"I wanted to get married and have twelve children," Gemma confessed. "We always were a big family. We always had a lot of people at our house, a lot of children. We had an open attitude. A lot of love was passed around. That's what I wanted to do was raise a family."

In a way, that's what she has done.

As I prepared to leave, the sisters loaded my car with tomato plants from their greenhouse and tried to give me homemade rhubarb pie. They pleaded with me to return soon. They invited me to bring my husband and children for mass. I had arrived as a journalist and was departing a family member. The sisters had fussed over me and hugged me at every prayer time. They had inquired about my life, my family, how I spent my day, how I picked out my clothes, and where I vacationed. They asked about how I cooked and whether I entertained. They had asked me nearly as many questions as I had asked them. And they were genuinely interested.

When I drove away, the cool evening breeze blew through my hair, and I couldn't stop smiling. I felt giddy and light-headed, as if I had emerged from a deep meditation. The little worries that I carry around like Post-It Notes seemed to have fallen away. I couldn't think of one bad thing in my life. I wished others could experience the same joy these women temporarily infused in me. I felt madly in love with life. I felt I had been madly loved. It was like I had discovered my own secret garden of grandmothers.

So often when I visited cloistered communities, I left feeling sad, remorseful that I was one of only a few people who had experienced such women so intimately, that for a few hours or a few days I was able to probe the depths of their souls, to get a sense of what all those years in silence and solitude had rendered. Though I understand and appreciate the dedication of such nuns and their need for uninterrupted focus, I also see the needs of women outside the cloister, women who spend their lives rushing from jobs to husbands to children and desperately desire to be nurtured as they have nurtured others. Such women often crave solitude, tranquility, and joy, aspects that many cloistered nuns have attained. Mothers need to hear that their role, often devalued in the modern world, is honorable and as worthy as that of women who devote their lives to God. I often heard nuns say that the true sacrificial life is being a wife and a mother.

The Hudson sisters, with their embracing, benevolent nature, provided the kind of thoughtfulness that I, as an adult woman, had rarely received. Even pampering at exclusive spas doesn't equate to the pleasure of being cared for by human beings who aren't paid to do so.

I was glad that the Hudson Carmelites had persevered, that they had connected themselves with people outside their small community, that their elastic cloister is allowed to bend and expand to include all those who need to be embraced. Their gift is seemingly intangible, yet they make people feel special, cared for. And I realized how empty many lives would be if these women had simply followed their order's ancient traditions and hunkered down for years behind steel bars. While strictly cloistered nuns may feel that the Hudson Carmelites have disobeyed the true spirit of contemplatives, the truth is that they have obeyed their vision of God, their conscience, and their calling.

These women have touched so many through their attention to the needs of everyday folk. Whether it is the few women and men who gather daily at their chapel for mass, or the gay couple who stayed at their hermitage and were welcomed for prayers, or the Jewish couple who stayed at the monastery and walked the gardens as they grieved the deaths of their daughters, the sisters open up their community to share themselves.

The number of relationships the sisters maintain often surprised me. One night after a talk at the local parish, several women surrounded the sisters, dragging adult daughters or friends to introduce. They hugged the sisters and talked on and on, clearly enamored. Gemma just smiled and held my hand. At Jane's Jubilee—the twenty-fifth anniversary of her vows—the sisters' backyard was filled with hundreds of people, many in wheelchairs and motorized carts, people Jane had befriended, several through the Internet.

Despite the cloister's eight-foot-tall fence, the sisters are not isolated. The monastery phone rings frequently. Occasionally people stop by to pick up food that the sisters donate out of what is given to them. Others come by for private consultation or prayers. Several have supported the monastery for decades. One man has paid their milk bill since they arrived—nearly forty years. Another man has provided toilet paper for twenty. Grocery stores and the community food shelf donate food. Most clothes come from a local retirement center after residents die. Nearly every china dish or knickknack in their parlor was given by someone they helped.

"We're not being disloyal," Gemma told me. "We've tried to build bridges with the other communities and say we're not that different from you. The only thing we've done is be a little bit more open and human. We know what is happening out in our world and we can pray for people and have closer contact with people. We don't keep our prayer lives to ourselves."

PART THREE

CHASTITY

THE SECOND VOW A SISTER PROFESSES INVOLVES HER PHYSICAL body, an area that, until recently, few religious orders wanted to deal with. While many people assume that chastity is simply the renunciation of sex, the vow encompasses a great deal more, including an intense loyalty to both the order and God. A woman pledges her absolute fidelity to her community. Even her thoughts are to remain pure. She promises to renounce sexual relationships with others—and herself. In some orders, the vow is interpreted as forsaking emotional intimacy with others, saving such intense communing for private prayer.

While many people outside religious life may think that chastity—or celibacy—is the hardest of the three vows, most nuns say chastity is challenging but usually something they deal with at certain intervals in life, not on a daily basis. Often when a woman enters religious life, her focus isn't on her physical desires. Only after several years does she become acutely aware of what she has given up. Many nuns say the struggle is most intense in their thirties and then again during menopause when they realize that having children is no longer physically possible.

Often, though, it's not the physical contact that a nun longs for, but a lifelong relationship with a partner who is human. Up until the last twenty years, close friendships were discouraged at most orders. Sisters were supposed to be equally available to all members of the community. Choosing certain individuals as close friends was frowned upon. These "particular friendships" were viewed as dangerous because it was thought they could lead to sexual temptations. If a sister wasn't emotionally intimate with anyone, the belief was she wouldn't be tempted to be sexually intimate with anyone either. Not only were women shutting off their sexual impulses but they were also shutting off their emotional needs. God and Jesus were the only ones they needed, they were told.

Now religious orders have greatly relaxed such rules. Most communities understand that friendships are healthy. Several communities, like the Benedictines in Ferdinand, Indiana, openly discuss chastity and the struggles of maintaining this vow. They encourage women to talk about their sexual desires and their losses. They try to help women accept themselves as sexual beings and to teach them how to channel this powerful, sexual energy. Other communities, such as the Trappistines in Crozet, Virginia, are teaching human sexuality but in a more sterile, less intimate atmosphere.

While close friendships are encouraged and expected at the Ferdinand Benedictines, they are seen as stumbling blocks at the Trappistines in Virginia. Both communities teach that it is normal to want sexual relationships, but the Benedictines go further in that they encourage their sisters to discuss these everyday sexual struggles with each other, whereas the Trappistines keep such intimate thoughts to themselves or share them only with the mother superior. To the Trappistines—who follow a much stricter interpretation of the Rule of St. Benedict—chastity means forsaking intimate friendships that could interfere with their relationship with God.

6

THE SENSUAL SISTERS

BENEDICTINES IN FERDINAND, INDIANA

"We've learned to find intimacy, and it doesn't have to be sexual. I can be sitting with another sister in conversation talking at a very deep level and that would be so intimate."

—SISTER TESS DUENAS

I n rural Indiana, near the Kentucky border, roads slither through fields like snakes through tall grass. Rows of corn toss in the hot wind. White clapboard houses and red barns flank family farms dating back generations. Atop Mount Thabor, a large hill overlooking the German-settled village of Ferdinand, stands a medieval-looking monastery, home of the Benedictine Sisters. Resembling a scene from *The Sound of Music,* this was the last place I expected to find nuns candid about their sexuality and their struggles with celibacy.

For decades, the monastery had drawn sister candidates from nearby farm families. But ten years ago, the sisters faced a dwindling future with no new recruits and benefactors reluctant to give money to a foundering monastery. Attract new blood or perish, the sisters were told.

So the Benedictines launched a jazzy advertising campaign, hoping to attract women from across the country. Using clever one-liners, the ads dismissed religious stereotypes and touted a new, improved nun: a cosmopolitan woman, openly flawed, endowed with a personality, and not timid about expressing her sexuality.

"OSB (Order of St. Benedict) seeks SF (Single Female)," began one ad, parodying personal dating ads. "21–45, Catholic, spiritual, w/sense of humor, ISO (in search of) LTR (long-term relationship). Ht./wt. open. Must love God/life. Photo not req. Reply ASAP."

One ad promised: "You don't have to be perfect to be a nun." Another touted: "Molds are for cookies, not nuns." Others countered the fear that a woman would lose her identity if she became a sister: "I thought I'd have to leave my personality behind. I didn't even have to leave my trumpet." A few ads targeted the void that successful women sometimes experience: "I've got the job. I've got the car. I've got the friends. Something's missing."

After launching their ads in 1992, the sisters received more than four hundred inquiries. By the time of my first visit in 1998, the Ferdinand Benedictines had transformed into one of the country's fastest-growing monasteries. That year alone the sisters boasted fifteen women in formation—preparing to become full-fledged nuns—and more than five hundred women on their mailing list.

Ferdinand's brazen ads draw a different kind of woman, one who is curious about religious life but who previously disqualified herself because she believed she was not prudish enough or pure enough to become an icon of perfection. Many were under the mistaken impression that nuns had to be virgins, rare among women in their twenties, thirties, and forties, ages the ads target. Advertising in a hip, daring way attracts hip, daring women. And while the ads project an image the monastery hopes to achieve, it is the new nuns who are making the commercialized portrayal a reality.

LIVING SINGLE FOR GOD

At 6:30 A.M. my first morning, I climbed the 110 stairs from the dorm at the foot of Mount Thabor to the domed cathedral atop it. The cathedral was dimly lit when I entered, huffing and puffing from the steep ascent. Light trickled in from stained-glass windows, casting spooky shadows along the alcoves. Sisters sat in rows of hand-carved pews near the altar, flanked by massive white Roman colonnades. Behind the altar, a giant wooden cross holds a lifelike statue of Jesus bathed in lights—the only man in the room had everyone's attention.

As the sisters started singing, two young women rushed in, their hair still wet from showering. One, a heavy-set woman wearing ratty jeans and a baggy shirt, was twenty-seven-year-old Sister Macy Jo Marshall. Her friend, sporting short black hair and sleepy eyes, was Sister Briana Craddock. At twenty-six, Briana is the youngest sister in formation, the five- to nine-year training period before a sister makes her final vows. Both work in the monastery's gift shop (called For Heaven's Sake), where they don't have to report until 10 A.M.

"I'm struggling getting up in the mornings," admitted Macy later at the gift shop. "I'm really mean in the morning. It was a hard adjustment for me. I'd worked nights, for six years, till two A.M. I really hope we get a prioress who wants to do morning prayers at nine A.M."

Macy grew up in Lansing, Michigan, with her mother and three sisters. Her parents divorced when Macy was young, and she didn't see much of her father. "When I was little I always wanted to live single for the Lord. I'd go around in my little dresses, praying over the dead worms and burying them," she said. "I carried around my little Bible."

Raised Catholic and educated at Catholic schools, Macy was among the first generation of Catholics taught by lay people. "I didn't know any sisters," she said. "I saw The Sound of Music and The Flying Nun. I didn't know what to think."

As Macy got older, she discovered boys and her interest in "living single for God" waned. She had several serious relationships, including one she was convinced would lead to marriage. But she was too demanding and he was too wimpy, she said.

While in her early twenties, Macy worked her way up to night manager at a McDonald's and took sign language classes at a local college.

Sensing something was missing in her life, she started attending church more frequently and remembered her earlier desire to live single for God.

Not long after, Macy called the local diocese office. "Hi!" Macy said. "I want to be a nun. What do I do?"

The woman who answered the phone happened to be a nun, the first one Macy had ever talked with. She sent Macy information on religious orders, including a copy of *Vision* magazine, geared toward people considering religious life. The magazine is laden with ads for various communities, including the Ferdinand Benedictines.

"In the magazine you'd see all these ads with old nuns playing guitars or old nuns taking care of children in Africa. But in the Ferdinand Benedictines there's just a dome and you want to find out more."

Macy narrowed her search to five orders. One was the Daughters of St. Paul, who run bookstores, publish religious books and pamphlets, and produce videos. An avid reader, Macy liked the idea of working in a bookstore. She didn't admire the Daughters' blue habit though; her McDonald's manager uniform had been blue. Fourth on Macy's list was the Ferdinand Benedictines, whose ads she found "catchy." Since she couldn't afford to visit all five, Macy prayed that God would help her decide. Two hours later, the Ferdinand Benedictines called her.

On her first visit, Macy was struck by the fact that the sisters were just as flawed as she was.

"I was so excited the first time somebody broke a dish," she said, laughing. "I thought: Wow! This is great! They even break dishes! Then somebody got up late and came running into morning prayers. Somebody had a hole in her pants. Somebody else got up [in church] to read and they messed up and got embarrassed. It was just little human faults. It's just like in real life. You have people who want to get out of church first, so they rush out after communion. And it was cool to know that you could still be human and be a sister. There weren't all these expectations of you being this 'holier than thou' person. You could be who you were and fit in."

Macy said she enjoys working at the gift shop because she feels less isolated from meeting people from outside the monastery. Occasionally customers come into the store upset about some tragedy—an accident, a death, a disease—and talk to Briana or Macy for hours. Customers frequently are taken aback when they learn the young clerks are nuns.

"This one family came in and they wanted to know if they could 'go look at the sisters,' like we're a side of beef," Macy recounted. "I asked, 'Look at the sisters? What do you mean?' They said, 'Oh, we just want to see what they look like.' I said, 'Well, you're looking at one! We just look like regular people.' They said, 'Oh. We thought you would look different.' I told them, 'This is as exciting as it gets.' "

The young women candidly talked about how they are lonely at times and struggle with desires to have children.

"For me, there's still a choice," said Briana, who was stocking a shelf with vanilla-scented candles. "Yes, I have maternal instincts. I was wondering: Gosh, if I had kids what would they look like? It's not like you come here and it ends. I don't dismiss it. It's still an issue. Still, I feel more strongly called to this than marriage."

Raised in an era of pervasive sexual images, Briana and Macy are not shy to talk about their bodies or their temptations or their lives before nunhood. It all seems very natural and honest to them.

"I liked the intimacy of sex," Macy said. "Since I've been here intimacy doesn't have to be physical. It can be a deep friendship."

Briana added, "You have to have relationships. I'm still trying to figure everything out. Yeah, it gets lonely. Sometimes deep down you feel: Nobody knows me. Nobody understands me."

Macy thought that once she became a nun, her physical desires would subside. "I thought I would have a special grace from God. I was very idealistic. He gives you what you need to deal with it. I didn't realize it would take as much work. I wish that once you became a nun, you'd stop getting your period—that's what I thought happened as a kid."

NO SPECIAL GRACES

Many religious sisters I met at other communities were loath to discuss sex and dismissed such yearnings as something that never affected them or that they got over, like a cold. They often gave lofty explanations that involve mysterious "graces" from God. The Ferdinand sisters are forthright: The hardest part about being a nun, many say, is not having an intimate, sexual relationship and not having children. I respect their honesty. They aren't being salacious or impertinent. They simply want to demystify religious life at every turn. They want to be seen as real women with real needs.

No one made this clearer than Sister Tess Duenas, a native of Guam. The sisters suggested that I speak with Tess. I would later observe that Tess and a handful of others the monastery had me seek out are the same confident, attractive faces that appear in nearly all advertising, brochures, and videos.

Tess is forty-two, but she appears decades younger, with her short dark hair, jade green eyes, and suntan from gardening and running; I did a double take when I first spotted her jogging in shorts around the monastery.

She had initially considered—but then dismissed—becoming a sister in high school. At age twenty-seven, as she was about to enter graduate school, she felt a deep pang and knew she had to seriously consider religious life one final time. Her parents supported her for a year while she sorted out the issue.

Her biggest obstacle was celibacy.

Tess asked various sisters how they dealt with the physical longings. Some sisters joked that they took showers; others said they went for walks or sought physical activities. Others confessed celibacy was difficult at first but became easier as they got older.

The sisters' honesty helped Tess see that living a celibate life takes courage, not belief in "special graces" or denying her humanity. For Tess, talking about her frustrations is more helpful than ignoring those feelings.

"It doesn't seem as intense," she said, then screamed: "*Ahhhh!* If I were to keep it in and be all quiet and secret about it, it would be frustrating. I find that it opens others to be free also and say, 'You know, I feel that way, too. So let's go for a walk, or let's go play tennis.'

"I'm not going to deny it. I'm not going to stuff it," she added. "It's a matter of going and sharing our story with each other. We joke about it. That's one tension-relieving way. We also cry about it and say, 'You know, I'm just having one of those horny days, so watch out!'

"We've learned to find intimacy, and it doesn't have to be sexual. I can be sitting with another sister in conversation talking at a very deep level and that would be so intimate. That's what intimacy is: getting to the very core of who we are and to be able to share that."

Not long after Tess took her first vows, she lived in a rural community near Ferdinand and taught third grade. One day while shopping with a woman friend, Tess pointed out an attractive man.

"Tess, you're a nun!" the woman gasped.

"And you're a married woman," Tess responded. "Do you agree he's cute?"

The woman nodded.

"Are you going to leave your husband and jump in bed with him just because you thought he was cute?" Tess pressed. "Can you just admire him from a distance and still stay committed to what you're doing?"

"Yeah, well, I just thought nuns didn't have those thoughts," her friend said.

Tess felt she had given the woman a new perspective on religious women, that she'd shattered the myth that nuns are somehow different, nonhuman, that they don't have sexual feelings.

"We're human beings and struggle through the same things married women do. It's that commitment. How committed are you to your marriage?" she asked me without waiting for an answer. "I'm as committed to my community. So there are times I do feel lonely. But there is also the consolation that there are sisters to support me, and we are all in this thing together."

The energy Tess might have put into a marriage or having children is channeled into her work and into her relationships with other sisters. As she has aged, her sexual desires, the pull to be a mother, have declined. What has helped her the most is reimagining God as a maternal being.

"God's more like the Crone, the old woman. She can sit there and say, 'Come here and tell me about it.' It's that kind of experience, that spirit of a mother, an elderly woman God. Kind of like your grandmother who lived life and has birthed children and has grandchildren and understands at the deepest level what that ache's all about."

At first I thought Tess and the younger sisters, Macy and Briana, were aberrations. I had never been to a monastery or convent where sisters talked so openly about their struggles with celibacy. The Ferdinand sisters, though, recognize that experiencing physical attractions is normal.

Some sisters even encourage their feelings of sexuality. They think it is healthy to flirt, that it allows them to feel more alive and to feel more fully their vow of chastity. Sister Rachel Neveu said that her need to be near men was why she quit teaching and became a parish minister.

"I was in the classroom all day and the only male people in the building were the janitor and the principal," said the forty-seven-year-old. "We were all female teachers, and I just missed the intimacy, the dialogue, the conversation, the encounters."

Attractive and statuesque, with cropped chestnut hair, a long neck, and an angular jawline, Rachel wears bronze oval glasses that heighten her intellectual aura. She looks more like a college librarian than a seductress. So how could this nun be such an avowed flirt?

Rachel laughed. Being around men causes her to have temptations, she said, but she has learned not to act on her desires. "Just because I have them doesn't mean I go out looking for that genital satisfaction," she said.

"I think it's healthy," she added, "because it calls me to womanhood and to look at the vows, and not to feel inhibited—to allow myself to have those feelings and acknowledge that I am a woman; I am sexual rather than dried up and not attractive. It energizes me."

Like Tess, Rachel equates her sexual attractions to men as those any married woman might have. She said the support of her sisters helps her break off friendships whenever they become too intense. The "breakup" might be painful, but then she just puts herself back out there, again making friends with men.

"You'd think it would be easier being in an all-women environment, then you wouldn't have that sensation," Rachel said. "I'm going through midlife, and it's worse now than it's ever been!" she shouted, then laughed. "I don't stifle my feelings. In years past the sisters were not allowed to even speak about it!"

In recent years, the Ferdinand Benedictines, like most religious orders, began accepting middle-aged women whose marriages have been annulled and whose children are adults. Whereas marriage and a sexual life prevented women in previous decades from entering religious life, now it is no longer a constraint, as shrinking monasteries raise their age limit and curb their requirements.

Kate Willegal was recently divorced when she happily discovered that her annulled four-year marriage no longer precluded her from religious

Left: Sister Briana Cradock (left) and Sister Macy Jo Marshall
Right: Sister Tess Duenas

life. Kate, who has no children, entered the Ferdinand Benedictines in 1993 at age thirty-nine. A slim blond with hunched shoulders and a sheepish demeanor, Kate speaks in a loud whisper. She was helping a frail sister put on her veil when I found her in the infirmary where Kate works part-time while attending nursing school.

Previously, Kate had been a mortician for twelve years, embalming the dead, planning and directing funerals, comforting the bereaved. Then, in her late thirties and divorced, Kate had grown bored with her career and felt drawn to "something God was asking me to do, something I couldn't concretely say what it was."

The answer came in an article about a woman like herself who had divorced and become a nun. After visiting several orders, Kate decided she wanted to spend her life in prayer and with a community of women. Kate's biggest challenge was accepting that she could never have children.

"It is painful when I see children, babies. There's a lot of grieving over that. It's also difficult to meet my intimacy needs. I'm in love with someone incarnate."

Kate doesn't hide that she's been married, but she doesn't announce it either. She doesn't want to hold her experience over the heads of sisters who have never dated or who entered young. Sometimes sisters ask her what marriage and sexual intimacy were like.

"I tell them truthfully it was a very happy experience," she said. "There is something about married love. I found that being sexually intimate was good, emotionally, spiritually. At first it was hard to give up that lifestyle. But now I know who I'm to be."

Her experience, though, has made it difficult to make friends. Most nuns her age entered religious life twenty years earlier. Occasionally women her age and older enter. "We find each other," she said. "And that's when I realize I'm not alone. It is so comforting to talk to women who have dated and who've known what it is like to have been close to someone."

GOD AS SUITOR

One afternoon, a young Philippine American woman interested in entering the monastery and I talked as we swung on one of the numerous monastery swings. Vivian had it all: a thriving veterinary practice in California, a beachfront condo, a strong parish community, and several boyfriends. She was making lots of money in a career of her choosing. So what was she doing at a monastery?

"There's more you can be, and it centers around God," she said. Even while dating she said she felt an outside interference. "I noticed there was always a ménage à trois. There was always a third person."

I looked at her, not sure what she meant. "For him?" I asked.

"No, for us. And that third person was God! It was so bizarre. In one way or another we would bring each other closer to God. It just always worked out that way."

Vivian was plagued by "the calling." She gushed. She glowed. She smiled constantly. Had I met her in another setting, I might have questioned whether she was taking drugs. Her laughter and her constant alliteration that she was "happy, so happy, her life is so happy," her constant references to Jesus as if He were sitting there with us, reminded me of the self-described "Jesus freaks" I had met at church youth conferences when I was a teenager.

Vivian's excitement was scary but also contagious. I longed to feel the way she did. I wanted something so powerful to take over my life. I wanted to feel the hand of God touching my forehead, calling me—that's how I imagined it, listening to these women who swore they never wanted to be a nun until, one day, they were "touched."

"God is a persistent suitor," Vivian explained. She could see in my expression that I was leery of her exuberance. "The thought is always there. And you try to put it on the back burner, but one time or another it will come to the forefront. Or as my spiritual director put it: 'If you truly have a call, you will be unhappy doing anything else.'"

Vivian's calling happened while she attended Purdue University, about a three-hour drive north of Ferdinand. She was completing a year of clinical rotations to obtain her veterinarian license. On the eighth anniversary of her father's death, July 4, 1994, Vivian awoke early and went to a nearby chapel, the first time she had attended mass in fifteen years. During the service, an intense aroma of roses overwhelmed her.

"It smelled wonderful, like someone was hugging me."

The experience haunted her for days. She began attending mass, sometimes every morning. She felt God was tugging at her to do something with her life, but she wasn't sure what it was.

"I was totally changed," she said. "It was as if my eyes were opened. You hear about scales being pulled away from your eyes. It totally changed me."

At a friend's urging, she explained to a priest what she had experienced and asked, "What the fuck is going on?"

"You said this to a priest?" I asked.

"Oh yeah!" she said. "I didn't understand what was going on."

The priest told Vivian that the rose aroma was a sign of the presence of the Virgin Mary and that she should consider religious life. He handed her a copy of *Vision* magazine.

Vivian dismissed the priest's interpretation. "I had it in my mind the habit, that you were locked away behind bars. And that's it. Adios! Put away the key," she said, pretending to throw a key over her shoulder. "I thought he was nuts."

The idea of religious life didn't go away, though, and after receiving materials from various orders, she decided to visit the Benedictines, probably because they were nearby. On her "come and see" weekend, though, she wound up in a snowdrift, alone.

"God, if you really want me to go, let's make a deal," she said, staring at the car ceiling. "Why don't you give me a sign? How about a rainbow? If you really want me to go let's make it a rainbow."

"I was being pretty smart: a rainbow at night," she recalled. "So I sat there for a while, bored; and I turned on the radio and this song came on." She hummed a verse—" 'I can see clearly now the rain is gone' "—then continued, "And the very first line that came on was: 'There's the rainbow I'd been praying for.'"

Vivian knew she had to keep her end of the bargain.

"It sounds flaky but it's just the way God works in my life. God has a sense of humor."

Vivian drove for six hours through the storm. The sisters saw it as a sign.

"There was no pressure. They weren't pushy. A lot of places are pushy."

Still, Vivian wasn't convinced she was nun material. She tried moving on with her life as a veterinarian. Yet, after setting up the California practice, she began visiting orders near her home. They aren't as progressive as the Ferdinand Benedictines and two years later, she again visited the monastery in Indiana, a state she detests. Since then, she's been coming back every few months in preparation to join.

"God radiates through these women and that is what draws me. It's a very dynamic, vibrant community. They're genuine. They each have their own thing. There's a sister who swears like a truck driver. And there's a sister who brews her own beer. There are a lot of characters here."

LIMITS TO PERFECTION

Later that week, I left Ferdinand elated that I'd discovered a religious community unlike any I'd ever experienced, one that I might have joined—if I were Roman Catholic and weren't married. I felt I could relate to the women on my own level. I admired how they didn't try to hide their difficulties, their flaws—or so I thought.

Over the next several years, I explored many other communities. While other sisters were candid about their sex lives, I never found another community whose members are as open about dealing with celibacy. I frequently bragged about the Ferdinand community. I told sisters at other orders how the Ferdinand nuns don't try to sugarcoat the trials of keeping their vows or flinch from answering questions that modern women want to know. I believed I had discovered the ideal modern monastery.

What I didn't know then was that there is a thin line between a sister admitting to her struggles with celibacy and admitting she had succumbed to her desires. Despite its advertisements about the imperfect nun, there is definitely a threshold to how imperfect a nun at Ferdinand could admit to being.

On my first visit, I hadn't seen the tension between older nuns who had entered straight out of high school and modern nuns who had joined after years of dating or marriage. Generational differences became obvious during a summer retreat several years later when the Ferdinand sisters invited me back to experience Benedictine Life Week, a time when women come to the monastery for a "look-see."

Having met many of the sisters who had joined five to ten years earlier, I was curious to learn more about the latest rounds of women interested in such a progressive community. What I didn't know before I arrived was that this visit would reveal a more calculating side to the Ferdinand Benedictines. While they had successfully marketed their "imperfect" nun image, they also had learned to skillfully manage that picture by controlling the imperfections revealed to outsiders. I was about to learn just how "flawed" a sister there could be.

The afternoon I arrived, eleven women who came for the Benedictine Life Week were gathered at the monastery's camp, situated on a pond amid thick woods. The visitors milled about, looking like college coeds attending a sorority rush meeting. They came from all over the country: Bethany, Connecticut; Brooklyn, New York; Vallejo, California; Mansfield, Ohio; State College, Pennsylvania; Gaithersburg, Maryland; Kansas City, Missouri; Boonville, Indiana; Chicago, Illinois; Milford, Indiana; Louisville, Kentucky. The group ran the gamut from jaded urbanites with leopard-skin print scarves to slow-speaking rural girls with bib overalls. Some were barely eighteen and naïve.

Before dinner, the visitors and sisters gathered inside the lodge's screened mess hall for evening prayers. The women sat on benches in two rows facing each other. During a quiet interlude, a van roared up to the building and out jumped a *Nightline* film crew. For two days, the crew had been trailing the visiting women. The *Wall Street Journal* had published an article about the community a year earlier, thrusting the sisters into the national spotlight and sparking numerous television stories.

The *Nightline* crew talked loudly as they decided what to film. Meanwhile, the sisters pretended they couldn't hear the racket on the other side of the screened porch. As the women sang psalms and religious songs, a cameraman wearing a T-shirt with a beer logo repeatedly slammed the screen door.

When prayers ended and the camera's bright lights were turned off, I found myself angry and tense. The sanctity of evening prayers, a time of contemplation and inner inspection, had become a staged photo op. The sisters were trying to accomplish too much by courting the media and the young women at the same time. The community's leaders were aspiring for as much media attention as possible. Each national newscast was another benchmark in their quest for publicity. Their ultimate goal, I was told, was an appearance on a national morning show, like *Good Morning America* or *The Today Show*.

Later we gathered around a large bonfire and the sisters passed out handmade songbooks. Two sisters strummed guitars as we sang tunes like "Take Me Home, Country Roads," "Blowing in the Wind," "Grandma's Feather Bed," and "Elvira," the young women and the gray-haired sisters laughing at the silly songs, which reminded me of childhood summer camps. The scene seemed so idyllic. The Ferdinand sisters were successfully attracting new members by relating to young women on their level, not in a nunny, religious way. This, too, seemed calculated.

As we roasted marshmallows, the sun started setting. Clouds diffused the light into brilliant shades of orange. A few young women paddled a dinghy across the pond, rocking it, screaming and laughing. These nuns really knew how to set the perfect picture.

The next morning I walked to Madonna Hall, a dormitory where the guests were housed. In the third-floor lounge women were sprawled on couches and a mattress on the floor. Bags of junk food lay scattered on nearby tables. Ice chests were filled with soft drinks. Thirty-three-year-old Sister Teresa Gunter was about to speak on monastery life. Teresa had led the singing the night before, dancing around the bonfire, looking more like a Girl Scout leader than a nun.

Teresa stood in the middle of the lounge in jeans decorated with flowers. Her face was freckled and her long, flaming red hair was braided down her back and tied with a yellow flower. On one wrist was a yellow sports watch and on the other was a peach sports band. Teresa used eighth grade lingo, sprinkling her choppy sentences with "it's cool" and mimicking the hip-hop, butter-churning dance to emphasize her thoughts.

"Your relationship with God," Teresa explained, "is like being with five friends, but you're closer to one than the others and you just need some time to be alone with God. It's like when you want to go to Taco Bell with only one of your friends."

On one hand I admired the sisters in their efforts to address modern women in their own language, to present them with sisters who weren't stuck in a 1950s nun mold. But on the other hand, their portrayal of religious life seemed to highlight more shallow aspects of their monastic lifestyle.

During a break, sisters showed the monastery's recruiting video. It reminded me of Nike ads: shots of women running, biking, mountain climbing, striking thoughtful poses. Several close-ups of mostly younger nuns are set against a deep blue background accompanied by these words: "There is a person inside of me who wants to be involved, to be challenged, to find inner peace, to belong, to find meaning in life, to be unique, to find God in every day, to be a Sister of St. Benedict."

Each woman in the video also shows up in printed brochures. There's the gray-haired Sister Jennifer, the oldest of triplets; Sister Maria Luisa, the Mexican American who dreamed of a successful business career; Sister Tess Duenas, who left her close-knit family in Guam for a monastery family; Sister Mary Claude, a recovering alcoholic who's become an addictions counselor; the "cool, athletic sister"—Sister Teresa Gunter—shown wearing shorts and an assortment of baseball caps while assuring viewers that she still plays loud music and whistles; and glamorous-looking Sister Susan, who entered at age thirty-four.

"It's a lifestyle," one nun explained. Another said she'd "answered a call to an adventure."

The combination brochure, ad, and video is like reading an edition of *Oprah* cover to cover. It is the women's magazine approach—making the most out of life and being the best woman you can be—mixed with a Nike "just do it" challenge and spiced with the Marine Corps's promise of "an adventure." The sisters in the video use words like "self-fulfillment," "peace," "feeling grounded," "being myself." This is not the old concept of suffering as a nun for the Lord. No one mentions what it means to live the vows of celibacy, obedience, and certainly not poverty.

"I have things available to me, amenities, a lifestyle that would be hard to achieve by myself," Sister Susan boasts to the camera.

I had always thought nuns in general live a higher quality of life than the average woman outside the monastery. Yet, I'd never heard any nun admit that—until now. I'd certainly never heard that used as a recruiting tool. Though sisters don't own anything individually, they indeed have access to cars, summer cabins, retreat centers, swimming pools, club memberships, extensive gardens, not to mention comprehensive health care benefits. "Amenities" include vacations and sabbaticals. Of course, I have encountered a few communities whose members live more frugally—never throwing away a sandwich bag, even washing used Saran Wrap. And while orders might have to do without a swimming pool, none of the orders I visited served ramen noodles for dinner.

After lunch, the young women were back slumped on couches and on the floor. It was a hot, humid day, and some were drowsy from the starchy meal and the snacks. A boom box blared and a couple of the young women got up and danced. Eighteen-year-old Diana DeFillippo lay on a mattress kicking up her hippie sandals. Her tie-dyed shirt exposed her pale stomach. She was telling anyone who would listen why she had decided to go to a Catholic university, that she had been named after Princess Diana, and wasn't Prince William just the cutest?

A few minutes later Prioress Sister Joella Kidwell arrived for her scheduled "chat." Diana sat up and yelled to Joella: "What's up, girl?"

Joella either didn't hear Diana or ignored her. The rest of us looked at each other and raised our eyebrows, then stifled our laughter. I couldn't imagine greeting a prioress like a high school girlfriend. But that was certainly the atmosphere the sisters had provided.

Joella, in her paisley silk skirt and ivory blouse, explained what attributes the monastery looks for and the application process. What were their impressions so far? she asked.

One woman said she was surprised that the sisters wear shorts and baseball caps. She thought she wouldn't be able to wear makeup or jewelry, which she clearly liked, judging from the mascara caked on her lashes and the many rings on her fingers.

One woman wanted to know why she should attain her college degree if she knew she was going to enter the monastery.

"Becoming a sister is not an occupation," Diana shouted across the room. "It is a lifestyle."

Another piped up: "I called my mom and told her, 'It's like a resort, but you pray. There's too much to do—tennis, canoeing. . . . ' "

Sister Jenny Schmitt (right) sharing a laugh with a possible candidate

Joella seemed annoyed by the woman's assessment. "You've been entertained thoroughly this week," she said, hardly concealing her disappointment. Despite her community's deliberate attempt to create a summer camp experience for the candidates, she clearly expected the women to have been impressed with much deeper aspects of religious life than the community swimming pool.

That afternoon, the women broke into work groups, cleaning and gardening around the monastery. After all, Benedictines don't just play tennis all day. With the dorm vacant, one of the nun recruiters, Sister Jenny Schmitt, and I found a cool room in which to talk.

Jenny relaxed on a bed while I pulled up a chair. She is probably one of the most attractive nuns I have ever met. At forty-seven years old, she resembles a middle-aged Jane Fonda. While most sisters keep their hair short, Jenny's flows past the middle of her back. She is thin and tan with penetrating blue eyes. She has an earthy aura about her, an adventurous persona, a look that communicates she's seen a lot in her life.

"By all rights, I should not be in community because I got so distracted so many times," she admitted early in our conversation. "I really struggled for a long time before and after entering the community with wanting to have children, wanting to have a husband, the affection and feeling of being honored by a man, having a relationship with a special someone. It wasn't like I entered the community and so that takes care of *that* desire."

The oldest of nine children, Jenny grew up on a farm in a German American community about forty-five minutes from the monastery. She attended the sisters' female boarding school and joined the community after she graduated in 1971 at eighteen years old. Hers was the last group that entered right after high school.

"My parents were of the opinion that if this was where I wanted to go in my life, then I didn't need to be dating," she said, looking pained as she wrinkled her eyelids. "I had to do a lot of the maturational things that are necessary after I got here, which was a really difficult thing to do. Now we encourage women to date before they ever make a decision about religious life, and for good reason!" she laughed. "I'm a classic case."

Jenny hadn't ignored the sacrifices required of becoming a nun. She knew she'd have to give up sex, a husband, and children. She also knew that she could be a devout Catholic without becoming a nun. But Jenny wasn't particularly self-disciplined and she believed it would be difficult for her to maintain a balance between her relationship to God and a marriage. She realized she needed to be with other people who had the same goal and desire to seek God, people who would help her stay focused and challenged. A child of the sixties, Jenny had a deep-seated need to make a difference in the world. And in her world of rural Indiana, religious life was the avenue most available.

Five other postulants joined the year Jenny did. By the second year, half the class had left. During temporary vows, one more sister quit, and Jenny debated whether she should leave as well. Finally she decided to tell her formation director she wanted to resign.

"I was trying to discern whether or not I wanted to pursue married life, and I was still trying to balance relationships and figure out how to be in a relationship and keep that in balance with community life."

Away at college, Jenny was supposed to return to the monastery but a snowstorm detained her. Feeling overwhelmed with her pending decision, she went to the chapel. In her mind, she constructed a list of the reasons she should remain a sister and the reasons she should leave. They turned out evenly weighted.

"I was just pouring my heart out to God," she remembered. "I received a gift that has continued to be a strength and an assurance even to this day. It was almost like an annunciation moment. All of a sudden, I knew, not in my head, but in my heart, that this really is the life that I both wanted for myself and felt called to do. But I would not say that I haven't had a myriad of temptations."

During our conversation, Jenny referred to "relationships" more than thirty times. At first, I was enamored with her forthrightness but when she repeatedly alluded to these mysterious liaisons, without any explanations, I became irritated. How could I understand her journey if she remained vague and cagey about her struggles and how she overcame them?

"Have you fallen in love?" I finally asked. "Have you had relationships with men?"

"I don't think I'm going to go there," she said, laughing nervously. "That's very personal."

I told Jenny I was interested in how she was able to work through her temptations.

"I haven't dealt with it real well," she eventually offered after much sighing. "The community did challenge me. The truth is I probably wouldn't be saying anything that everybody doesn't already know anyway," she said, but declined to fill in the gaps of her story.

"The struggle for most of my life was not knowing for sure if God could be enough for me."

Just before celebrating her Jubilee anniversary, twenty-five years as a vowed sister, Jenny took a thirty-day retreat. There, she said, she became "friends" with the biblical Mary Magdalene, a woman who, according to popular legend, was Jesus' girlfriend. Historically, Magdalene was also the title conferred upon a penitent prostitute who had been placed in a religious community.

"I felt she was truly alive and I journaled with her," Jenny explained. "We conversed with each other. We shared stories of our lives with each other. She became very real."

"Why did you pick her?" I asked.

"She was the one with seven demons. It's like the demons of my life, you know, and her intimate relationship with Jesus, her intimate love."

During that retreat, Jenny had another "God moment." It was a healing epiphany where she realized that not only is God enough for her but she, with all her shortcomings, is enough for God.

Though Jenny had come to peace with her flawed past, it was clear that she couldn't admit her mistakes publicly. Even if they had happened decades ago, the sisters wouldn't see them as old mishaps, she said. There is a limit to the admitted imperfections of nuns in the Ferdinand Benedictines, and I had just met it.

The next morning I was summoned to the monastery. Sister Rose Mary Rexing, the sister who had been the nun recruiter for eleven years and responsible for much of the monastery's press coverage, met me at her office door frowning. She led me inside and we sat in her large office decorated in Laura Ashley colors and stripes.

"I've heard you've been asking inappropriate, personal questions. Is it true?" she challenged.

"What?" I said, surprised at the question.

"You've been asking people about their personal lives," Rose Mary insisted.

"Yes, that's what I do," I said. "That's why I've come here, to tell the personal stories of nuns."

"Well, why are you just talking to young women? Why aren't you interviewing older nuns?" she asked, as though there were some conspiracy regarding which women I talked with. Somehow portraying only young, hip nuns was alright for candidates but not a balanced portrayal for the media.

I explained that I had interviewed the women the monastery had selected for me.

Rose Mary glanced at the *Wall Street Journal* article hanging on the wall above my head. "We've worked too hard to build our image to have someone come in and with one bad report ruin years of hard work. I won't let you do it," she said, her voice trembling.

"I'm here to write about the truth," I responded, feeling defensive. "I won't cover up the truth. I'm also not here to ruin you. If anyone feels uncomfortable by questions I've asked or answers they've given, I can throw out those interviews. You have to understand that if a woman continues to allude to 'relationships' in an interview, I'm going to ask her what she's talking about. I can't write about people's lives in the abstract.

"I can leave right now," I continued, anger building as I scooted to the edge of my seat.

"No. That won't be necessary," Rose Mary said, more calmly. "We should have had somebody with you. All media have to have an escort when they are at the monastery. It's our policy. Either myself or [the public relations director] will have to be with you when you interview women from now on."

"I don't understand," I said, astounded. I pointed out that the last time I visited no one sat through interviews with me, no one escorted me around the monastery. None of the monasteries or communities I'd visited had anyone sit through interviews with me.

"These women are adults. Why don't you trust them?" I asked.

"It's not that I don't trust them," she said, softening her tone. "It's that we don't trust the media. We've had some media who've asked inappropriate questions, and we're not going to ruin years of hard work," she repeated. "We have an image to protect. This has nothing to do with you. It's just our policy."

Rose Mary explained that several years earlier a television film crew had asked a young sister "inappropriate questions." The sister felt "compelled" to talk about her sexual experiences. Rose Mary, who happened to be standing nearby when the TV cameraman asked the question, stepped in when she heard the sister's response—that she had enjoyed sex before becoming a nun. Rose Mary told the cameraman that she wanted a written promise that he would not use that interview. She also told him that if he asked any other "inappropriate questions" he would be kicked off the monastery property.

I understood that sometimes the media go too far. I also knew this particular sister had said the same thing to me—unsolicited. The young woman wasn't ashamed of her background, nor was she boasting that she had a sex life before she became a nun. She simply presented herself as a normal, modern woman. Her message is: You can be as imperfect as I was; a woman doesn't have to be virgin to be a nun. Her point was echoed by other nuns who wanted to make it clear that sisters aren't frigid women who dislike men or sex. They are women with normal urges and desires.

After the morning with Rose Mary, I felt uncomfortable at the monastery. I felt the sisters, particularly Rose Mary, were trying to control how I portrayed them.

For the rest of my interviews, I was trailed by either Rose Mary or the public relations director and sometimes both. As a journalist, I had seldom been subjected to such Big Brother tactics. People tend to be less than authentic and feel pressured to give certain answers when someone of authority hovers over their every word. At this modern monastery, where the prioress bragged that nuns are treated as adults and responsible for their own decisions and actions, opinions suddenly had to be monitored.

CELIBACY IN A MODERN ERA

I had always wondered if sisters feel more powerful or more confident because they are celibate, if not having sex frees their minds, if it makes them feel like extreme feminists, totally independent of men. I know that celibate women on the outside intimidate some people; they just can't understand why anyone would purposely give up sex.

I felt I could relate to the newer nuns who had chosen celibacy in an era overdosing on sexuality. I took a personal promise of celibacy for two years in my twenties. At the time, I had just broken up with my fiancé.

From the moment I committed to celibacy, men seemed to be more attracted to me. Suddenly I was seeing several men, and not perpetual bachelors, but decent, good-looking men with impressive careers. Still, they pressured me to have sex, but the more they pushed, the more I became determined not to give in. Not surrendering to my own lust made me feel in control. Even though I couldn't control the chaos that surrounded my everyday work world—I could control my body. Not getting wrapped up in the moment forced me to look at the person, the relationship that was building or not.

During my years of celibacy, I met other women who had made similar promises. They wanted to know that they were in control of their sex lives and not the other way around. I remember that time fondly, as a period when I looked within and gathered strength. I don't think I ever felt as confident, at least not as a single woman.

As a married woman, I have taken on the same vow of chastity that the nuns have—theirs to God and their community and mine to my husband. The longer I am married the more I understand the deep commitment that the chastity vow requires. I relate to the parallel that Sister Tess draws between a married woman admiring a good-looking man and a nun doing the same. Neither of us has severed our sexuality. Like Sister Rachel, I know how working with men can awaken feminine energies, how discovering a mutual attraction can be intoxicating. And, like Sister

Jenny, I know that temptation must be tempered when inspiration curdles to lust. In many ways, nuns and married women share a great deal in common: Neither has buried their sensuality and both are willing to sacrifice for their relationships, be it with a community or with a spouse.

I can say firsthand that living with a group of celibate women meets many emotional and intimacy needs that a relationship with one person can't. It's a connection that many women crave—often more than they crave sex. Some of the most intense conversations I've ever had have been with nuns.

In light of the healthy attitudes displayed by the young nuns at Ferdinand, I was disappointed that the older regime was still enforcing old prohibitions. Rose Mary, who entered the monastery at age eighteen in 1968, failed to understand that young women entering the monastery now have grown up in a society inundated by sexual images; even the president's sex acts are prime-time news. And when a woman takes a vow of celibate chastity, she is, of course, taking a public stance about sex whether she wants to admit it or not. Asking her to explain the struggle behind that countercultural decision is hardly salacious.

The sisters under age fifty who hadn't entered the monastery right after high school seemed less hesitant to discuss sex and celibacy. I believe the monastery encourages young nuns to speak about their personal issues among themselves. Perhaps that was why they each felt so unfettered to discuss them candidly with a stranger, a journalist no less. Younger nuns perceive themselves as normal people who grapple with their passions and desires and want lay people to know they are just like them. For the older sisters, like Rose Mary, who had just turned fifty, there is only so much of an imperfect picture they are willing to reveal. For them, certain subjects, like sex, are still verboten. They have an image to maintain, a pedestal to stand on.

7

A DIVINE INTIMACY

TRAPPISTINES IN CROZET, VIRGINIA

"My loneliness is part of my celibate life; it's part of the reality. . . . When I'm not attending to my relationship with Jesus, and I'm seeking friendship or distractions, what I'm doing is evading my loneliness. When I'm seeking to have my needs fulfilled by other people, I'm prostituting myself."

—SISTER JO ANN DOANE

I n the foothills of the Blue Ridge Mountains, just fifteen miles from the Appalachian Trail, eight Cistercian Nuns of the Strict Observance—also known as Trappistines—live austerely amid the opulence of million-dollar estates and thoroughbred horse farms. These are the Green Berets of religious life—an elite order who live like medieval monks.

When the sisters moved from Wrentham, Massachusetts, to the countryside of Charlottesville, Virginia, in 1987, they garnered much attention in a region where there are few Catholics and even fewer monasteries. Quickly the nuns became a study of contrasts and were besieged with visits from women, many of them Protestant, curious about their monastic life.

Part of the Trappistines' appeal is their simple lifestyle. They rise at 3 A.M. every day, read in the dark early morning hours, chant or pray together seven times a day, and talk only when necessary, often using their own sign language. The rest of their days are interspersed with prayer and manual labor—growing vegetables and every eight days transforming 6,200 pounds of milk into 626 pounds of Gouda cheese, which they sell primarily by mail order.

When they make cheese or work in their garden, the sisters dress in jeans and work shirts, their hair tied back in brightly colored bandannas. Their uniform, though, is a white, long-sleeved, monkish smock that hangs to their ankles with a black scapular, or vest, and a black veil that partially covers their hair. Most wear leather belts with knots that drape down to their knees and leather sandals. They are vegetarians and retire by eight each evening. Their modern monastery is spare except for more than ten thousand books stacked in hallways and community rooms.

The sisters look to each day as another step in making themselves better Christians. They believe their disciplined lifestyle forces them to be less selfish and more loving; their isolation and loneliness allows them to seek God. The order's twelfth-century French founders called their way of life the School of Love. While most communities, even some of the strictest monasteries, exhibit a camplike camaraderie among sisters, this monastery seems more like a collection of hermits who live together for financial and practical support.

It's difficult to imagine why sisters would cut themselves off emotionally—not just from the world, but from each other, denying themselves deep friendships and intimacies, reserving their loneliness only for God as a part of their chastity vow. At first, I thought such women must be cold and incapable of relationships. Like other assumptions I had about nuns, this one, too, proved to be unfounded.

Trappistines are strict adherents to Benedict's Rule—the seventy-three-chapter handbook for monastic living written in the sixth century by an Italian hermit. While there are numerous Benedictine orders—St. Benedict was the father of Western monasticism—there are only a handful of Trappistine monasteries in the United States; Crozet is the newest and smallest. Whereas most Benedictines are known as the moderates of religious life—a sort of Social Democrat—Trappistines follow Benedict's way of life with a fundamental zeal. Theirs is a course for enlightenment and an attempt to perfect themselves, to shed distractions and focus on God. As part of that pursuit, they give up physical intimacies and the mental equivalent as well—their innermost thoughts, their soul searchings, their longings, their epiphanies. Those they save for God alone.

THE PROTESTANT HERMIT

When Janet McCoy joined the monastery, a day after her forty-first birthday in 1993, she expected that the friendships she'd given up on the outside would be replaced with even deeper relationships with the sisters.

"It's kind of shocking to stumble across this vast wilderness that you thought you were going to be able to share with everyone, and you'd share in theirs," Janet said, speaking of her interior life as though it were a place others could visit. "Everybody would fully know me and I would fully know them."

I found Janet inside the refrigerated rooms at the cheese barn where she was turning aging five- and ten-pound cheese discs, about the size of a man's outspread hand. It was a boiling July afternoon during my second visit, and since the monastery is not air-conditioned, I welcomed the walk-in cooler's temperatures, chilly enough that I could see my own breath.

Tall and thin, with ivory skin and pale yellow hair, Janet speaks in a buttery Virginia drawl. I discovered that nearly all the sisters speak with accents, some with distinct regional flairs, the result of talking so seldom. Since speaking is rare, the sisters place a high emphasis on the quality of a conversation. Like everything at a Trappistine monastery, words are not wasted but are sparingly spread like homemade jam and savored.

Like some women who enter later in life, Janet had had a successful career, only to feel hollow in her accomplishments. A successful veterinarian with a thriving practice in Virginia Beach, Janet, who was raised Baptist, spent several years searching for a spiritual connection. As a

Protestant, there were only so many options available and by 1988, she was even dallying with becoming a minister for her recently adopted New-Age congregation.

Eventually Janet realized that her heart really wasn't into becoming a pastor. "I just hit a blind alley of despair," she said, looking back. "At that point, I threw up my hands and said, 'Well, maybe I'm supposed to get married.' And right on cue this guy walks in and tells me that God has sent him."

Sister Janet McCoy in the cheese freezer where the Gouda cheese is aged.

There was a problem with her relationship, though. Janet liked spending time alone. She had lived alone for so long that she had become accustomed to luxurious amounts of solitude. One Sunday morning Janet craved a "hermit day" so she could pray, but her boyfriend wasn't eager to leave. After they argued, he fumed out of the apartment, only to return ten minutes later lugging a newspaper.

"This is where you belong," he said, throwing the paper in her lap.

The front page that February 1988 featured a story about the cloistered Trappistines.

"It hit me like a ton of bricks," she remembered. "I didn't know anything about Catholics, but I knew immediately that I needed to talk to these sisters."

The next weekend Janet drove three hours from Virginia Beach to the Piedmont hills of central Virginia. She drove past a horse racetrack, through tunnels of towering trees, across a one-lane bridge, and down meandering unmarked dirt roads. When she couldn't find what she thought a monastery should look like, she phoned. The superior informed Janet that the monastery hadn't been built yet; and furthermore, they were not receiving guests.

"You don't understand," Janet said into the receiver. "I've driven a long way to talk to you, and I need to talk to you today."

The superior and another sister met Janet at the gate to what had been a 507-acre cheese farm. They showed her where the monastery foundation was being laid.

"This is nice. I think I'll stay," Janet said, half jokingly.

The sisters stiffened.

"Well, first of all, we don't have any room," the superior told her. "Second of all, you're not Catholic."

"I can fix that," Janet promised.

Driving home, Janet couldn't believe she wanted to join a monastery. She kept repeating to herself: "You've got to be kidding! You've got to be kidding!"

They are Catholic, and they dress funny, went the argument in her head.

Still, she was hooked. She had felt it when she turned down the narrow driveway leading to the cinder blocks of what would one day become the Lady of the Angels Monastery.

"At that point, I understood my whole life—which up to then had never made a bit of sense," Janet reflected. "All of a sudden, it made sense—all those crazy twisting turns and the decisions, the tragedies, the crises I had barely survived. It came clearly into focus: This is where God wants me. I was stunned."

Three months later, Janet broke up with her boyfriend. She then devoted herself to bridging her Protestant beliefs with Catholic theology. Unsure exactly where her spirituality lay, Janet attended three different churches each Sunday: her New Age church, then an Episcopal church—which she saw as her bridge to Catholicism—and a Baptist church.

"I didn't know enough about Catholicism to make any logical decision that this is the set of beliefs that I will adhere to for the rest of my life," she said.

In fact, the first time Janet entered a Catholic church was after she quit her job and went to live at the Trappistines' mother house in Wrentham in an effort to commit herself full-time to converting. Janet was attracted to the life of prayer and solitude that the monastery offered, and, initially, her conversion was about attaining that lifestyle.

Her first morning at the monastery, Janet was sitting in the chapel praying when she noticed two sisters kneeling before the Blessed Sacrament. Janet stared at them, trying to figure out what they were doing.

"Then suddenly it dawned on me," she said. "Here's a group of people who believe so strongly that Christ is present in this bread that they will sit and gaze at it and adore it for half an hour. Now that was stunning!"

Suddenly Janet was presented with a faith that was contrary to all her Protestant beliefs and even her scientific nature. Whereas Protestant churches operate under a symbolism of the Divine, Catholic theology insists that the Eucharist—the bread, the crackers—is literally Christ's body.

"There was a big fork in the road. Could I swallow this or not?" she said. "At this point, I had to stay or go."

She decided to assume, at least for the time being, that what the sisters believed was true. During her stay at the monastery, Janet took catechism and instruction from a priest, but it was watching the sisters that made her a believer more than her theology lessons.

"Here are people who have walked away from everything else to live this life, come to church seven or eight times a day, and spend at least half an hour gazing at this bread. Jesus must be real. Why else would people do this?"

Six months later, Janet returned to Crozet and celebrated her first communion and confirmation in the sisters' new monastery. Four years later, she joined.

"In the beginning, I was afraid that I had converted to religious life and that Catholicism was an appendage, something I'd have to go through to live the lifestyle that I wanted," she admitted.

By the time she reached her confirmation, though, she realized that the monastery was merely the magnet that drew her to Catholicism, even if her vocation as a nun didn't work out, her conversion would.

While converting had been a struggle, adjusting to life in a religious community demanded much more. The biggest barrier was bridging a culture gap with women who hadn't lived in a modern world for decades. "You realize that you're living with a house full of people who wouldn't even recognize the Beatles if a song came on the radio and we were allowed to listen to it. They missed the Vietnam War, the Rolling Stones, the Grateful Dead, the years of streakers, the sexual revolution, drugs, even television. A lot of them didn't even have a television at home when they entered. Occasionally you'd try to make a connection or make a joke and it just fell flat," she said.

As the years passed, Janet's connection with the outside world decreased, too. Now when Janet stands at the grocery store checkout line, she doesn't recognize the hottest new actor or actress on the cover of *People* magazine, a shock to a woman who once prided herself in keeping up with the latest movies and music.

Although the sisters own a television, they watch mostly educational videos. About three times a year they rent movies. Recently they watched *Schindler's List,* and several sisters, including Janet, had to leave during the more graphic parts.

"Because of the silence and the solitude, whatever you see impacts you greatly and stays with you a lot longer. After a few years, I lost that yearning to see everything on the billboards. There's only so much space to allow before movies start spilling over into prayers and dreams."

Though she had initially anticipated that her relationships with her sisters would mirror the intensity and intimacy she was forming with God, Janet came to accept that her romantic vision of monastic life doesn't exist in this Trappistine community where the sisters believe that exploring the depths of a nun's inner world is a private quest. Here, sharing one's spiritual intimacies is akin to kissing and telling.

"There is a sense of family, belonging, and community; you may not have had anything else in common but you have this in common," she said. "The community just gives you enough courage to face what seems like a much more vast area of the heart that is reserved for God alone."

THE MARINE NUN

In January 1994, four months after Janet entered, she was joined in the postulancy by a thirty-four-year-old former marine. Jo Ann Doane had spent more than a decade drinking and carousing. Now at age forty-one, she was the monastery's youngest nun. Despite her evenly plucked eyebrows, Jo Ann struck me as a perpetual tomboy. Her copper bangs are cut at a slant and her voice has a deep, masculine Southern twang, a Loretta Lynn drawl compared to Janet's Scarlett O'Hara version.

Jo Ann's transformation from marine truck driver to monastic nun is a complicated, mythical tale. She'd been baptized Catholic but her parents didn't attend mass. As a teenager, she studied Eastern religions and was captivated by a book about monks.

"God touched me through that book," she said one afternoon as we sipped ice water in the monastery's study cooled only by a ceiling fan. "I wanted to be a monk on a snowcapped mountain in Tibet. That image carried me through eighteen years of living out in the world."

Her desire for the Divine, however, was outstripped by her weakness for partying. After high school, Jo Ann joined the marines. Her father had been a career navy man and she felt comfortable with military life. Her marine job was in motor transport—driving jeeps, buses, and dump trucks. She also played left field for the Marine Corps slow-pitch softball team, traveling around the country competing against army, navy, and air force women's teams.

"I still drank and partied. I was having fun," she said. "Nobody was living the spiritual life in the Marine Corps. Sometimes, when I would get drunk, I would talk to people about God. There was just an inner yearning that I was more free to express when I was drinking and wasn't so inhibited."

Though men outnumbered women—and Jo Ann could have had her pick—she preferred not to date.

"I grew up fighting and playing with guys, so I knew I would never want to marry a guy. They were my friends. I didn't need to make one my husband. Having children wasn't an issue for me because I knew I couldn't take care of myself, so I certainly didn't want to take care of somebody else."

After her six years of active duty ended, Jo Ann tried to maintain her wild life while she worked jobs in lawn care, furniture refinishing, and construction. When she was fired from her full-time construction job, she began delivering newspapers. Her new job forced her to go to bed at 6 P.M. and to rise around midnight. The work prevented her from partying and, while on her paper route, she began listening to a Christian radio program. Soon Jo Ann started reading spiritual books. One day while reading about Eastern religions, Jo

Sister Jo Ann Doane studying religious texts early in the morning

Ann remembered her earlier desire to become a monk in Tibet and she was flooded with sadness.

"It really buried me in that moment, relinquishing a long-held memory, a dream that I wanted to fulfill since childhood that got swamped under the partying."

For six months Jo Ann continued listening to the radio announcer's invitation for listeners to fall on their knees and ask God to instill Christ in their hearts. Then one night she stopped the car in the middle of a country road, kneeled on the gravel, and prayed with the radio evangelist.

Afterward Jo Ann prayed on her own and began classes to become a member of a local Catholic church. She also read *Seven Storey Mountain,* written by Trappist monk Thomas Merton. She didn't know there were Trappist nuns, called Trappistines, but she knew she wanted to lead the life of a Trappist monk.

She confided her desire to her parish priest, who directed her to the nearest Trappistine monastery in Crozet. In 1990 Jo Ann came for an interview and liked the nuns' lifestyle of prayer, work, and meditative readings.

While she "discerned" whether she should become a nun, Jo Ann took a job driving dump trucks for the Virginia Highway Department and worked in an elastics plant. Every three months, she visited the monastery.

When she finally entered, she struggled with loneliness, like Janet, but decided that friendships would only distract her from her relationship with the Lord. "My loneliness is part of my celibate life; it's part of the reality."

"Loneliness is part of celibate life?" I asked, incredulously.

"Oh yeah! That is something one accepts," Jo Ann said. "When I'm not attending to my relationship with Jesus, and I'm seeking friendship or distractions, what I'm doing is evading my loneliness. When I'm seeking to have my needs fulfilled by other people, I'm prostituting myself."

SILENCE AS A BOND

Compline, the last prayer time of the day, begins the "Great Silence." No one is allowed to speak from 7 P.M. until 7:30 the next morning. Before retiring to their cells at night, the sisters line up single file in front of the superior, Mother Marion, who sprinkles holy water on their bowed heads. That night, Mother flashed a playful smile before showering my head and face.

The sisters walked silently to their cells; I headed to the guest parlor. I'd spent two scary nights alone at one of the sisters' cabins deep in the woods, where growling bears kept me awake and worried. When the sisters suggested I stay at the monastery so it would be easier to rise for 3 A.M. vigils, I eagerly agreed. The sleeper bed was already pulled out, and I crawled beneath the crisp sheets, trying to convince myself it was bedtime. It was 7:30 P.M., and the sun was still shining. I pulled down the shades. When the alarm buzzed at 2:45 A.M., I was exhausted, having lain awake most of the night. I pleaded with my body to get up. I wanted to prove that I, too, could be among the spiritual elite.

The sisters filed silently into the chapel, which is starkly decorated with a burgundy marble altar at the front and the sisters' prayer stalls, two rows of seats and prayer book holders facing each other. Walls are a shade of vanilla with chocolate-colored brick floors. A Russian icon of the Madonna adorns the front wall, next to a gold tabernacle. The sisters kneeled next to their pew stalls and began singing psalms. Their soprano voices worked like a lullaby for a woman with little sleep.

"A voice cries out: Watchman, what of the night?" one side chanted. "Stand up and come to our help! Redeem us because of your love."

The other side responded: "We preach Christ crucified, the power of God and the wisdom of God to those who are called. Come to me, all who labor and are heavy laden. And I will give you rest, says the Lord."

After forty minutes of singing interspersed with meditative silence, we filed into the back corridor, carefully stepping over two dogs, and climbed the stairs. We passed by the monastery's enclosed courtyard, where the moon shone on rows of lettuce, green beans, tomatoes, and flowers. At the end of the hall, the kitchen refectory was dimly lit. Sisters took assigned seats at tables arranged in a U-shaped pattern so they can all look out the windows at the fields and trees. The sounds of nature floated in the open windows. But the country vista, still shrouded in darkness, couldn't offer much mental escape. So the sisters sat staring down at their place mats, drinking coffee or juice; breakfast would be served more than an hour later.

Each sister appeared deeply immersed in thought; it was like a room full of mathematicians trying to crack the same code. After several minutes each sister quietly washed her cup, walked to the library, and practiced lectio divina, meditative scripture reading.

Jo Ann motioned for me to come closer. Standing over her shoulder, I saw she was reading from a large gold-leafed Bible. Nearly every sentence was underlined in red, blue, or green. She pointed to a passage in Jeremiah about whores. In the margin in red pen she had written: "I prostitute myself when I try to get attention." My eyes widened, stunned that she would write something so personal, so damning in the Bible. She looked up and smiled, proud that she had found a scripture verse that emphasized her own beliefs.

Outside on the monastery's front balcony, a full moon lit up the grounds, nearby fields, and pastures. I could see for miles, including the little house on the edge of the sisters' gravel road where a retired hermit Trappist priest lives. Cicadas buzzed loudly, and in the distance dogs barked and a catbird cried. I breathed deeply the cool country air. Not a morning person, I could see why the nuns take advantage of the peace and calm before the sun rises and the world gets busy, before the air becomes thick and muggy. The darkness provides a quiet, cool cocoon.

Later that morning, I met with Mother Marion Risetto, superior since 1992. Mother is a young-looking fifty-eight, with thick white hair, stunning blue eyes, and large pearly teeth. Her most distinctive feature, though, is her voice: sonorous and stilted with exacting pronunciation, sounding almost British.

Mother Marion and I drank coffee from white china cups like dignified ladies. I was unnerved by Mother's highbrow diction, but she quickly put me at ease with her toothy grin and her frequent laughter. Although educated in Latin and trained in Gregorian chants, Mother Marion still has a humble spirit.

Marion entered the monastery in 1959, at seventeen years old. Having grown up in what became SoHo, Marion attended a Catholic high school in Manhattan and went to Columbia University on Saturdays to study engineering. She competed on the debate team. She frequented Broadway plays and read many books, including *Seven Storey Mountain*. She was drawn by the simple daily life of a Trappistine monastery and the idealism such a life suggested.

In those days, Trappistines practiced strict fasting, silence, flagellation on Fridays, and ran a farm and a candy factory in Wrentham, Massachusetts. The sisters' large dormitories offered no personal space. Sisters were only allowed to speak to the mother superior. There were, however, ways of getting around the silence rule. Some sisters communicated through sign language or notes or talked if they took a trip in a car away from the monastery.

Like breadcrumbs in a forest, sisters frequently left clues for other sisters on how to deal with the trials young sisters faced. One day, Marion pulled a book off the shelf in the library. It was earmarked to a chapter entitled "The Dark Night of the Soul." Marion believes that a sister had left the book in such a way so that another sister might open the book and find the answer to her problems.

Mother Marion pointed out that the sisters didn't talk or share personal details not because they were angry or coy but because they had sought out their life of silence.

"We chose this silence. So it is a bond," she explained. "If you did make use of the signs or if you carried on and acted like a nut, you were really betraying the other person's silence. You were infringing on her quiet. The point was that you could work for two and a half hours sitting beside somebody, and she could be praying, saying ejaculations, or just reflecting without having to leave and go to the chapel."

Although the sisters didn't speak, they communicated through body language, she said. A look could convey whether a sister was troubled.

After Vatican II, the order initiated more group discussions. Today private conversations are still arranged with permission of the superior. Still, the Trappistines remain one of the few religious orders that do not have "recreation," a set hour when sisters can converse. The penance and discipline that first attracted Mother Marion were toned down in the late 1960s. Now fasting constitutes keeping a vegetarian diet and not eating between meals. Penance is maintaining silence and not disturbing sisters.

While Trappistine life has gotten "easier," Mother Marion sympathizes with women entering today. "We suggest that people stay out and get more experiences in life, but they are not always good experiences. So they come in wishing they could tear that page out of their lives. The so-called evil world was less threatening in my day."

Mother Marion said many women come to the monastery troubled by their "mistakes." "They are the ones who would call themselves tainted," she said. The danger is when these women develop self-hatred in the monastery, or when they seek out monastic life in order to compensate for the errors of their previous lifestyle.

I wondered how the sisters dealt with the subject of celibacy and the Church's position that even masturbation is sinful and a violation of religious as well as marital vows. These younger nuns, many like Jo Ann and Janet, who weren't raised Catholic, might have learned a worldlier concept toward "self-love," especially since psychiatrists and even a former U.S. surgeon general have publicly stated that masturbation is a healthy, normal practice. Tactfully, I tried to ask Mother Marion, using several euphemisms.

"Are you referring to masturbation?" she asked, unabashed.

"Yes," I said sheepishly, afraid she would expel me for asking "inappropriate personal questions."

"When people come to realize how much that trivializes sex, they are open to a deeper understanding of celibacy," she explained.

For many years, Mother Marion has had an elderly Marianist brother from Australia, a psychiatrist, teach periodic two-week conferences about sex and celibacy, including discussions about masturbation.

"It was all right out there," Mother Marion said. "The root causes and how to deal with it and the blame, the guilt. He portrayed it as an end result of a lot of other factors, like depression."

In one course, the brother explained how religious men and women often believe they have fallen in love when, in reality, they are simply attracted to qualities they wish they had themselves. "Whatever qualities we are projecting on another person," Mother Marion said, "we should retrieve those and see that they are developed in ourselves."

Unlike the older Ferdinand Benedictines, who frowned upon questions regarding celibacy, Mother Marion welcomed such inquiries. It was a chance to explain her sisters' dedication, to demystify some of the stereotypes.

"Your questions are thought-provoking," Mother Marion said after I'd closed my notebook. "You must have a strong meditative life."

SEEKING SANITY

While the sisters ate spaghetti with tomato sauce and an iceberg lettuce salad for lunch, Sister Janet read aloud from the book *In Search of Van Gogh*. The sisters occasionally read nonreligious books at meals. The main character was just about to break into a French monastery, which had once doubled as an asylum, to view the room where Van Gogh had lived. As she read, Janet's lullaby voice drew out each vowel in a dramatic soliloquy. The sisters, especially Mother Marion, laughed when the author met up with a scowling nun.

" 'Let me show you out,' " Janet read, capturing the mother superior's terseness. *"Sister Marie-Florentine took me by the arm and walked me back down the corridor. We stopped at the door.*

" *'Goodbye, sister.'*

" *'Goodbye, my son,' she said with a smile as sweet as a razor.*

"To hell with this, I thought as I trudged down the drive. Looking back, I could see the sun reflecting off the nun's glasses behind the peephole. I wondered how long I would keep sane in there."

★ ★ ★

I, too, wondered how the sisters kept their sanity, how they were able to live all these years in silence without developing personality problems or lunging into some revealing "girl talk." After all, that was one of the aspects that I found most alluring about women's religious communities—the intense relationships and the deep conversations between nuns that I'd experienced at many other orders. I'd read somewhere that humans need so much physical touching to maintain their sanity, something akin to eight hugs a day. So how were these women, who didn't regularly connect either physically or mentally, able to keep from going crazy? I would soon learn from a sister who'd had to confront her own disorder.

I found Sister Kay Kettenhofen meandering the grassy paths between the monastery and the cheese barns, reading a book about saints without lifting her eyes from the page. Kay is a quiet, studious woman whom I often noticed sitting in front of the computer cataloguing the monastery's ten thousand books. At fifty-one, she had been the youngest at the monastery before Janet and Jo Ann arrived. Shy and frequently stooped, Kay has an appealing honest face with hazel eyes.

"This is a difficult life but not for the reasons people think," she offered as we walked. "It's not difficult to get out of bed early in the morning. After a while, your body gets used to it, and you wake up automatically. You try to sleep in, but you can't. Assimilating to the way things are done in a monastery is a culture shock: learning to appreciate silence, learning how to read and how to pray."

The monastery and its silence, Kay explained, are about allowing nuns to feed their inner lives, to provide an atmosphere where they can continue an uninterrupted conversation with God. The quiet simply inspires intense meditation and provides long stretches of time when sisters can work out their "problems." Instead of fostering a hunger for conversation, though, Kay said the silence creates a peaceful atmosphere that everyone appreciates. Such space allows the mind to open up and release thoughts.

"It's a funny thing, but even in the silence, you're with people all day long, you're just not communicating with them on a superficial level."

After her first two and a half years, though, Kate left the monastery.

"My problem was that I was getting scrupulous," she said. "I was making a sin out of everything and worrying about everything. It's self-centered and being so concerned with yourself that God's not getting anything out of it. It's turning common critical thoughts into major sins."

"Hmm. So it's like being too strict of a nun?" I asked.

"Yeah, right. There are a lot of causes for it," Kay said, embarrassed. "You can almost get a sort of addiction to religion just as people can get addicted to anything else. Fortunately, I had good guidance, and, through counseling, was eventually able to get over that."

Kay is the first sister I'd ever met who had left the monastery because she was trying to live religious life too rigidly. I'd encountered many nuns who are obsessed with things like maintaining good posture, keeping their eyes lowered, never questioning an order, and reciting litanies. For them, religious life is more about following a list of do's and don'ts and less about achieving a personal relationship with a divine entity.

"What are the signs of being scrupulous?" I asked.

"They're silly really," Kay said. "It's making mountains out of mole-hills. It's not having enough trust in God's mercy. It's thinking that you can save yourself."

She compared her former condition to a kind of obsessive-compulsive disorder. She might ask forgiveness over and over again for errors, not sins. Kay worried about her own salvation, about the slightest infraction, about typical human thoughts. Part of her problem, she said, was that she aspires to be a saint. Of all the nuns I'd met, no one had ever confessed such an aspiration.

WHEN REAL LIFE INTRUDES

The next morning I caught up with Sister Mary David DeFeo just before she headed to the hospital for her radiation treatment.

"Only six more burns to go," she said, smiling, her angular face gaunt, her cheeks red. Where gray hair would have been peeking out from under her veil, there was a white headband that hid her bald head.

Sister Mary David is the subprioress and, at sixty-nine, the sisters' oldest member. Earlier in the year, she had been diagnosed with stage three cancer that had spread from her breast to her lymph nodes. Instead of becoming a tired, discouraged nun battling cancer, though, Mary David has found new meaning in her monastic life.

A late entrant, Mary David joined the Trappistines in Wrentham, Massachusetts, at twenty-eight years old in 1959, giving up a career as an operating room nurse. She had smoked one and a half packs of cigarettes a day for nine years, inhaling her last at the monastery gates the day she entered.

During my first visit here two years earlier, Mary David had revealed, in her strong Boston accent, what her life had been like as a cloistered nun. Refusing to play the monastic exemplar, she complained about the days she doesn't feel holy and doesn't want to pray. The life of silence and meditation forces her to deal with her own imperfections.

"This life is not an escape. You are faced with yourself," she had said. "You still have your bitchy moods. You do centering prayer and you go off and get in a better frame of mind."

Now, she faces cancer with the same bluntness. Instead of letting the cancer discourage her—her mother died of breast cancer when she was the same age—Mary David finds inspiration even from a disease that she says will most likely kill her.

After her mother's death twenty-five years ago, Mary David became vigilant about examining her breasts every month and getting a mammogram once a year. As the monastery infirmarian, she insists the others do the same.

So that January when Mary David was removing a tick embedded under her right breast and felt a bump, she didn't hesitate to get it checked out. A mammogram confirmed her worst fear: like mother, like daughter.

"I went through all the things that women go through," she said. "I may have a veil on my head, but I'm all woman underneath."

At first she was shocked and angry. She'd done everything she was supposed to do: no caffeine, living a balanced life. For four decades she hadn't eaten meat or drunk alcohol or smoked a cigarette.

"I thought: 'Oh, God, where does this come from?'"

She had a mastectomy and a month later began chemotherapy. While she was going to the hospital for her follow-up treatment, a nurse asked if she would speak to a woman who had just been diagnosed. Soon, she was talking with three women who had breast cancer. She called it a "spontaneous support group." The nun who'd spent her life in silence was suddenly finding comfort in human connections—with women who weren't even nuns, let alone Catholic.

"All of a sudden there's a sisterly bonding. There's a sisterly concern for each other," she said, surprised to find a connection with women outside her monastery.

Mary David deals with the disease by spending even more time alone, sorting out her feelings and reading about how others have survived, mentally and physically. The more she reflects on what is happening to her, the more she feels she's able to help others get through their diagnoses.

Whenever negative feelings well up inside her, Mary David gives herself permission to be angry, even with God. She doesn't write her feelings in a journal because she doesn't want anyone else reading them after she is gone. But if she did, her words would be "ugly" and "unholy."

Mary David opted not to have reconstruction surgery and was fitted for a prosthesis, which she said makes her feel better about herself.

"All of a sudden, I rediscovered my body. It was such a new feeling for me. When I grew up in a family of six boys, what made me different was my long hair and my boobies. Now I only have one boobie! It hurts every time I undress and look at my chest. Every once in a while, I'll say: 'You look a mess!'"

The first time she tried on her silicone breast, she went to Mother Marion's room and struck a pose.

"Notice any difference?" she asked, pushing her fake breast out.

The two nuns laughed and cried together. Even in her loose-fitting habit, Mary David appeared "caved in" after her surgery.

"If I can find humor, I will," she said, then her face turned stiff. "You can't imagine how prevalent cancer is in our society. Cancer affects women of every age, young women with young kids. Oh, my God, my heart goes out to them."

As she spoke, I thought: if only you knew how much it has affected my life. I remembered Pat, my husband's first wife, who died at age forty-two after fighting breast cancer for four years, who left a six-year-old daughter and a barely nine-year-old boy—children I had adopted and spent the last several years struggling to raise as my own. I thought of my mother who, at age fifty-three, had just had surgery to remove the lump in her breast and was facing possible surgery to determine if she had uterine cancer. I thought of all the health books and journals I had pored over trying to help my children avoid their cancer heritage, and now mine.

When I revealed my own situation, Mary David pulled a piece of paper and pen from deep within her habit pockets and began asking me questions, jotting down notes. I guess I shouldn't have been surprised when I started hearing my mother's name mentioned at prayers. Weeks later, my mother's uterine cancer turned out to be a false alarm.

While solitude and reaching out to other patients helped Mary David overcome her anger with cancer, it strained her friendship with Sister Barbara Smickle.

"I had to pull back from her because she wanted to take control of the disease," Mary David said of her friend.

Although such intimacies are generally frowned upon, Sister Mary David and Sister Barbara are permitted to have a close friendship because they are older nuns and presumably understand the limits of such a relationship.

"I think everyone realizes that there is a special bond between us," admitted Sister Barbara. "She's one of the greatest blessings of my life. She's my best friend."

I was stunned by Barbara's admission, not just because such relationships are generally suppressed, but because the two nuns are complete opposites. Barbara and Mary David are the only remaining sisters left who founded the Crozet, Virginia, monastery. The nuns had lived much of their early monastery years in Wrentham separated by class distinctions: Barbara was a choir sister, a nun who spent the majority of her time in the chapel, while Mary David had entered as a lay sister, charged with manual labor. When Mary David learned she was going to live with Barbara at the Virginia monastery, she cringed. "Oh, my God! We're going to have to work on that," Mary David told herself.

While Mary David's frankness borders on irreverence, Barbara is the picture of gentility. Gray-haired and tall, Barbara has large round cheekbones that make her eyes squint when she smiles. Her voice is soft and Pollyannaish, the kind teachers use when speaking with children. Whereas Mary David is down-to-earth, practical, Barbara is more cerebral, idealistic.

Through the years, they've been able to point out each other's flaws, much like a married couple.

"Mary David can tell me I can be pretty controlling," Barbara said, smiling. "To have someone who can see your faults and tell you because she loves you, that's a great gift. I really do love her more than I love myself," she said, sounding like a misty-eyed young girl.

Still, Barbara believes a nun's loneliness in her early years is necessary.

"At that stage, you need more from God than you need human companionship. There is a certain loneliness but that is fruitful because it sends you to prayer more often. Young nuns don't achieve that if they have human support too soon. Real spiritual friendships aren't for the very young."

While Barbara and Mary David don't hide their friendship, they are also careful not to exclude others. They are discreet about their private conversations. And they try to give each other the space they need.

That has been particularly true since Mary David's diagnosis. Mary David has sought out Mother Marion since her surgery because she seems to find the humor in the disease more easily. Meanwhile, Barbara has taken Mary David's cancer hard. Her own biological sister died of cancer in 1997 and she fears it will also claim her best friend. When her sister was diagnosed, Barbara prayed—with permission from the superior—that God would take the cancer from her sister, who had children and a husband, and give it to her.

"God didn't take me up on it," Barbara said, disappointed.

While often the picture of composure, Barbara lost her temper one day when she saw how sick the chemotherapy was making Mary David. "Damn chemotherapy!" Barbara yelled. "Damn these treatments making you like this!"

Later she tried to make her own deal with God, pleading him to spare her friend the suffering she has witnessed in others. Most days, Barbara tries to focus on what she can do for Mary David, often reading to her, making her tapioca, collecting a bouquet of flowers, or just listening to her talk about her experiences. Facing her friend's cancer is the single hardest struggle of Barbara's life.

"In a good sense, life will never be the same," she said. "Had this not happened, I still would have lived my religious life the best way I could. But life would not have been so intense, so demanding, and so rewarding. Life just seems so much more precious. Priorities become so clear. You understand the importance of making loving choices because you may not have a chance later."

TRAINING FOR THE GREAT SPIRITUAL MARATHON

Aside from Sisters Barbara and Mary David, no one else at the Trappistine monastery appears chummy. Theirs is a different approach to religious life, a purist's pursuit for an ethereal connection. Intimacy interferes with that mission, especially early on in the life. Their ambition is about disconnecting from a worldly culture and transferring the closeness of earthly relationships to an unseen deity. In many ways, their goals are no different from those of nuns and monks of other religions who separate themselves for the intense purpose of meditating and praying and connecting with the universe—or their own minds. The Trappistines just find solitude amid the company of others.

It's difficult to conceive a life with such boundaries, yet in a secular society we routinely set limits on relationships outside of marriage. Most spouses are distrustful—or jealous—if their partners have emotionally intimate relationships with others, especially with the opposite sex. The fear is that an emotional connection could lead to sex or detract from the marriage's intimacy.

From a practical standpoint, maintaining a close relationship with anyone—male or female—requires a great deal of time and energy. If a nun's primary relationship is to God, then it is understandable that she would want to conserve her time and energy to foster that bond. And who are we to dismiss that relationship, since few of us can say we know what it's like to achieve an intense communion with the Divinity? Perhaps the feelings of bliss or satisfaction or even the reported ecstasy would outweigh any desire to connect with another human being.

In some ways, the sisters' intensity reminded me of dedicated athletes, marathon runners or triathletes who pursue disciplined lifestyles and rigorous training schedules to attain their goals. The sisters are, in essence, training themselves for the Great Spiritual Marathon. They are the elite religious, those who put themselves through incredible tests and deny themselves much in order to achieve what few do. Unlike some orders and monasteries where nuns separate themselves because they fear being tainted by the world, Trappistines separate themselves to avoid distractions.

I envied their intensity and wondered what it would be like to go days or even months never speaking to anyone, forming conversations with God or saints in my head. I wanted to go to that part of the brain the sisters routinely inhabited, that unclaimed territory, the last frontier. To me, their interior life with God sounded like a tropical deserted island, a place so beautiful and so remote that they could only transport themselves there by preventing their mental energies from escaping elsewhere. At least that's how I imagined the "vast wilderness" that Sister Janet described. I saw their solitude as a sort of step-down to nirvana, each year in seclusion allowing them to reach another level but always dangling dangerously above madness. It was as if they needed to exfoliate the world from their memories. And the only reason they required each other was to remind themselves that they were still on earth.

PART FOUR

POVERTY

BEFORE TAKING FINAL VOWS, A SISTER DIVESTS HERSELF OF ALL personal property, houses, cars, and stocks. Family inheritances are given away or signed over to the order. Aside from clothes and a few personal mementos, a sister usually does not own anything. If she works outside the monastery or convent, her salary is deposited into her order's coffers and she is provided a monthly stipend—often fifty to one hundred dollars—for personal expenses.

As with the other two vows, poverty is defined differently from order to order. For some, it is relinquishing personal possessions. For others, especially Franciscan orders—like the Franciscan Sisters of Mary, who run a birthing center in Weslaco, Texas, or the Franciscan Sisters of Christian Charity, who run schools on Arizona's reservations—a profession of poverty is intricately tied to the order's core beliefs. They often live poverty to the extreme: refusing to buy clothes or food unavailable to the poor, residing in modest houses or apartments, driving old cars—as do Paula Vandegaer, a Sister of Social Service, and her Volunteers for Life, who run pro-life pregnancy clinics in poor areas of Los Angeles. They frequently forgo luxuries that most Americans take for granted, like air conditioning, restaurant meals, and cable television.

Still, the vow raises questions among religious women because they are provided housing, food, and health care—and that suggests that they are in no way living in poverty. What's more, some sisters feel that true poverty is not a virtue and certainly not a lifestyle that anyone should strive to attain. They believe the vow makes a mockery of those who are truly struggling to get out of poverty. Some monasteries stand as great palaces on prized properties. So while these sisters themselves may not own anything, they live in palatial splendor and have access to amenities that impoverished women would not have: the ability to travel, access to extensive education, entrée to national conferences, the security of extensive health-care benefits, and the enjoyment of annual vacations at spa-like retreat centers, not to mention the access to rich benefactors' houses, cars, boats, and cabins.

Yet, many newer sisters argue that giving up their financial freedom is one of the hardest demands of religious life. In a modern feminist culture that values independence and self-reliance, relinquishing a paycheck and possessions is seen as the ultimate sacrifice.

8

THE LAST OF THE MONJITAS

FRANCISCAN SISTERS IN WESLACO, TEXAS

"You just never look at the world again the way you looked at the world before you were poor."

—SISTER ANGELA MURDAUGH

She looked like a human crucifix—arms outstretched, left hand grabbing the wall while the right hand grasped the door, legs clamped. Maria Guadalupe Aranda was in labor. At twenty-six and bearing her seventh child, Lupe had walked alone into the Holy Family Birth Center in Weslaco, Texas. She carried no satchels filled with clothes, no diapers, no video camera. She arrived that cool October night wearing only donated clothes: a maternity shirt, pants, and scuffed white tennis shoes.

I didn't know Lupe when I put my hands on her belly. I didn't even speak her language. When a contraction hit, she stopped in front of me, took my hands, and showed me how to lessen her pain. The folds of her stomach rolled like gelatin between my fingers, and I could feel the coarseness of her private hair. As the pain lingered, she squatted on the floor, spread her legs with her toes turned under her feet, and quietly groaned as she pushed.

The nuns who run the birth center know Lupe well; she birthed two other babies there, and even named her last child after Sister Angela Murdaugh, the center's founder and nurse-midwife who delivered the baby, barely two years earlier. Lupe and Sister Angela developed a friendship, with Lupe nicknaming the heavyset Sister Angela "Gordita," meaning "little fatty."

Holy Family Birth Center is known as one of the few places where being poor or an illegal alien doesn't dictate the kind of care women are given. Eleven miles from the Mexican border, on an old cucumber field, the center consists of a series of bright yellow buildings that form a makeshift commune in a neighborhood of dilapidated estates. At the center's edges, horned goats eat overgrown thistle and chickens pick at rotting vegetable rinds. Renowned in midwifery circles as one of the premier places to practice natural childbirth, the clinic is highly sought for its medical internships, even though the sisters can do little more than feed and house its volunteers.

Founder Sister Angela Murdaugh is a charismatic Southerner whose personality and vision dominate the clinic. A large, handsome woman with slight buckteeth and curly blond hair, Sister Angela's presence would be intimidating if it weren't for her folksy, down-home attitude reflected in her twangy Arkansas accent and her casual, baggy attire. Though she is sixty, her energy, coupled with a face dotted with freckles, makes her seem much younger.

While Angela is a member at the Franciscan Sisters of Mary, a health-care order based in St. Louis, Missouri, most of the other sisters at the center come from various religious orders all over the United States. Several are from Franciscan orders, known for their devotion to living poverty. The nuns room side by side with volunteers who are Jewish, Protestant, or even atheist. The center's clients are largely Hispanic, 90 percent live below the poverty level, and the majority are undocumented aliens who dwell quietly in shacks and substandard housing throughout the Rio Grande Valley, one of the poorest regions of the country.

After eighteen years and 5,108 babies, Sister Angela and her clinic sisters understand the power, exhilaration, adrenaline, and even the rare moments of peril when women help other women give birth. They have aided girls as young as twelve years old who are pregnant or women like Lupe with multiple children with different fathers and no means of support. Yet, they don't criticize the women or express exasperation when they continue to get pregnant. Mothers say the sisters treat each baby's birth as a joyous occasion, offering heartfelt congratulations. The sisters teach natural family planning, the Catholic Church's approved method of birth control. But they also make women aware of their options and where they can obtain birth control pills or condoms. Still, they understand that in Latino culture the man often dictates when a woman will have sex and when she will get pregnant.

I had come to the birth center to watch the sisters work with the illegal immigrant women in South Texas. A little more than an hour after my arrival, Lupe staggered in the door. When the sisters suggested I stand in as Lupe's personal support, they nodded to each other with a quiet acknowledgment. They knew what they were asking of me, but I did not. Lupe's labor was expected to be long and arduous. She was anemic and had bled dangerously during her previous births. Her first baby had miscarried at seven months. She had carried her second child to term when she was seventeen years old. Each delivery after that proved increasingly difficult. The older midwives knew what was happening: Lupe's uterus was tired and giving up.

Even though Lupe was the same age as the young, smooth-skinned, unmarried volunteers at the clinic, she didn't readily trust them. Sister Angela had never carried a child of her own, but she had delivered more than fifteen hundred babies in her twenty-eight years as a midwife; Lupe trusted that kind of experience. Sister Angela, though, was not the midwife on duty the night Lupe went into labor. It was Kamala Krakover, a thirty-three-year-old volunteer nurse-midwife who had arrived in August fresh from midwifery studies at New York University.

A Jewish woman, Kamala had never met a Catholic nun before she was introduced to Sister Angela at a midwifery conference earlier that year. Kamala found Angela to be an intelligent, forceful, and committed midwife—so much so that she convinced Kamala to endure three months of Texas heat as a volunteer midwife.

Kamala has a dark, exotic look—like an emaciated Brooke Shields. Long and gaunt, her face looks like it could barely support the thick black hair extending down the back of her turquoise scrubs. Her voice is that of a child—breathy and high-pitched.

Before arriving, Kamala imagined the sisters as strict, rule-oriented people, women who weren't independent thinkers. Though other interns had told Kamala that the nuns at Holy Family don't wear habits, she still expected the stiff prim figures she had seen in movies. What she found, however, were sisters in sandals and shorts.

When women came to the clinic with a venereal disease for a second and third time, Kamala watched as the sisters made no judgments, just mild threats that they would castrate the men who continued to infect them. She was amazed at the nuns' accepting attitudes toward sex and how they don't condemn or preach.

Though other Jewish interns had difficulty adapting to the crosses on the walls and the icons of Our Lady of Guadalupe, they didn't trouble Kamala, who thought the spiritual atmosphere at the clinic—enhanced by noontime prayers, the feel-good Christian poetry adorning every room, and the tiny one-room chapel—added to the overall birth experience.

When Lupe arrived at the clinic that Tuesday evening at six claiming she was in labor, Kamala could find no physical sign confirming what Lupe was saying. She wasn't dilated, and her cervix wasn't open. But Lupe insisted Kamala admit her anyway. Against her own experience, Kamala admitted Lupe. Within two hours, Lupe dilated to six centimeters and was having regular contractions while walking around the "Mary" birthing room. Kamala was amazed that Lupe could feel the onset of labor before it happened. She was glad she hadn't sent Lupe home. It wasn't long, though, before Lupe voiced her reluctance toward Kamala and asked that Sister Angela deliver her baby. Kamala knew she needed to quickly gain Lupe's confidence.

Lupe, wearing only a light blue hospital gown, sauntered around in her bare feet. Pacing from the birth room to the adjacent bedroom and bathroom, she spoke in Spanish and broken English. The waiting reminded her of her exodus from Guatemala six years earlier when she rode a bus for four days and four nights to escape from her common-law husband.

Guatemala was not her home. Lupe was born in Mexico and lived for the first few years in Cruzeros de Flores, near the Texas border. She was eight years old when her family floated to Texas via inner tubes along the river Americans call the Rio Grande and Mexicans call the Rio Bravo. She met her husband when she was just fourteen years old. Her parents were opposed to them marrying, so they ran off to Guatemala, where they lived with his parents on the outskirts of Guatemala City.

It wasn't long before she became pregnant. She lost her first child, she believes, because she was unable to get enough food. Within the next couple of years, Lupe's living conditions improved. She and her husband moved into a house, and Lupe gave birth to two daughters.

But then Lupe discovered her husband was having an affair. At that point, she made up her mind to go home. However, Lupe couldn't take the girls—Sedy Linette, then age two, and Claudia Carolina, then age three—without proper government papers. Lupe was too distraught to wait the months or years that might take. So she placed the girls with their *madrina,* or godmother. Then she rode the bus to the Mexico-Texas border, she said, holding up four fingers to emphasize the duration of that journey. To reach her family in Progreso—a town on the Texas side of the border—Lupe swam the black waters of the Rio Grande underneath the border's barbed wire by the cover of night.

A few years later, her husband visited Lupe in Texas and begged her to come back to him. During his visit, Lupe conceived her fourth child. After the birth of Juan, Lupe met a Mexican man who fathered her son Rene and daughter Angelica. That man was also unfaithful to her. Now she was pregnant with her seventh child, by a third man, a Puerto Rican, who also had left her.

When Lupe tired of walking, she sat on the toilet trying to push the baby while Kamala held her hand. Between contractions, Lupe asked if I had children. Kamala acted as translator. I told Lupe I have two children, at that time a thirteen-year-old son and an eleven-year-old daughter. Lupe's eyes lit up and her lips formed a half-moon smile. She seemed to take comfort that she was delivering her baby with another mother.

"Then, you know what it's like," Lupe said through Kamala.

I shook my head. "My children are adopted," I said.

Lupe's smile faded a little. She patted my arm, as if to give comfort. "It's okay," she said in English; then she asked me in Spanish: "You want to have babies?"

Suddenly, a contraction hit and Lupe doubled over, grabbing her stomach.

"*Respira mas profundo,*" Kamala said, urging her to relax.

"*Tengo dolor,*" Lupe responded and grabbed Kamala's hand to massage her. Kamala gently rubbed and talked to Lupe in her whispery voice.

After a couple of contractions, Lupe pushed away Kamala's hand and reached for mine.

"She says you have bigger hands and can rub harder," Kamala said, smiling.

I grinned back. For the first time since I'd entered the birthing room, I felt I was needed. I was supposed to be Lupe's physical and emotional support, yet I couldn't even speak directly to her. I hadn't ever given birth, so even relating as a mother was limited. Still, I sensed that Lupe liked my being there, if only because of my big hands. But I wanted to believe it was more than that.

When the contraction had finished, Lupe continued our conversation, suddenly feeling the need to share her life story with the stranger easing her pains. She was hoping for a girl. That way she would have two boys and two girls at home. Lupe was eager to hear my guess of the baby's gender. She moved my hands around her belly, then asked me what I felt. I tried to discern whether she carried the baby high, which meant a girl—according to the old wives' tale—or low, meaning she was carrying a boy. Lupe said she thought the baby was a girl. I said it felt like a boy.

"I hope you are wrong," she said in Spanish, smiling.

Before midnight, Sister Angela stopped by the "Mary" birthing room—a cigar-shaped building with a bedroom for visitors on one end and a birthing room on the other, with a bathroom sandwiched in the middle. Sister Angela sat on the edge of the birthing room bed and waited. Lupe was taking a hot shower, trying to ease her contractions.

"An indoor shower is a real luxury to her," Sister Angela said. "Normally she just sprays off with a hose in their yard. She's one of our poorest clients."

Kamala told Angela how she was trying to win Lupe's trust but Lupe kept asking for Angela.

Angela nodded. "In their culture, they really trust their elders," Sister Angela explained. Then she turned to me. "Kamala here looks like she's fourteen."

Growing impatient, Sister Angela knocked on the bathroom door. The water had stopped for a while. A wet-haired Lupe came to the door, and when she saw Sister Angela, she threw her arms around her neck.

The two women talked excitedly in Spanish. Angela touched Kamala on the arm and told Lupe that Kamala was a professional and that Lupe was in good hands.

Lupe looked somewhat relieved. Then she told Angela, "Go home and get some sleep. You work hard."

A COMMUNE OF CULTURES

Growing up Catholic in the Protestant Bible Belt of Bryant, Arkansas, Sister Angela knows firsthand the plight of the poor. At the Catholic high school she attended, Angela worked for her tuition and ate with the help staff. When her nun teachers asked who wanted to be a nun, Angela was always among the first to raise her hand. Even though her family lived on the margins, Angela was determined to do something for "the poor."

With eight kids, her mother's salary as a nurse and her father's paycheck from the local aluminum company barely covered their family's basic needs. Although Angela needed braces to fix her teeth, her parents didn't have the money, and Angela began to see that access to health care was determined not by need, but by wealth.

At twenty-two years old, Angela entered the Franciscan Sisters of Mary. In 1972, after obtaining her master's in nursing and a specialty in nurse-midwifery, Sister Angela began delivering babies at a government clinic in Raymondville, Texas. Her first delivery was the tenth baby of a woman named Maria de la Luz Salinas. The father asked Sister Angela what the birth cost. Angela told him it was twenty-five dollars. The father looked at Angela and said, "For you, thirty dollars," then laid out three crisp ten-dollar bills.

Sister Angela quickly garnered a reputation among the Mexican women as a skillful *pantera,* the Spanish word for midwife. In Mexican culture, delivering a baby by a midwife is the rule rather than the exception. Women feel more comfortable when other women help them give birth, which is more commonly done at home.

Sister Angela's practice gained national attention in 1981 when she was elected president of the American College of Nurse-Midwives in Washington, D.C. While in Washington, Sister Angela envisioned opening a birthing center in the Rio Grande Valley. Unlike government clinics, this one would be run by sisters—*monjitas* in Spanish.

By 1983, Angela had convinced another sister who was also a nurse-midwife to join her. Shortly thereafter, two sister nurses joined them. The Catholic diocese in Brownsville loaned the sisters four acres in Weslaco that at one time had been a retreat center. The only building on the property, though, was falling apart; the roof leaked, and raccoons and possums lived in the walls and ceilings. The rest of the property had been leased out to a cucumber farmer. Sister Angela would literally have to build her clinic from the ground up.

Initially, it was difficult to lure sisters who were nurses to the hottest and poorest area of the country, especially when the center hadn't been built yet. When one sister, who was an accountant, came to interview, there was only a plowed field on the property. Sister Angela walked around in the mud with arms outstretched showing the woman where they planned to build the main buildings. The woman couldn't envision the center that Angela described. She didn't stay.

Eventually, Sister Angela and her Holy Family clinic attracted other sisters who were nurses and midwives. The clinic became known as a place where nurses could perfect their midwifery skills. The onslaught of different cultures—Protestant, Catholic, Jewish, Mexican, South American, Texans—helped Sister Angela conceive of her clinic's varied mission: to care for the poor mothers and babies of South Texas, to help others learn midwifery and to provide a healing environment where discouraged nurses and midwives could go to revive their self-confidence.

Soon it became clear that the clinic's biggest influence wasn't on the clients, but on the workers. When young nurses and volunteers worked closely with impoverished clients, the abstract plague of poverty took on real names.

"We allow these new young nurses to be stung by the poor so they know what it's like," explained Angela. "You just never look at the world again the way you looked at the world before you were poor."

I knew what Angela meant. On my first visit to Holy Family, I followed a volunteer midwife on several home visits where I saw families crammed into suffocating shacks in abandoned subdivisions. I watched as she examined mothers and babies in homes with open ceilings, junkyard furniture, and gas stoves that had only tinfoil for oven doors. A hot plate served as a stove for a family of six. The stench of sewage became as common as the mangy mutts that could barely stagger to greet us. Upon seeing two or three families living in filthy two-room hovels, I had to hold back tears so hard that my throat hurt. How could people be living like this in the United States? What I saw on the back roads of Texas was as bad or worse than the slums I'd visited in third world countries. And I've never been able to forget it.

Sister Angela believes everyone at the clinic should live as simply as their clients, a concept that not everyone appreciates. Incorporating convent-style living with a clinic structure, Angela designed the center so that sisters and volunteers lived together. The living quarters are dormitory style, small cell-like rooms equipped with a dresser and desk and a single bed, but no air conditioners. Only clinic offices with computers and the birthing rooms have window air conditioners. In the prickly summer heat, which is more commonly above one hundred degrees than below, volunteers, many from Northern states, sleep practically naked with fans blowing in their faces and tears of sweat rolling off their bodies.

Though she is clearly the clinic's de facto mother superior, Sister Angela insists that she sleep in the same quarters as everyone else and receive the same amount of money as everyone else. The sisters pool their salaries—those who receive salaries from their orders—and give the money to the clinic. If there is anything left over after the bills are paid, the sisters divide the money equally to pay for personal expenses.

Originally Sister Angela envisioned the clinic more as a working commune in which the sisters and volunteers would raise their food. She discovered that managing a birthing center twenty-four hours a day with limited staff didn't leave much time to farm. As the clinic gained more staff, Sister Angela devoted more of her time as an advocate for the poor and midwifery. For six years, she fought to get Medicaid to pay for midwifery births. It was only when she and Texas Rural Legal Aid threatened a lawsuit that the state relented in 1989. Sister Angela and the clinic own the first Medicaid number for birth centers. Later, Sister Angela became part of a team that redrafted the state rules and regulations for birth centers.

"People have a right to health care," Sister Angela said. "It's the same right as housing and food and love. Every unborn baby has the right to come into the world with the best of medical care. There shouldn't be a river that changes that. We take care of human beings—not Mexicans or Indians or Americans. Human beings."

Sister Angela Murdaugh

Late that night, Lupe wearily pleaded with Kamala to break her water. Kamala struggled with whether she should induce birth. The baby's head was positioned high in the uterus; breaking the water too soon could cut off the baby's supply of oxygen before it was born.

If a woman suffers complications in her pregnancy or labor, the sisters refer her to a doctor who has agreed to take on such cases without knowing how or when she will get paid. The birth center itself only handles normal pregnancies—no twins or breach births. "Normal" for a poor population can often include anemia and high blood pressure. Yet, deaths at the clinic are rare.

Midwifery is incredibly low-tech. Midwives don't use electronic fetal monitors and don't cut the women. They lessen labor pains by massage or warm baths. And though they can administer painkillers, they do so sparingly. Midwives emphasize that birthing is a natural experience and not a "medical experience." Like many midwifery clinics, Holy Family encourages family members, including children, to participate. The sisters and midwives stress that going through natural childbirth increases a woman's self-confidence.

By 2 A.M., we had bathed Lupe in a warm bath and were trying to get her to rest. Lupe lay across the double bed in the birthing room, her legs bent, the bottoms of her feet grabbing at the edge of the bed. Underneath her were large blue plastic squares, like huge adult diapers, to protect the bed. Kamala strapped on a pair of sterile gloves, then reached between Lupe's legs, trying to feel the baby's head in her uterus.

"It's still really high up there," she said to me, then translated for Lupe.

Kamala took out the fetal heart monitor and its long steel probe. She squirted lubricant on the probe's flat end and began moving the instrument around Lupe's bulging stomach. The box squelched like a bad radio transmission as she moved the probe. Normally, the high-pitched screech turned into a soft beating that became louder and louder until it emitted an eerie rhythmic thumping. This time, though, all we heard was the squawking of the machine.

THE LOAVES AND THE FISHES

More than once the sisters have questioned whether God was telling them to close the clinic. In the fall of 1997, welfare reform and a more vigilant border patrol caused the clinic to lose two-thirds of its clients.

"The poor got poorer and those who were trying to become legal went more underground," explained forty-eight-year-old Sister Kristine Vorencamp, who, as office manager, often was the first person patients saw when they came to the clinic.

Before that year's crisis, the sisters required women to make a seventy-five-dollar down payment, then pay twenty-five dollars upon every visit. They credited clients five dollars an hour from their bill for each hour they worked as volunteers, often cleaning and cooking. When the immigration authorities learned that pregnant Mexican women were crossing the border and going to the clinic to "work," they gave the sisters a stern warning.

The sisters fasted every Monday for weeks and prayed about what they should do. Eventually the answer seemed clear, if perhaps risky. The sisters decided they would have no set costs. Women would pay what they could and volunteer on their own. Sister Angela believed that if the clinic was meant to exist, then it would. She wouldn't worry about trying to maintain her legacy.

"We built this place because too much of Catholicism is about brick and mortar, and they worry themselves to death about what they can do with it," she said. "We don't owe a single penny to nobody. If we can't afford it, we don't get it. That's the way it is."

The sisters estimate that each birth costs the center $1,500—in contrast to the average uncomplicated vaginal birth at a hospital, which costs $7,090. More often than not, the waiting room at Holy Family is filled with Mexican women who don't speak English and have nothing more than a few wadded-up dollar bills to give. Though the clinic receives sizable donations, Medicaid and patients paying out of pocket make up about 70 percent of the clinic's annual budget of $490,000. The clinic's accountant estimates that the sisters and the volunteers contribute more than $380,000 in professional services each year because they receive a greatly reduced salary or none at all.

Over the years, the clinic frequently seemed headed toward bankruptcy; then another donation or grant would appear. The sisters needed $6,350 for building insurance; then the clinic received a bequest from an estate for $6,385. The sisters ran out of diapers; the next day a hospital donated boxes of diapers. They ran out of supplies used in delivery; then a friend of a friend gave them a box. One of the clinic's cars fell apart, and a local obstetrician donated a car.

"It was like the loaves and the fishes, and it has just never ended," Sister Angela explained. "There's something bigger than you guiding things here. And every time it happens, it's like faith building, faith blocks you stand on because you more and more realize that you can depend on God the next time and the next time."

For that reason, Sister Angela refused to pay malpractice insurance after the diocese stopped carrying her. She said the clinic has nothing to protect, and she can't afford the premiums.

Sister Angela's faith is backed by some surprising statistics. The National Center for Health Statistics has found that babies delivered by certified nurse-midwives are less likely to die than those delivered by doctors. The risk of death in the first twenty-eight days, in fact, is 33 percent lower if the baby is delivered by a midwife.

Midwifery isn't without risks, though. Holy Family has been sued three times. The first case involved a mother who died before giving birth. The woman suffered an amniotic embolism, a rare occurrence in which the amniotic fluid around the baby flows into the mother's bloodstream.

"It's extremely hard to diagnose. They do it postmortem," Sister Angela explained.

The sisters transferred the mother to the hospital and the doctors performed a C-section, but the mother and the baby died on the operating room table. After two lawyers rejected the case, the father decided he would represent himself, Sister Angela recalled. At the first hearing, he didn't show up, and the judge threw out the case.

The second case involved a stillborn. The center was covered under Catholic Charities at that time: The organization's malpractice insurance company settled out of court.

The last time they were sued, the sisters put the lawsuit on the altar in their chapel, and it stayed there for years until it was settled. The case involved the birth of a child who suffered from cerebral palsy. The family eventually decided to pursue the Catholic Charities' insurance company and signed an agreement that Holy Family's assets would be protected.

Not all the women who seek out the sisters are impoverished. One night, twenty-four-year-old Elizabeth Jordan sat on the arm of a vinyl chair in the peach-colored waiting room, her arms resting on her stomach. Seven months pregnant with her third child, she had chosen to have the baby at the clinic instead of the hospital where her two daughters were born.

"I had bad experiences in the hospital," she said. "They always took the baby to the baby ward and wouldn't let me have her in the room long enough. The women I know who had their babies here, they tell me that kids can come to visit. I want him to be there," she said, touching her husband's leg. "And the babies," she said, looking down at her two young girls with dark eyes and pageboy haircuts.

Mrs. Jordan is Anglo but her husband is a Mexican American who spent most of his life as a migrant worker. Because the Jordans didn't have health insurance, Medicaid paid for the hospital births of their daughters. Now, they pay the sisters what they can afford.

"I didn't come here for the religion," said Mrs. Jordan, a nonpracticing Catholic. "But the *monjitas*—they treat you better. They have softer hands than the doctors."

If it weren't for the sisters, the poor and the undocumented mothers who don't qualify for regular Medicaid would not be able to seek medical care until the actual birth of the baby. U.S. Emergency Medicaid doesn't pay for routine visits, only emergency care. Without the clinic's prenatal care, the baby is at greater risk of having long-term health problems.

Some people mistakenly believe that the clinic, often referred to as "La Clinica de las Monjitas," only serves Hispanics. The few Caucasian women who seek out the clinic are usually referred by doctors or government offices.

A case in point is thirty-five-year-old Cheryl Gray, who had recently moved to Weslaco from Dallas and wanted her child to be born by the hands of a midwife just as her last two children had been. She was unaware of Holy Family until her gynecologist referred her to the clinic. Gray, a confident, blond-haired, blue-eyed woman, had Medicaid and could have gone to virtually any doctor, but she chose Holy Family.

"My first child was a premature baby who was born in a hospital room that looked like a garage," explained Gray, who lost that baby. "It turned me off to doctors and hospitals."

Now Gray deals with the pains of labor by putting on headphones and listening to soothing music and by taking hot showers. As soon as this baby was delivered and placed on her stomach, she would call in the children; her nine-year-old daughter would cut the umbilical cord.

"It's nice to come here and be treated like a queen, even though you're destitute," Gray said. "It's not because they're one religion or another. It's because they're women. Midwives don't get into it because they love the money. There's no such thing as a rich midwife."

THE ANGRY HOURS

Back at the birthing room, the probe in Kamala's hand slid across Lupe's skin, leaving a trail of grease in its wake. Kamala adjusted the knobs on the fetal heart monitor, then pushed the probe to the outer portion of Lupe's stomach. The machine's squelching began to soften, and we heard a quiet thumping that grew louder and more clear. Kamala sighed.

"I was really worried for a while there," she admitted.

She carefully wiped the lubricant from Lupe's belly and helped her lie back on the bed. Kamala picked up several fat orange envelopes that contained Lupe's medical records and read details that disturbed her. During her last two births at the clinic, Lupe had lost an unusual amount of blood. She also had uterine atony, when the uterus doesn't contract.

"I wish she would stop pushing," Kamala said. "She's determined to have this baby right now, and she's tiring herself out. She's going to need that strength later."

At 3 A.M., Kamala's shift ended. She phoned the next midwife on duty, Abigail Reese, a twenty-eight-year-old with long, dark, curly hair, cat green eyes, and perfectly arched eyebrows. In September, having graduated from Yale with a master's in midwifery, Abby had signed on as a paid staff member for two years at a salary of one thousand dollars a month. She is the first staff midwife who is not a sister.

Although Abby had placed the hall phone on her pillow, she didn't hear the ten shrill rings and had to be awakened by head nurse Sister Lori Sills, whose room was next door. Abby reluctantly pulled on her pink scrubs and rubbed the sleep from her eyes. Outside, she walked under the sway of the willow trees, the night breeze blowing her hair. She opened the screen door to the kitchen and didn't notice when the door slammed behind her. She heated some coffee, and then headed over to the farthest birthing room at the center.

By the time Abby reached the room, Lupe had returned to her feet and was pacing around, stopping only to pester Kamala to check whether the baby had fallen into the birth canal. Kamala put her off.

"I'll let someone who is coming into this fresh make that decision," Kamala said sleepily.

Kamala explained Lupe's situation to Abby. Then she hugged Abby and wished her luck.

Abby helped me rub Lupe's belly during contractions. When the pain started, Lupe could barely stand. She wrapped her arms around our shoulders, and we held her up. Abby checked Lupe frequently. The baby's head was still too far up the birth canal. Lupe's contractions continued to increase in frequency and duration. She pushed harder, her face strained, her red cheeks mashed up to closed eyes. Her teeth ground together as she sucked in air and sprayed out spit.

I had expected Lupe's labor to last a couple of hours, as it had when I helped my sister-in-law give birth in a hospital. As the hours passed, I grew more frustrated in trying to relieve Lupe's escalating pains. I also felt angry that the father of Lupe's baby had left her alone at such a critical time.

As I watched Lupe suffer through the contractions, my admiration grew. I questioned whether I could ever endure such agony. Was it through this pain that mothers bonded quickly with their children, as Angela argued? I felt torn by the experience; while there was so much warmth and love expressed by the nuns, midwives, and nurses who tried to ease Lupe's pain, there seemed to be such needless suffering, too. I wanted Lupe to have an epidural so that she could enjoy this moment without immense exhaustion.

At about 4:30 A.M., Lupe sat on the edge of the bed and cried, her face in her hands. Abby kneeled on the floor with her hands on Lupe's legs. These were the crazy hours before birth when women in labor tend to become irrational. Abby took Lupe's increasing moodiness as a good sign. Then things got ugly.

Lupe screamed that if Abby wasn't going to break her water, she wanted to go to the hospital. Through exhausted tears, she begged for sleep, for food, for an end to the pain. When Abby tried to explain the dangers, Lupe demanded to see Sister Angela. Abby looked up at Lupe. They were only two years apart in age but thousands of dollars apart in education and life experience.

"I'm a product of circumstances like anyone else," Abby said. "I can't minimize that privilege got me where I am, and the lack of privilege got her where she is."

NEEDING *MONJITAS*

The clinic has a hard time attracting qualified sisters. Many sisters who are trained midwives are not available because they're working in foreign countries. When they return to the United States, it's usually to retire.

Twelve-hour shifts that start or end at 3 A.M., with only one day off a week, are daunting—especially for sister midwives and nurses who are in their late fifties and sixties or older. That summer, two sisters left, saying they could no longer handle the pace.

"A lot of people have gotten very drained," said Kathy Buchheit, a Franciscan sister planning a year-long sabbatical. As she sat in a dark examining room, the light on the desk illuminated the dark fleshy circles under her eyes. She has a soft, tanned face; dark cropped hair; and a habitually intense expression. Occasionally she erupted into spontaneous laughter, and a huge toothy grin spread across her face, hinting at her lighter side, which had been strained by the taxing schedule. The stress of the clinic, menopause, and the declining health of her mother all took a toll on her.

"I got very tired here," she said. "I'm real grateful for the time I had here, but I've had no time to reflect. I was always out there giving to everyone else. That's not healthy."

It wasn't until the succession of baby deaths last year—two stillborn at the clinic, one at a hospital, and one late miscarriage—that Sister Kathy realized she couldn't continue.

"I was feeling like the funeral midwife," she said, having arranged several of the funeral details. "You expect that joyous aspect of birth, but it's death. And it's very, very painful."

One of the mothers Kathy knew well had a two-year-old son who died of leukemia, and Sister Kathy arranged his funeral, too. "Babies and children aren't supposed to die. I was real involved with the families, and it seemed like for a while—God, I just don't want to do this anymore."

Along with the long hours, sisters who come to Holy Family have to adjust to a unique living situation. Most Catholic nuns live either in a convent or monastery or with other sisters, usually from their own order. Sharing a house with nonreligious women who are several decades younger and with sisters from different religious orders quickly became problematic for some sisters.

"For sisters to be living with nonsisters is a progressive idea," said Sister Lori Sills, head nurse at the clinic, "but it's not as ideal as it's made out to be sometimes. It's not religious life as I have lived it nor is it strictly religious life. I feel I'm asked to compromise the kind of time I need for silence."

Others found the heat overbearing and couldn't understand why Angela wouldn't allow air conditioners in the bedrooms. Some sisters, like Lori, wanted more quiet time, less noise, and fewer phones ringing in the hallways. Whenever she complained, the other sisters told her she needed to adjust.

"I didn't like the phone ringing at midnight and people on and off the phones with their boyfriends," she said of the interns. "It's being surrounded by other things and other conversations that I just don't relate to. If it's not that, it's talk about work all the time. I often say, 'Can't we talk about something else besides stitching somebody's perineum?'"

Last summer, after a year at the clinic, Sister Lori fixed up a room at the old house on the property that serves as an occasional guesthouse. Her room looks much like a cell at a convent. She painted the walls plain white, and inside there is little more than a single bed. The other sisters, she said, don't understand why she needs more privacy than the rest of them.

"Some [of the volunteers] come here to be healed," she said. "They've had professional disasters. There's the expectation that you always should be able to listen to someone. You can't do it all the time. It's like living in a therapeutic community. It's expected that we should just continue to absorb all the baggage that comes here."

She added, "Angela's personality is what made this place. She maintains this idealistic vision of how it runs, and she doesn't tolerate it well when there's another idea."

BETWEEN BIRTH AND DEATH

At about 6 A.M., Abby checked Lupe and found that the baby's head had moved farther down the birth canal. She could now safely break the water bag, which had ballooned up against the side of Lupe's uterus. Abby called Sister Mary Thompson, a redheaded woman with freckles, fair skin, and a nasally Wisconsin accent. Mary is Angela's second in command and was the backup midwife that morning.

The Texas sky was beginning to lighten from black to dark blue when Mary walked over from her room just a few buildings away. She was sleepy but accustomed to rising early after her years at the convent and decades as a labor and delivery nurse and then as a midwife.

Mary checked Lupe herself, then reviewed with Abby how to insert the amniohook that would prick the water bag.

At 7:03 A.M. Abby squatted beneath Lupe's legs and followed Mary's instructions. There was a rush of fluid, and within minutes, the baby's head crowned. Sister Mary lay on the bed next to Lupe and held her hand while showing her how to breathe. Lupe pursed her lips and gulped short, exaggerated breaths.

Abby crouched below Lupe's legs with her gloved hands holding the baby's head.

"Okay, stop pushing!" Mary said, in English and in Spanish.

A brown little head appeared, then a shoulder, a belly. The long yellow umbilical cord appeared between the baby's legs.

Abby held the wet, wrinkled baby. Her tired eyes sparkled and her mouth brimmed a proud smile. The nurse noted the time: 7:15 A.M.

"It's a girl!" Abby said.

"It's a girl!" we all repeated.

Lupe, smiling, lifted her head to see her baby. The infant's eyes were barely open but the baby strained to turn her head, her mouth forming an O, wanting to suck. Abby wrapped the red and brown newborn in a blanket and the nurse suctioned the baby's nose. Then she placed the baby, with the umbilical cord still attached, on top of Lupe's stomach. The healthy baby girl weighed eight pounds, thirteen ounces. Lupe named her Maribel.

Two hours later, I was sitting on the bed next to Lupe, practicing my Spanish. Wearing a turquoise beanie and wrapped tightly in a wool blanket, Maribel was nestled between Lupe's arm and stomach. Lupe was relaxing, having eaten breakfast and breast-fed the baby. Her eyes were half open.

"Do you have pain? Are you bleeding?" I asked in Spanish, reading from an English-Spanish baby delivery book that I wished I'd had hours ago.

Lupe smiled. She liked it when I tried to speak Spanish to her. She answered in long sentences, strange words that flung from her tongue. Then she put her hand on her vagina and tensed her eyebrows.

"*Sangre, mucho sangre.*"

I understood that much.

"She says she's bleeding a lot," I told the volunteer nurse, twenty-seven-year-old Nicole Lassiter, the only one in the room with us. Everyone else had gone for breakfast or to take showers or to check on patients crowding the clinic's waiting room.

Nicole pulled back the covers to reveal a large puddle of blood beneath Lupe. She rushed to the phone and pushed the intercom. "Mary, Abby, stat!" she said.

Nicole checked Lupe's pulse and felt her stomach, which seemed bloated. When Sister Mary and Abby ran into the room, Nicole pointed to the blood. Sister Mary told Nicole to push hard on Lupe's stomach: "Even to the point of hurting her," Mary said.

Nicole pushed hard. Blood gushed between Lupe's legs. Lupe fainted.

"Oh, shit!" someone yelled.

Sister Mary inserted an I.V. into Lupe's arm, while Nicole kept checking Lupe's pulse and blood pressure.

"It's now fifty over twenty!" Nicole said.

Just then Sister Anita Jennissen, a tall, tanned, silver-haired woman with deep-set dark eyes, sauntered into the room beaming a large smile.

"Anita, this is not a good time!" Mary said. "If you want to help, start praying for her."

Anita hurried to the head of the bed. Brushing back the hair on Lupe's forehead, Anita prayed quickly to Our Lady of Guadalupe—Lupe's patron saint. *"Vamos a pedir a Dios por la intercesión de la Virgen de Guadalupe."*

Lupe wasn't responding.

"Let's give her some oxygen!" Sister Anita said.

Mary wheeled over the oxygen tank and handed the mask to Sister Anita. Then Mary took the baby and handed her to me.

The room filled with the eerie sounds of foreign words accentuated with medical terminology.

Lupe came to and began moaning.

Anita held her hand and prayed: *"Dios te salve"*—God save you.

fOLLOWING ST. fRANCIS

Sister Anita had spent nearly her entire adult life praying over young women like Lupe. At nineteen, Anita joined the Franciscan Sisters of Little Falls near her family's farm in Minnesota with a dream of becoming a missionary sister.

She waited ten years for God to answer her prayer. In 1962, Sister Anita was sent to South America and, as a nurse, was assigned to a fifty-bed hospital in the mountains of Peru. Later she was dispatched to Colombia, then into the bush of Africa. She worked as a nurse practitioner, delivering babies, stitching up injuries, and diagnosing diseases—doing the same labor as the few overburdened doctors.

In 1991, Anita was called home. Her father was dying. After the funeral, her mother begged her not to return to Africa. When Anita learned that Sister Angela and Holy Family were looking for a nurse, she applied. Anita was eager to get back in the field and work with the poor and speak their language. A year later, Anita became the clinic's social worker.

One night, Anita took me to the Mexican border town of Nuevo Progreso, a town that sprang up a few years ago as a tourist trap, to give me a broader perspective of life here. We passed through the heavily guarded border gates and drove up the narrow bridge over the Rio Grande and descended the other side into what looked like a modern Wild West. Two-story storefronts, many with fake facades, line the dusty road. We walked past a plethora of pharmacies where overweight Americans buy diet pills, dentists' offices where a cleaning costs ten dollars, hordes of T-shirt and jewelry stores, and warehouses full of ceramic knickknacks. Along the way, beggar women held out their Styrofoam cups, jiggling change. Anita pulled out a plastic grocery bag from her purse and handed chocolate Power Bars to those who asked for money, even to the boys sitting on the sidewalk smoking cigarettes.

That night we shared the sidewalks with other Anglos, many of them so-called Winter Texans who had just arrived that week. They were gray haired, bejeweled folks, who traveled in chartered luxury buses and sat in roped-off sections of restaurants clanking their cocktail glasses while mariachi bands serenaded them. Their opulence seemed so gaudy in light of the poverty I had become immersed in at Holy Family.

Anita, a Franciscan, exemplified the passion—or charism—that her order has for living poverty. St. Francis of Assisi, the order's thirteenth-century founder, valued poverty over all other virtues. Born into wealth, St. Francis renounced his inheritance and even his clothes. Like Francis, the few clothes in Anita's closet came from the donation box in the clinic waiting room. She said God always provided.

Recently, a young, pregnant Mexican woman came to the clinic with her husband. The woman wore a thin, short-sleeved dress, despite fall temperatures in the fifties. When Anita asked if she had any clothes, the woman pointed to her dress. Then Anita asked when she last ate. The woman looked at her husband and bowed her head, embarrassed. It had been three days. Anita gave the woman boxes of food and clothes.

Just minutes after birth, Lupe holding
Maribel on her stomach

"She sat there cold and starving but would never ask for anything," Anita said, dabbing a Kleenex to her eyes. "The pain of the people's suffering gets to me," she continued, slowly trying to stop the tears rolling down her cheeks. "The poor here have so much to teach me. They remind you that you don't have to have all this stuff."

LIMBO LAND

Two days after recovering from her dangerous hemorrhaging, Lupe was driven home, and three days later I set out to check on her and Maribel. Navigating the narrow back roads half a mile from the U.S.-Mexican border, I marveled at the *National Geographic* scene in front of me: a descending afternoon sun casting intense orange light on wild grasses and big-horned cattle grazing next to Lupe's house. I pulled the car into the weeds where the blacktop ended and walked past the neatly painted, soapbox houses next to Lupe's family compound of scrap metal shacks. A fence around the property was crafted from fragments of barbed wire, wood, and aluminum. Beyond the gate, filthy dogs lay around a yard scattered with odd machine parts: an old washing machine and something that looked like a lawn mower.

Angela had warned me that Lupe probably wouldn't allow me inside her house because she was too embarrassed. "She always meets you in the yard," Sister Angela had said.

Instead, Lupe's sister, Rose, met me at the gate and led me through the yard where chickens and roosters marched like proud landowners in the dried dirt. Her brothers and Lupe's children were in the field burying a dog that had died of starvation that morning, she said. Rose showed me around her family's property and explained the function of each tiny scrap metal building. Across from Lupe's house stands a small one-room house where Rose, her two adult brothers, and her parents sleep. "There's just barely enough room," she said. "My brothers sleep on the floor."

Outside the door of Lupe's aluminum house, an old washing machine churned clothes as soap suds bubbled down the vibrating legs. I ducked inside the doorway. Lupe's three children followed. Juan, age five, and Rene, age three, were barefoot and shirtless. Angelica, age two, looked like a boy. She had big brown eyes and short curly hair tangled with straw.

Lupe's side of the house is divided by a partition, with a stove and boxes in the "front room" and two small cots in the "back room." Hard dirt forms the floor. Extension cords and thick cobwebs hang from the ceiling. Lupe, breast-feeding Maribel on one cot, grinned when she saw me and offered me a seat on her bed.

A few fleas jumped from the polyester blanket that neatly covered her bed, and mosquitoes buzzed around the dark room, occasionally lighting on the arms and legs of their next victims. Lupe shooed them away, concerned that the mosquito tracks on my arms had come from her home.

At the head of Lupe's bed was an old television set.

"Does it work?" I asked.

She nodded her head and proudly turned on the machine; it piped in *Oprah* with an amazingly sharp reception. For a few minutes, we sat in the dark house staring at the television with the blue light shining in our faces. Then Lupe turned off the set and opened a wooden window, flooding the room with the rays of the western sunset. In the field, her parents were cooking dinner over an open fire.

Lupe finished breast-feeding and handed me the baby while she went to the outhouse. Maribel's brothers and sister lovingly patted her head as they smiled big, baby-tooth grins beneath mustaches of mud. Occasionally, a chicken ran into the house; the kids, laughing, chased it out.

I watched from the window as Rose swung a butcher knife in the sugar cane field, and not long after, she returned carrying long, thick greenish canes. The kids ran into the house sucking on them like lollipops. Rose handed me hers and instructed me how to rip out the yellow threads with my teeth, suck out the sweet juices, and then either swallow or spit out the remaining pulp. The meat was thick and coarse; the juice reminded me of pineapple.

When Lupe returned, she took out a stack of pictures from a box and showed me her daughters who live in Guatemala. In one photo, they were impeccably dressed in matching red-and-white dresses with their hair braided and tied with ribbons. In another, they were dressed like Hawaiian hula girls wearing grass skirts and flowered necklaces. The house where the girls lived with their godmother resembled nothing of what I saw around me.

Her own house, Lupe said, was eight years old. When it rained, water poured through the slats where sunlight now filtered. One night, a board fell down and hit Juan in the head, giving him a black eye. Lupe shrugged off the problems with her home. "For someone who's poor, this is nice," Lupe said in Spanish and her sister translated. "It just needs to be fixed so water won't come in."

As I was leaving, Rose and Lupe offered me tamales their parents had just made. The kids ate theirs in their hands. At the gate, Lupe hugged me and said, "Thank you," in perfect English.

BARBIE AND ALL HER ACCESSORIES

I began to understand what Sister Angela meant when she said the poor have much to teach us. When I asked her what she learned from Lupe, she immediately responded: "Pure love."

"She has nothing else to give. She is someone who is simple, who recognizes you. And she never begs." Then she stopped for a minute, cleared her throat, and wiped tears from the corners of her eyes. When Sister Angela spoke again, her tough-as-nails exterior softened, and her voice cracked. "She's just someone who gives you love. And worries about you. It's being centered on others. Those are the kinds of lessons the poor teach."

Sister Angela had bragged that a stay at Holy Family changed people's lives. She was right. Back in my comfortable suburban home, I couldn't stop thinking of Lupe and other women like her whom I had met at Holy Family. At night, I wondered how Lupe was sleeping with the monster

Texas mosquitoes swarming around her, how she could shut her eyes when snakes slithered under her bed, inches from her four sleeping children. When storms cracked the sky and rained down pellets of water, I wondered if Lupe and her family were getting wet. A rainstorm in my life was no longer a break from the heat, the pattering droplets no longer a sonnet to sleep. They were reminders of all that I had and all that Lupe didn't.

I began noticing all the excesses in my life, the luxuries my family and I took for granted. When my daughter decided she had outgrown the dozens of Barbie dolls she had collected over the years, I packed them in boxes with a growing sense of guilt. Besides the pile of Barbie dolls, there were Barbie clothes, Barbie accessories, Barbie penthouses and cars. Barbie and her accoutrements were glaring reminders of the waste in my own life: the closets full of clothes I never wear, the china we eat on twice a year, the crystal goblets that sit like priceless artifacts in the buffet cabinet, the expensive dinners out that could pay for Lupe's monthly rent. My experience with Lupe and the sisters initiated a running argument in my head that hasn't stopped yet: How much is too much? How much is too much house, too much car? When have you crossed the line between what is need and what is greed?

Although the sisters have spent their lives surrounded by poverty, its sting hasn't lessened. They aren't cynical or hardened, but, in fact, continue to be touched daily by the flood of cases they see. Unlike their clients, though, the sisters at Holy Family have chosen their poverty, not out of a desire to "redeem" the unsaved through their sacrifices, but in solidarity with those they serve. For them, each dollar they eschew means one more dollar for the needy. While I don't think their clients know whether or not the sisters and their nurse-midwives sleep with air conditioners—most probably assume they do—the point is that running dozens more units would inflate the sisters' electric bills. It also makes the sisters and their volunteers experience in their skins the kind of deprivation that the poor live with daily. For these Franciscan sisters, their sweat is just one more humble reminder that, in God's eyes, they are no different than the beggars.

9

TEACHING ON THE REZ

FRANCISCAN SISTERS OF CHRISTIAN CHARITY ON ARIZONA
INDIAN RESERVATIONS

*"Working with the poor has grounded me in the Gospel and helped
me to value people more than things. There's more to life than stuff. It's
our relationship to God and to each other."*

—SISTER MARTHA CARPENTER

I t was nearly high noon, and the Arizona sun reflected off shiny
buildings and colorless cars, leaving no shadows, allowing no re-
prieve. On an empty road in the desert, where Indian tribes have
lived for thousands of years, a giant white mosque materialized like an ap-
parition, its image shimmering in the hot haze. Up close, the mosque
transformed into a Spanish mission with gleaming white bell towers and
seashell-shaped domes.

Called the "White Dove of the Desert," the San Xavier Mission
Church has become a tourist magnet in an otherwise forgotten and deserted landscape known as the Tohono O'odham Nation Reservation.
Outside the church, visitors snap pictures and stand in line for "authentic"
Indian burritos made over open fire pits. Adding to this exotic ambiance
are the brown-robed Franciscan priests who run the church and the
veiled nuns who direct the elementary school next door.

At San Xavier Mission School, a long, narrow adobe building, most students are from the Tohono O'odham tribe (pronounced toh-HO-no o-O-dahm), formerly known as the Papagos, whose vast 2.7-million-acre reservation—about the size of Connecticut—lies at the western edge of the mission. *Tohono O'odham* means "desert people," a name the natives chose over *Papagos,* which means "bean eaters" and was bestowed upon them by Spanish explorers in the 1500s. In the late seventeenth century, a black-robed Jesuit priest named Father Kino Christianized the Indians and taught them how to grow wheat and fruit trees.

Nuns and monks started mission schools on Arizona's reservations in the late 1800s. Though Catholic schools were once part of a shadowy movement to strip Indians of their culture and language, some tribal leaders now look to religious schools as purveyors of Native American culture and spirituality. With less than 1 percent of Indian children in some villages able to read and write native languages, Catholic schools are preserving a dying culture as well as teaching morality and self-discipline in a society afflicted with alcoholism and diabetes.

To the 150 students at San Xavier Mission School, the fact that nuns teach half the kindergarten through eighth grade classes seems unremarkable. Yet, a Catholic school run by habited nuns is rare; while the image of a teaching nun wielding a ruler persists in the American mentality, less than 5 percent of Catholic school teachers today are nuns. In fact, most Catholic school students don't encounter a single nun teacher from first through twelfth grades. With the average age of nuns rising into the seventies and the nun population as a whole shrinking, nun teachers may soon become another piece of history.

Among the nun teachers left, many prefer to serve minority students, which make up 25 percent of the Catholic school population. These nuns feel that Catholic schools for the middle class and the wealthy can afford qualified teachers; they'd rather work with indigent students whose schools have difficulty attracting and retaining highly educated instructors. Often nuns forgo salaries or accept reduced pay because they believe poverty is not just a vow or a way of life; it's their ministry.

OUT Of POVERTY TO PROfESS POVERTY

Like a scene out of a Clint Eastwood western, I opened the front door to the school and desert sand blew in behind me. Temperatures had soared to 110 degrees, a record for Arizona in mid-September. The school is small, with most classrooms combining two grades. I found Principal Sister Jackie Koenig hunched over her cluttered desk in the front office.

Like many of the Franciscan Sisters of Christian Charity who run reservation schools, Sister Jackie comes from a poor German-Dutch farm family in rural Wisconsin. With ten siblings, Jackie had never slept alone in her own bed until the night she arrived at the Franciscan mother house in 1963. Unlike many of her fellow sisters, who entered at fourteen, Jackie was eighteen. She graduated from a one-room public school and decided to become a nun after watching a visiting Franciscan sister hit a baseball over the fence and into a cornfield.

"We never did find that ball," Jackie remembered nostalgically, clearly enamored with the nun's seemingly mystical powers. "That's still with me."

Based in Manitowoc, Wisconsin, the Franciscan Sisters of Christian Charity is mostly composed of teachers who run Catholic schools in the northern Midwest and the Southwest. They arrived in Arizona in 1935 wearing heavy wool serge habits but adapted to cotton and white veils. The order remains one of the few apostolic or active orders that retains some form of the habit; they believe it is a statement of their simple lives.

Jackie wears her order's modified version: a white blouse with a black skirt and a white cotton veil held on her head by a black headband. Instead of the traditional black lace-up shoes with sensible heels that most sisters wear, Jackie sports white sneakers, necessary for the 5 A.M. walks she takes for exercise.

Having been raised in large farm families in Wisconsin, many sisters knew poverty firsthand before they ever took a vow of poverty. In many ways, the sisters' meager childhoods, enriched only by their faith and their families, mirror the lives of their impoverished students.

"Because of a lot of the destitute situations, their faith is the only thing that gives them any reason to want to live," Jackie said of the Tohono O'odham. Earlier she'd made a similar observation about her own family. "They just depend on God to provide. They have to go out and sell their food or do things like that to provide for their family. But it's such a family thing, everybody does their part."

Many houses on the reservation still have dirt floors; some lack indoor plumbing and few have more than a bedroom or two. So they scatter mattresses on the floor at night and pile them in the corner during the day. Most live below the poverty level and depend on government food supplements. Seventy percent of San Xavier students qualify for the federal food program. Nearly half the students eat breakfast and lunch at the school. For some, those are the only sure meals they have each day.

Because of the high fat content in the modern Indian diet, diabetes is at epidemic levels, especially among children. About 2,150 of the 18,000 O'odham have been diagnosed with the disease. For the past decade, the Tohono O'odham have had higher diabetes death rates than any other tribe in the world.

The importance of family is one reason so few Indian women ever become sisters. While joining a religious order would provide security to a young woman and honor to her family, it also would mean leaving her family and culture for several years of formation at the mother house in Wisconsin. Because the sisters are missioned to dozens of schools and hospitals all over the country, a sister might not be assigned to the Southwest for many years. Still, the sisters try to overcome this obstacle by inviting girls to their convent next door and encouraging them to consider religious life.

"They hear our prayer schedule and they go: 'Ugh! I could never do that!' " Jackie said.

The schedule is exhausting. Most rise at 4 A.M. for an hour of private prayer. At 5:50 A.M., they gather in their chapel for communal prayers and mass. They arrive at school by 7 A.M., where they pray again with their staff and a few lay teachers. Though school lets out around 2:50 P.M., the sisters stay after, grading papers and preparing lessons for the next day. They return to their convent at 5 P.M., where they again pray, eat dinner, and resume grading papers until late evening. Most nights, after reading the newspaper, Jackie returns to her school office, where she stays until long after the others have gone to bed.

"This is pretty much our life," Jackie said, looking around her crowded office. "We have to go home and cook, but we don't have children like a lot of teachers have—children and family and a husband to take care of—that whole angle. So we are blessed with having more time to prepare."

PEACE AMID POVERTY

That evening I met the other San Xavier Mission sisters as we gathered around the dining room table for a simple meal of Crockpot roast and potatoes. Eldest is sixty-four-year-old Sister Patrice Walsh, the house superior, who stands just barely over five feet tall. Sister Patrice has a manner about her reminiscent of a little girl. With diminutive features, including a pug nose and short arms and legs, she speaks in an eager voice with a slight lisp. Despite her white hair and oversized glasses, Patrice hasn't lost her childlike enthusiasm and interests, such as her preference for reading children's books. Sister Patrice no longer teaches at the school but runs the catechism program for public school kids. Next to her sat Myra Sweigart, the youngest sister at forty-three, who had just arrived three weeks earlier. Beside her sat Sister Karen Suhr, an energetic, bright woman who, at fifty-seven, still manages to teach first grade with a zeal usually accorded to much younger teachers.

After dinner, Myra and Karen took me up to the top of the mission church roof to watch the sun set behind the mountains. It was easy to see how the San Xavier Mission, with its blend of Moorish, Byzantine, and late Mexican Renaissance styles, has become southern Arizona's most famous architectural landmark. By the time we arrived, the church was locked and the tourists were gone. Karen unlocked a back door and we meandered through dark hallways until suddenly we were standing in the middle of a shadowy nave lighted by hundreds of candles left by visitors. The three-foot walls normally keep the church cool, but at night they retain the heat. Sweat poured down my face. The walls, dating to 1783, are painted with brilliant scenes. Angel statues with golden wings attached at the nave's arches appear to be flying in midair. Dozens of niches hold saint statues. There also are carvings and other figures. Such artistry was designed to serve as a religious classroom for people who could not read.

In a side chapel, the Madonna is portrayed as Our Mother of Sorrows wearing a blue silk dress, white lace veil, and a gold crown. With golden hair and clasping a long white strand of rosary beads, she seems more like a European aristocrat than a poor Jewish peasant. The opposite chapel houses a reclining Saint Xavier statue believed to have healing powers. Visitors often line up to pin *milagros*—little metal charms depicting body parts that need a cure—on the blanket that covers the saint in his clear coffin.

Myra tugged at my sleeve. She and Karen were eager to climb the long twisting attic stairs to the roof before the sun descended. With her flashlight, Sister Karen led the way as Myra and I tried to follow through the narrow staircase, a claustrophobic space with uneven steps and a low ceiling. We crossed an unfinished choir loft, entered through an unmarked door, and climbed yet another set of stairs. The climb was rough in the choking heat, but when we arrived at the roof we could see for miles across the valley, a landscape dominated by prickly pear cactus, paloverde trees, creosote bushes, and buckhorn cholla. The Santa Catalina, Rincon, and Santa Rita Mountains lurked in the near distance.

An orange glow bathed everything in sight.

"Oh, why don't I come up here more often?" Karen said with a long sigh.

Myra closed her eyes and enjoyed the sun's last rays. "This is my favorite spot," she said. "I'm promising myself that I'm not going to work every night this year. I'm going to get out and do some things, see what's around here."

Karen agreed. "Oh, I wish I could make myself do that. But there's so much work. I just don't want to work all the time."

The next morning, Karen put me to work in her first grade classroom. The sisters didn't seem to understand my role as observer. To them, I was a healthy body, someone who could grade papers, read to and instruct students, create skits, and tell stories. Though at first I was reluctant to become a teacher's aide, the tasks gave me a close-up look at how modern nuns teach.

I had asked virtually every sister I'd ever met whether she had experienced the legendary nun who whacked students on the knuckles with a ruler, but no one ever admitted to having encountered such a teacher. And Karen's answer was no different. The most common explanation was that all teachers before the 1960s, whether nuns or not, "ruled" their classrooms with a ruler. I had come to believe that the women who became sisters must have done so because they had pleasant teachers. Most sisters—and especially Karen—describe their own nun teachers in quixotic terms, admitting they wanted to be just like them. I doubted that those who had experienced severe nuns would have aspired to spend their lives replicating that image.

Many believe the stereotype developed because sisters for decades were overworked and overwhelmed with large classes. Before Vatican II, most nuns were assigned to be teachers regardless whether they felt at ease in the classroom. Many also were not well prepared. Until the nun educational reforms of the 1950s, which demanded that nuns receive the same training, education, and certification as their lay counterparts, sisters seldom had a college degree when they entered the classroom.

Karen's own Catholic school education sounded enchanting. Although she is fifty-seven years old, Karen still remembers the name of every teacher she ever had, and she aspires to be just like them, she said. Her challenges today, though, are certainly different. Despite hearing dire stories over her three decades of teaching, each new tale from her students seems to horrify her anew.

During prayers that morning, one student asked that her mother return home. Another prayed for a baby sister who died. One girl prayed that her father would stop drinking. A boy asked blessings for an uncle who had died; another student asked that a classmate be nicer. One boy requested that his new baby sister stop crying so that he could sleep.

"Heidi prays every day that her real mother will come back," Karen told me during a break. "And somebody else will say: 'Well, at least you've seen your real mother. I don't even know what my mother looks like.' Or someone else will say: 'Somebody hit somebody in our house last night.' And we'll pray for that. It's those awful heart-wrenching things, and you can't help but want to put in extra time for them."

Thin, with short gray-white hair, blue eyes, and silver glasses, Karen uses animated voices to capture the attention of her fidgety students. Sometimes she brings out a Jesus puppet or a tambourine to sing lessons. Karen mixes religion into all class subjects. Doing homework and paying attention are marks of a good student but also of a good Christian.

"Don't you want to grow up and be better disciples for Jesus?" Karen asked her wide-eyed, eager-to-please students. "What if Jesus was coming in the bathroom after you? You wouldn't want to leave toilet paper on the floor."

At lunch, I sat with the students in the cafeteria, which also doubled as the kindergarten room. We ate Indian beef tacos. Several fourth grade boys took swigs from milk cartons, pretending they were beer cans. "When I grow up," one boy announced after a particularly big gulp that left him with an impressive milk mustache, "I'm going to drink beer." The other boys agreed as they took swigs, then swayed in their seats, their eyes bulging and their tongues hanging out. Later Karen told me that one has an abusive, alcoholic father.

At day's end, Karen placed a banner on the threshold of her classroom. Depending on which picture the students stepped on, they received a high-five, a hug, or a handshake from Karen. They almost always chose a hug.

"You just try to give them a really happy day with some solid learning," Karen said. "They live in undisciplined little worlds at home so naturally they're going to jump out of their seats and not wait for their turn to talk. If they had real structured environments to live in, they might have all their things together. But they're sitting in their greasy little corner at home, trying to do their work, or they're trying to sleep and the TV's blasting, people are over there drinking."

While alcoholism plays a major role in domestic problems on the reservation, drinking seemed to be a quick scapegoat for every problem, including poor academics or lack of discipline. As a mother, I know that kids are easily distracted and not always responsible about completing or turning in homework, regardless of whether their parents are teetotalers or not. The sisters' biggest disappointment, I thought, derives from their assumption that students want to be as self-disciplined as they are. Yet, the kind of ordered environment the sisters strive to provide at school—and hope that families will adopt at home—is exactly what they have taken to the extreme in their own lives.

Often Karen doesn't even have time to entertain visiting relatives. Although she's lived at several Arizona missions, she has seen few area attractions. After several nights watching Karen grade papers—and helping her—I asked why she feels compelled to work night after night.

"It's hard to say: 'Well, tonight I'm not doing any papers, I'm not doing any planning. I'm just going to go to school and wing it.' I'm trying to ask myself this year if I'm working too hard. I only have sixteen kids. I've never taught just sixteen kids before. I've been here two years so I should have most of the material made. So I'm wondering why these days are getting to be this long.

"In the older days, we used to take forty-five minutes to an hour of recreation every night," she said. "We'd come up from the dinner table, and we'd either go outside and play tennis or sometimes we'd sit around and play cards. I think it's because I've been in this pattern, and a lot of people in our community are in this pattern, of—all we do is this schoolwork. I've never been in a place where we didn't work this long and this hard."

When a priest asked her to play tennis, she told him she didn't have an extra hour in her schedule. When friends call on weekends and ask her to join them hiking, she almost always declines because she feels she needs to prepare for upcoming classes. On the occasions she does go, she feels so guilty that she promises herself she won't do it again. She even feels guilty talking on the phone to sister friends because that is time she could spend grading papers.

"I'm trying to cut back on my work," she said earnestly. "It's like Myra; she's really trying to not let school be all-consuming because then you really have no other life. And when I look at those other [lay] teachers—oh, they're not doing that! They don't have four hours every night to work on preparation!"

Yet, fifteen-hour workdays appear to be the only aspect that sets the nuns apart from teachers who haven't taken vows of obedience, celibacy, and poverty. The long hours define them. It justifies their lifelong sacrifices. It provides them with the strength to watch counterparts rush home to families and husbands and grandchildren. They know lay teachers can't compete. Nuns often describe religious life as a balance of work and prayer. But these sisters work so intensely, they tip the scales. I began to question whether the sisters subconsciously interpret their poverty vow as a deprivation of life experiences, a lack of time spent on themselves, that working for the poor means denying themselves the only thing they possess: their time.

A CATHOLIC IDENTITY

One day I tagged along with Sister Myra Sweigart, who teaches a combined class of seventh and eighth graders. Myra was raised in Ohio, the seventh of ten children. At sixteen, she entered the convent in Wisconsin. Catholic institutions have schooled her from first grade through graduate school.

"As a child, I remember thinking only nuns could teach," she said while her students were in gym class. "The lay teachers were not good teachers. We never had the respect for them that we had for the sisters. The sisters always had more control of us. We had a lot of younger lay men teachers, and they screamed a lot. I remember one throwing a book across the room. But the sisters were firm, and you knew they meant business and you knew your mom and dad would back them up no matter what. So you did what they said."

Myra's strong, authoritative voice rules her classroom, discouraging laziness and curtailing the guffawing so common among junior high students. Often she demands her students speak up. Typically her young teenage students speak softly, heads bowed, hair covering shy faces, voices muffled. In their Indian culture, drawing attention is viewed as bad manners.

With her short black hair starting to gray and ivory skin decorated with brown freckles, Myra stands out as the youngest sister at San Xavier. "I'm forty-three. But don't tell my students!" she said, laughing. "That's the big secret this year for some reason. They are always guessing. It's gone anywhere between twenty-five and sixty."

Myra made her permanent vows at twenty-eight. Today the average age of the 456 Franciscans of Christian Charity is seventy-one. About 40 percent of her sisters are retired or in assisted living, she said.

Now Myra sees Catholic education from a different vantage point. "There's definitely a difference in the way kids greet you and talk to you," she said. "Like when I go outside—all the little kids run by and say, 'Hi, Sister! Hi, Sister!' But if they run by Ms. Christianson or Ms. Rodriguez, it's like they don't even know they're teachers." There are other distinctions. Usually sisters have master's degrees and lay teachers generally have bachelor's degrees.

But the Catholic identity that nun teachers bring to Catholic schools is now almost extinct. Myra is particularly concerned about the trend in hiring public school employees to run Catholic schools. While the teachers and administrators are Catholic, they haven't grown up in Catholic schools, haven't worked in Catholic schools, and don't know how to reinforce a Catholic identity in students, she said. She fears that eventually Catholic schools will become no different from other private schools.

So what makes a Catholic school have a Catholic identity? I asked.

"Prayer life in the school is essential," she said. "The kids pray on a daily basis—as a school sometimes and in the classroom other times. Students participate in the sacramental life of the Church, meaning the Eucharist. They have the opportunity for reconciliation [confession]. Honest, I've seen people forget about those things. Even simple things like having a cross up in the room or having bulletin boards that have a message about the Lord in it. You know, I've been on accreditation teams, and I've walked into schools that are supposed to be Catholic and gone: 'Uh-uh, not this one.' You know there's that flavor of Catholicism. It's a subtle thing. But you know it when it's not there. It's like what do you see when you walk in the front door? A cross or a patron saint or do you see sports trophies?"

At San Xavier, crosses adorn the walls, alongside the letters of the To-hono O'odham language. There are also religious statues in all the classrooms. The Mary statues are older versions that portray her as a light-skinned woman with blond hair.

As a student, Myra viewed nun teachers as trustworthy women who

Left: Sister Karen Suhr
Right: Sister Martha Carpenter wearing her Packer's cheese wedge

would lead their students to God. "I always felt the nuns cared for us, and I hope I give that message to the kids."

Myra, however, doesn't believe devoting endless hours to schoolwork necessarily makes her a better Catholic teacher. She is determined to carve out more personal time but finds herself falling into a familiar pattern of working more than praying.

PUNISHMENT AT THE HANDS OF NUNS

A few miles from San Xavier looms the 2.7 million acre Tohono O'odham reservation, otherwise known as the "Big Reservation," the second largest in the country. A two-lane highway traverses the vast desert land, lined on both sides with little altars or grottos adorned with white crosses and plastic flowers erected to remember those killed in car accidents, mostly caused by drunk drivers.

Alone on the highway that sunny morning, I was mesmerized by the hills covered with tall saguaro cacti. The O'odham believe these cacti are their ancestors because buried relatives nurtured the soil. Indian children are taught to treat the tall, prickly plants with reverence, never to throw rocks or puncture their pleated skins. Growing only half an inch a year, the large saguaro are more than two hundred years old. The cacti, some over fifty feet tall and weighing up to several tons, look like mythical people, their crooked branches resembling outstretched arms, hats, and legs. Suddenly I saw more than just cacti amid the endless vista of mountainous hills but colonies of spectators staring at the stranger passing through.

At the public high school run by the Bureau of Indian Affairs, I met Regina Siquieros. Regina, who has a mystical air about her, likes to say she was born forty-eight years ago under large trees and fell from her mother's womb into her grandmother's hands. Through storytelling and language, Regina tries to keep alive the Tohono O'odham culture.

Regina described a Catholic education far different from what I'd heard from the Franciscan nuns. Like most Tohono O'odham of her generation, in the 1960s she attended St. John's Indian School on the Pima Reservation, about a two-hour drive away. The large school educated Indian children from thirteen tribes all over the state. Because their homes were hours away and few families had dependable transportation, the students lived at the school for months, returning only during summers and holidays.

"It wasn't a very positive experience for me," Regina said. "I didn't speak English when I went into the school and they pushed us so hard to learn English. I rebelled very strongly. In those days there was a lot of physical abuse done to us. The nuns spanked us, pulled our hair, slapped rulers against our fingers and legs. We were punished quite a bit."

Even outside the classroom, students weren't allowed to speak tribal languages. If caught, they were disciplined, even paddled. Nuns feared that if they allowed students to speak their native languages it might reignite tribal feuds. But Regina believes the nuns were just paranoid.

"They thought we were talking about them," she said, laughing. "They thought we were going to do something to them."

Back then, Regina felt alienated and flouted the rules, often speaking her language in defiance. As punishment, she was forced to clean classrooms. The goal of old Catholic school teaching was to mainstream natives into the dominant Anglo way of life, she said.

"It was kind of like taking away our culture and our religion."

When I asked what the tenets of the Tohono O'odham religion are, Regina said her people don't have an organized religion but a spirituality expressed through songs, stories, and ceremonies.

"You're going to hear the same thing as the Bible in every Native American creation story," she said. "There's a lot of similarity. We have a Creator; we have a Maker who wants us to live in harmony with everything about us. We are here for a purpose. All our values are right in line with the commandments—just living right. And being happy and being in balance. Our spirituality is just a part of us. We live it."

Yet, today few Tohono O'odham people have heard the tribal language spoken, even near the "city" of Sells, the Tohono O'odham Nation's headquarters and largest city, with a population of four thousand.

The tribe is also fragmented spiritually. Though there are more than forty-five Catholic mission churches on the reservation, few students regularly attend, Regina said. And while about 85 percent of the Tohono O'odham identify themselves as Catholic, more and more have converted to become Baptists, Pentecostals, or Mormons.

Despite her negative experiences with nuns earlier in her life, Regina remains a devout Catholic and often works with the nuns on the reservation. She said today there is a greater respect for native culture and a deeper understanding of their spirituality among the sisters. She especially appreciates how nuns interweave Tohono O'odham traditions and Christianity at the mission schools. Regina wonders whether there would be less alcoholism, gangs, and dysfunctional families if the larger Catholic schools had survived. Her alma mater, St. John's Indian School, closed in 1994.

"No matter how much I rebelled against the Catholic school at the time, I realize it taught me a lot. It helped me go on to college, the university," she said. "There's a breakdown of the family and a lack of family spirituality. And you wonder what is happening to us."

AN ATHLETIC MISSION

North of the Tohono O'odham reservation is the Gila (pronounced HEE-la) River Reservation and St. Peter's Indian Mission School, also run by Franciscan Sisters of Christian Charity. Gila River is the home of the Pima Indians, cousins to the Tohono O'odham. The two tribes share the same basic language and similar customs and symbols.

Compared with the sprawling Tohono O'odham land, the Gila River Reservation, south of Phoenix, is small—just 374,000 acres. Dirt roads with a scattering of adobe houses lead from the highway to the mission school. Plumes of sand and dirt whip up without warning. Despite the Estrella Mountains in the distance, the Gila land seems flatter and contains fewer trees than the hilly terrain of the "Big Reservation."

The mission school looks like a vibrant village. At its heart is a church and a modern ranch home—the sisters' "new convent"—donated by a builder after the sisters outgrew their old adobe. In the center of the school cluster is a courtyard converted into a basketball court. Outside the complex are a volleyball court, football and soccer fields, and a running track with grandstands. Students seem thinner than their counterparts at San Xavier who don't have the fancy athletic fields. To counteract rampant diabetes, the school pushes athletics. Despite hundred-plus–degree temperatures the afternoon I arrived, boys were practicing football and girls were playing volleyball.

That night at the convent, while one sister cooked dinner, another set the table. Sister Juana, an Indian woman, was resting in an enclosed back porch flanked by the sisters' two black Great Danes, named Shotgun and Danger. A short Hawaiian sister and one who had recently arrived from Wisconsin were watching the news on television when Sister Martha Carpenter, the school principal, burst into the house, recounted a story she'd heard earlier in the day, then rushed back outside to lock the fence that wrapped around the mission, which had been vandalized several times by area gangs. When the sisters heard Martha talking in the carport, they decided to start dinner without her.

"It's so rude for her to engage in a conversation when everyone is waiting on her," one sister complained.

We'd just said the dinner prayer when Martha walked into the house bubbling over with more stories and details from her day. She'd started to pile her plate with mashed potatoes and green beans when the phone rang. She'd barely ended that conversation when the phone rang again. And again. Tension mounted. Later I would learn that this was typical Martha: too many demands on her to-do list to pay attention to them all.

That night, two sisters escorted me to the old adobe convent where I would be staying alone. They warned me about scorpions, more prevalent on the Pima reservation than the Tohono O'odham. A few years ago, a scorpion bit Martha's middle finger, which provoked numerous jokes from students. Normally the sisters don't even like to walk at night or in the early morning for fear of stepping on scorpions or snakes; they even drive a donated golf cart the several hundred feet between their home and the school.

Just three weeks earlier, Martha was in her bedroom praying, when at about 4:30 A.M. a sister knocked on her door in a panic. The sister, who had been praying her morning office in the house chapel, had spotted a diamondback rattlesnake, the size of a nine-inch pie plate, curled up underneath a chair across from her.

Martha ran to the garage, grabbed a shovel, and began scooping up the snake. As the rattlesnake lifted its head, Martha recited the rosary: "Hail Mary, full of grace; the Lord is with you; blessed are you among women," she chanted as she carried the snake into the yard and tossed it over the fence.

Later, she learned rattlesnakes can strike a target twice the distance of their length. At the end of a three-foot shovel, Martha was well within the snake's reach. Martha chalked up not getting bitten to God and the Indian spirits protecting her.

The next morning, the sisters and the students gathered for mass in the mission chapel. The ceiling of the Spanish-style adobe church is painted with the Indian symbol of the Man in the Maze; the simple human figure represents humankind and the circular maze represents life. Pima students acted the homily that day: the story of how Jesus turned one boy's lunch of bread and fish into loaves and fishes to feed a multitude.

As the teachers and nuns corralled students back to class, a sister suggested I talk to Juana Lucero, the Indian sister, who was home recuperating. Normally she would be teaching Indian culture and language, but the doctor had ordered Juana, who is diabetic, off her feet for several weeks to drain fluid from her legs.

When Juana came to the door, she looked as if she had just woken up; her face was swollen and her veil askew. She was the first Indian sister I'd met. I was eager to speak with her because I wanted her to explain how she integrates Indian spirituality with Catholicism. Seventy years old, Juana is short and squat, with a large square face, tired-looking eyes, and dark, leathery skin. She struck me as feisty, defensive, and somewhat withdrawn. Still, she has a strong Indian spirituality, a mystical sieve through which she interprets life's events.

The daughter of a Pima mother and a Santo Domingo father, Juana grew up on the Gila River Reservation at Santan, about seven miles south of St. Peter's Mission. Her mother converted from the dominant Protestant religion to Catholicism. Unlike the Tohono O'odham, Presbyterian missionaries had Christianized most Pimas. Juana didn't attend a Catholic school but had grown up hearing her parents and parish priest predict she would become a nun. One day Juana had a vision that convinced her they were right.

"I looked up and saw a little boy come out of the lightbulb; it looked like the boy Jesus," Juana recalled. "He had on a little turban and a white robe, and he was up there smiling at me. Then behind him were two people. I kept looking and I got so scared and I started moaning. My mother and sister were in the kitchen getting supper, and they came running and asked me what happened. I said, 'There's somebody up there.' My older sister got up to the lightbulb and said there was nothing there but fly specks. Then the picture faded. And they took me and put me in bed. I couldn't sleep. I felt like I was going to die. And I lay there, and that's when my vocation came on strong."

At the time, Juana was in the eighth grade and was old enough to enter the convent. But she decided to wait because she'd overheard her parents say they really wanted one of their children to graduate high school.

The week after her high school graduation, Juana was sent to the Franciscan mother house in Wisconsin. Juana had no desire to become a Franciscan; she found the sisters at St. Peter's too demanding. Besides, she wasn't interested in teaching. But Juana didn't know enough about religious orders to know she was in the wrong place.

"I wanted to go to some other community," she said. "But in those days, I thought there was only one mother house, and then you came out and joined whatever order you wanted."

When she arrived at the mother house, Juana was the lone Indian in a room crowded with young, white postulants.

"I turned around from the door we came in and there was a big picture of the little boy Jesus, the exact picture I had seen on that lightbulb. When I saw it, I felt right at home."

Juana was sent to college, then out to teach. She's been teaching ever since—more than forty years educating children kindergarten through the eighth grade. For a few years she taught in Catholic schools in Iowa and Wisconsin but has spent most of her life at the sisters' Arizona missions.

While Juana knows little about the Pima religion, she does respect her ancestors and believes they intervene with the living. It is just as conceivable to Juana that she would be visited by God in dreams as by Indian spirits.

The most profound of such spirit visitations occurred several years ago when she and her fifth grade students visited an Indian burial ground for bones inadvertently dug up during freeway construction. As Juana prayed, she felt overtaken by a spirit.

"I started speaking in Indian," she said. "And all of a sudden, I felt myself out of the prayer. I mean I'm here, my mouth was talking, but some other spirit had come in and was saying all these words. It was beautiful. Some of the words I didn't understand because they were old Pima words. And it just went on and on."

Then it stopped abruptly. Everyone slowly looked around to see if any others had had the same bizarre experience.

"I knew something, someone, some spirit had taken over me," Juana said. "I always think about that experience and how the spirits are alive. And I keep telling the children about that."

When other bones were discovered, Pima elders asked the sisters if the school cafeteria could be used to prepare them for burial. Indian legend claims that bones possess spirits, sometimes friendly and sometimes mean. Disturbed bones could mean angry spirits. Although other schools had turned down the request for fear of attracting angry spirits, the sisters agreed. For six weeks that summer the elders gathered at sunset and prayed for hours over the bones while wrapping them. At night, the men left glasses of iced tea and fruit for the spirits.

That's when strange things began to occur. At one-thirty each morning, the outside security lights would flick on for no apparent reason. After a few weeks of such incidents, the village medicine man told the sisters that spirits were tripping on the lights during early morning strolls. The spirits, he said, like the early morning hours because it is quiet. The medicine man also said the spirits had told him that they were curious about "the women who wore rags on their heads."

"They said we were doing good for the people and the children and that we would be blessed," Juana recounted. "And from that time on, we were blessed."

Juana even attributed the school's recent turnaround—in part due to donations from wealthy benefactors—to the spirits' blessings, which she called miracles. The first miracle, she said, occurred when Bill Bidwill, owner of the Cardinals professional football team, replaced the school and convent roofs. The second miracle, she said, was when a monsignor died and willed the mission money, which was used to replace the school's old kerosene heaters with heating and air-conditioning units. The third miracle happened when the Williams Air Force Base near Phoenix was closing and volunteered to build a new wing for the school. Subsequent miracles involved ex–baseball player and former *Today Show* host Joe Garagiola, who persuaded companies and friends to donate money and time to build a basketball court, outdoor track, and irrigated grass football field. Then came vans, buses, library books, and the new house for the sisters. On and on the list went. Countless deeds by volunteers, companies, professional sports teams.

"It's been going on ever since that blessing," said Juana in a quiet, eerie voice. "We never ask for anything. It just comes."

THE CHEESE HEAD NUN

Getting a few minutes alone with Sister Martha was nearly impossible. A tall, big-boned woman with tanned skin, gray hair, and a teenager's energetic voice, Martha stands out among the more reserved nun teachers. She gives so much of herself that there is little time left. She goes to bed around 8:30 P.M.—shortly after dinner and evening prayers—and rises at 2 A.M. She spends the early morning hours praying and jotting to-do lists. Martha teaches seventh grade and runs the school, but often complies with the local broadcast media for various video clips, including a promo she did that week for Catholic Charities and a sports prediction she filmed for the Fox affiliate on the upcoming Packers-Cardinals game. Martha predicted the Cardinals would win, 24 to 10. (They lost 29 to 3.)

Martha's office is covered with Green Bay Packers and Phoenix Cardinals pennants, decals, and signed photographs of football players like Chris Jones and Bart Starr. *Football is not a matter of life and death: It's much more important,* reads a bumper sticker tacked to her wall. Nearby hangs a large photo of Martha and other nuns wearing cheese wedges and cheering at a Packers game.

"I'm a born cheese head, but a born-again Cardinals fan," Martha said proudly as she placed her Packers cheese wedge hat over her veil, leaving her black veil sticking out like a stylish ponytail.

Martha, whose conversations are peppered with arcane sports dates and history, grew up in Green Bay, Wisconsin, within walking distance of Lambeau Field. Her mother's three brothers played for the Packers, an NFL record, Martha noted proudly. While her father attended virtually every home game with her uncles, Martha went to the Packers practices in the summer.

"I just thanked God over and over," she said, remembering her childhood prayers. "I had such a wonderful family and Vince Lombardi was the coach of the Packers and they were winning all the time and the Braves were doing well."

In Martha's household, there was always some game, some competition to root for whether it was football, basketball, bowling, car racing, or the horses. "We did a lot of betting in my family," Martha said. "And you had to know what you were talking about to be a part of it."

Taught by Franciscans in seventh and eighth grade, Martha entered the convent's high school aspirancy program at thirteen. Her principal had told Martha that she was destined to become a nun. Such stories underscore the extent to which nun teachers have been recruiting machines for the Catholic Church. It is incalculable how many nun teachers have prompted students to choose religious life. With so few nuns in Catholic classrooms today, it is apparent that women's religious orders have lost much more than devoted teachers. They've lost their ability to replicate themselves from generation to generation.

After graduating from the sisters' college in 1971, Martha received her first mission—St. Peter's Indian School, where she is now principal. At the time, Martha didn't even know her community had Indian missions. Since then, Martha has spent her entire teaching career on Indian missions in Wisconsin and Arizona.

Indian people and their closeness to God and one another have inspired her. "I see Jesus here," she said. "Working with the poor has grounded me in the Gospel and helped me to value people more than things. There's more to life than stuff. It's our relationship to God and to each other. Those are the things that count. We struggle with people; we struggle to keep the school going and keep families together, putting families back together."

Because she loves to talk sports, Martha has become the darling of Arizona's professional sports community, regarded much the same way that art lovers adore Sister Wendy. Martha uses sports trivia to warm up crowds when she talks about the mission school.

Appearing at Cardinals games alongside owner Bill Bidwill and leading prayers for a few team events, Martha drew the attention of a Fox network producer, who asked Martha to pick the weekend's winners on air. Martha picked twelve. The producer excitedly called Martha the following Monday and told her that her accuracy rate was twice as high as their regular sports predictor.

"I don't want to sound arrogant," she told him, "but some weeks I get all of them right." As her success at predicting games became well known, fans began calling the station asking for "Sister Martha's reaction." The station offered Martha a contract for a Monday morning quarterback show, but she declined. Her reasoning could have been a bumper sticker for the mission sisters: "I'm a busy sister, and my kids come first."

WORKAHOLIC NUNS

The main difference today between modern teaching nuns and those who taught most baby boomers is their connection with students.

"You just didn't get involved then," explained Sister Carol Mathe, who began teaching in 1959. "You were in your classroom costume and after that you went to your little convent and barred the doors. Whereas today, we are free to go out and mingle with the people and be a part of their families, if we need to be."

Now, sisters are beginning to question whether they are too involved in their students' lives. The needs on the reservation are so overwhelming that the sisters often find it difficult to extricate themselves for down time.

"The sisters have become workaholics," said Carol, a stout sixty-three-year-old with chestnut hair and tortoise-shell glasses. "They have become so involved in their work that they never really learned to just plain relax and get some time for themselves. This is our life," she said sweeping her arms around her fifth grade classroom. "It's a real commitment to the poor. And not everybody can do it. It's not easy out here."

After staying with the Franciscan Sisters at three Arizona reservations— trying unsuccessfully to keep up with their schedules—I couldn't help but agree with the sisters' own assessment. They did, indeed, strike me as workaholics. Their devotion to work is so single-minded that its pursuit becomes a sort of poverty of self, a complete giving with nothing left in reserve. Some sisters see the unhealthiness of their situation but feel helpless to break out. After all, their culture encourages selflessness.

The sisters also pride themselves on their devotion. It is what distinguishes them from their lay counterparts. It is also what fills their otherwise undemanding lives. They don't have children or husbands or even traditional bosses to take up their time. And, unlike their monastic counterparts, they don't have a taxing prayer schedule. What they have are impoverished students whose needs make their own pale in comparison. After all, how can a sister refuse a hungry person so that she can meditate to be closer to God? Yet, the sisters are so overburdened with rescuing their students from poverty, providing them an education—a future—that their focus has admittedly left their own spiritual lives lacking.

I questioned how these sisters achieve a sense of community when they devote so much time apart, teaching and preparing for classes. Facing reassignment every year doesn't help the feeling of impermanence. Few sisters stay at a mission for more than three or four years. Perhaps that's why apostolic—or active—orders have had the hardest time attracting new women. No matter how worthy or altruistic an order's mission is, it may not be enough to entice a woman to sacrifice her freedom—or her paycheck. Today most women can find equally meaningful and dedicated professions outside religious life. They don't need to take vows to work with the poor.

Attracting modern women requires more than a mission. While most successful women would applaud the work these Franciscans are doing, I doubt many would want to swap their consuming ladder-climbing corporate world for an order than offered the same imbalances. Women interested in religious orders today are seeking a spiritual life and connections with other women. They want a culture that enriches, not absorbs.

10

AMONG THE DOWN AND OUT IN L.A.

SISTERS OF SOCIAL SERVICE IN LOS ANGELES, CALIFORNIA

"I feel the Lord started this agency. It's just common that we don't have any money."

—SISTER PAULA VANDEGAER

A mentally disabled woman and her Chihuahua escorted me from the wrought-iron gate to Sister Paula Vandegaer's cramped one-bedroom apartment. Clustered near her doorway were two members of Paula's pro-life organization and her best friend, Kathy Hochderffer, a former lay Franciscan, wearing a miniature police badge on her starter jacket and a pistol strapped to her waist. Hovering over the kitchen counter, Paula ate dinner while navigating the group's schedules.

After the women dispersed, Paula prepared me a plate of food and sat down at her tiny dining room table crowded with books and pamphlets—all connected to her organization, whose tentacles extend from promoting pro-life issues to fighting euthanasia and physician-assisted suicide. A tall, hazel-eyed woman with thick gray hair and bushy black eyebrows, Paula's face appears on nearly every leaflet and brochure as a noted psychiatric counselor and social worker. A publishing and speaking mogul, Sister Paula has her own series of videotapes, appears on television talk shows, and goes on speaking tours around the world.

But her tiny apartment near downtown Los Angeles seems a long way away from that glitzy milieu. Furnishings look like 1970s garage sale items: worn green velvet chairs and a sagging couch. A previous tenant—a gang member—had left a huge hole the size of a foot in her yellowed walls.

"Our poverty here is in the lack of privacy and the noise," she said, looking around her apartment. "We hear music blasting at all hours. But really we're quite comfortable."

Apartments next door and across the hall house the two female Volunteers for Life. The women each dedicate a year at Paula's pro-life operation, International Life Services, which loosely connects twenty-seven pregnancy clinics across the country, including twelve in California.

While she seems like a one-woman corporation, Paula is part of a religious order, the Sisters of Social Service, founded in 1926 in Los Angeles by a group of Hungarian nuns. An original member was the first female elected to the Hungarian parliament; other members were arrested and killed scheming against the Nazis. In the United States, the nonhabited nuns, known by their official gray suits, work mostly as social workers and number about eighty.

I had come to observe Paula's pro-life ministry because it is the only one of its kind supported by a progressive order. Conservative orders, such as the Sisters of Life in New York, do promote pro-life counseling and pregnancy centers, but reproductive issues tend to be discussed with grave discomfort at many progressive orders. Privately, some modern sisters voice a pragmatic view that an impoverished woman or teenager aborting a fetus is, at times, making the better choice. While most progressive sisters I've met believe in contraception, they respect that others are uncomfortable going against Church teachings. As a result, many progressive orders stay clear of ministries that deal directly with pro-life issues. Not Paula's.

She believes contraception and abortion victimize women. Paula has counseled hundreds of women whom she says are mentally and physically damaged by using birth control pills or by having an abortion. She says society pushes women to accept a myth that pregnancy can be managed through modern medicine and if that fails, abortion is merely a medical procedure to extract tissues, not children. Paula contends that contraception, especially birth control pills, hurt women's health by making them more susceptible to sexually transmitted diseases and by making it more difficult for them to become pregnant later on. She also contends that by controlling pregnancy through artificial means couples are robbed of the sexual intimacy of natural family planning.

At one time, Paula had considered breaking away from her order and starting her own pro-life religious community. But her sisters assured her that such a ministry fits within the order's mission of serving the needs of women, children, and families. Aside from that outward show of encouragement, I suspected many sisters privately are less approving. Indeed, I would discover just how divisive the issue is among Paula's sisters.

AN URBAN COMMUNE

That night, Paula and I attended a pregnancy center board meeting. The clinic, little more than a small storefront a couple blocks away, had opened seven months earlier. Besides its doctor and Sister Paula, the board consisted mostly of neighborhood Hispanic men and women. Two were Volunteers for Life: Gloria George, a small, studious-looking twenty-nine-year-old Indian from Canada, and Marcela Figueroa, a glamorous, dark-eyed thirty-three-year-old Hispanic who'd grown up in a wealthy L.A. suburb. Both agreed to work within Paula's pro-life ministry for at least a year in exchange for an apartment and a small stipend.

The discussion that night centered on seven area abortion clinics that were advertising on Spanish-speaking radio stations. Board members hoped to counter with pro-life messages on the same stations. While Paula's center doesn't provide adoption services or contraceptives, it does offer counseling, clothes, diapers, food, furniture, and money for pregnant women. It also acts as a resource, helping mothers find better jobs, apartments, and child care.

After the meeting, Paula sat quietly listening to the young volunteers ecstatically sharing their ideas. She was proud of her protégées' passion. Gloria had only been a volunteer for three months. Marcela, the program's first volunteer, had been with Paula for more than three years and was managing the new center.

Like the volunteers and sisters who work together at Holy Family Birth Center on the Texas-Mexico border, these women have formed what is essentially a modern convent with a mix of lay and vowed women working with the poor. In Paula's group, though, there is much more of a religious connection; its volunteers are devout Catholics and pray together each morning and evening in their chapel; they accompany each other to morning mass at the neighborhood cathedral. Unlike Sister Angela's scattered buildings on an old cucumber field, Sister Paula's commune is in an unlikely urban setting, with apartments forming a contemporary convent: Paula's serves as the central kitchen; Marcela's doubles as the chapel; Gloria's functions as guest quarters. Even the apartment of Paula's best friend has a classic function: Kathy Hochderffer serves as a modern portress, watching over the volunteers and Sister Paula.

Paula, her volunteers, and three other nuns moved to the Rampart building in 1997 as part of an unusual plot to rid the building of drug dealers and gang members. The neighborhood has long boasted the city's highest crime rate, and shortly after the L.A. riots, gangs had taken over the apartment. By installing the chapel and positioning nuns throughout the building as spiritual sentinels, the drug dealers were eventually guilted into moving elsewhere.

"It was much better than calling the police," remembered Kathy, who concocted the plan. "The gangbangers got so upset because they were all Catholic, and they were not going to mess with God. Even the police officers were laughing. I'd go down the hall with a gun in one hand and a rosary in the other, whichever worked."

DRAWN INTO THE PRO-LIFE MOVEMENT

Despite her impoverished surroundings, Paula sustains an idealistic vision of how people's lives can change. She isn't afraid for her own safety and frequently follows Kathy on her neighborhood patrols. Against great odds, she pursues her pro-life ministry, even at the brink of financial and medical collapse: Paula has suffered from diabetes for decades. Yet, she rarely seems discouraged, even when most people would have given up. Her optimism doesn't stem from a sanguine disposition but rather is born of a Midwestern determination; through prayer and hard work, she can achieve anything, even the unreasonable.

Paula knew she wanted to be a social worker long before she knew she wanted to be a nun. Growing up in Kansas City, Missouri, Paula was sheltered from real-world problems at her Catholic girls' school until one summer she got a job as a carhop and began meeting troubled people.

"This girl came in pregnant and then somebody else came in drunk. I thought, Gee, these people are trying to be happy, but they're not. They don't know how to be happy. So, I'll be a social worker and explain to people how to be happy."

She joined the Sisters of Social Service the summer after her high school graduation in 1956. Two years after she'd started working as a social worker, Paula became involved in the ministry that would consume most of her adult life.

The year was 1967 and the California legislature was considering a bill that would legalize abortion in that state. Paula didn't believe the bill had a chance, but she halfheartedly handed out a few flyers opposing it.

"I thought, Oh, that's ridiculous. I'd never heard of such a stupid thing. Nobody would legalize the abortion laws. No state in the union had legalized it."

When Gov. Ronald Reagan signed the bill, Paula was devastated.

"I couldn't believe it passed," Paula said, her face rekindling the shock she felt at the time.

The law allowed abortion up to twenty weeks into a pregnancy in cases of rape, incest, or to protect the health of the mother. "All of a sudden, all these women said they were going to commit suicide if they had to have their baby. It became abortion on demand," she said.

Paula didn't know what she could do. She attended grassroots meetings of antiabortion supporters, but it wasn't until two years later that she began working as a social worker at a Catholic adoption agency. Then in 1970, her order's superior asked Paula to help start an antiabortion hotline. So, in her spare time, Paula developed a manual and trained social workers to teach other volunteers—many of whom were former Girl Scout leaders—how to counsel women against having an abortion. Her instruction manual was mimeographed and sent out to pro-life groups all over the world. Pretty soon, pregnancy centers started opening around the country in response to the Supreme Court's *Roe v. Wade* decision, legalizing abortion in the United States, and they sought Paula's help.

"I was so convinced that women were being victimized badly," Paula said. "There's lots of money in abortions. My passion has always been about the women."

In 1972, Paula joined the International Alternatives to Abortion and began counseling pregnant women. One day while she was in a counseling session, Paula had an epiphany about contraception, a subject about which she had been ambivalent. The young woman in her office that day had delivered her baby and was considering whether she should start dating again and go on birth control pills.

"All of a sudden, the room was filled with spirits: There was a terrible fight going on between heaven and hell over her decision to go on contraceptives," Paula recounted. "I realized that this was a really important thing. God did not want her to do this. Contraceptives was really an instrument against women. It was really a big deal."

Paula was so stunned by what she saw that she could barely speak. She knew she could no longer take a passive stance toward contraception. But the National Right to Life Committee had asked pro-life groups to stay away from the contraception issue, she said.

Eventually, though, Paula felt compelled to speak about the dangers. After one of her first talks, a woman came up and asked if white birds meant anything to her. Paula was befuddled by the question but nodded. The woman told her she'd had the strangest experience while listening to Paula speak: She saw a white bird sitting on a branch dangling above Paula's head. The bird was singing and chirping.

"I took that as a sign God was happy I was teaching about contraceptives," she said.

Not long after that, pro-life pregnancy clinics were told not to refer women to doctors who could prescribe contraceptives but to encourage chastity and natural family planning. Paula began collecting medical information that further convinced her contraceptives were devastating to women's health.

"I'm not doing this because the Pope told me," she said. "I'm doing this because it's based on science. The Pill is the golden calf of our time. It is very, very destructive. I think it will be years before we realize how destructive it is."

I'd heard many nuns oppose contraceptives because Church law forbade it, but I had rarely heard any claim that it was physically harmful to women. Paula explained that when women go on the Pill, their vagina changes from an acidic environment that is hostile to pathogens to a warm, moist place like a petri dish where mutations can occur. Since 1960, the year the Pill came out, there have been twenty-two new sexually transmitted diseases, including herpes, AIDS, and the human papillomavirus, which can cause cancer of the cervix. (Stunned by Paula's assertions, I later consulted my own gynecologist and numerous medical texts, none of which could confirm that the Pill was harmful. My doctor said there were more sexually transmitted diseases because the Pill had instigated a sexual liberation, not because it somehow changed the vagina's chemistry.)

Paula promotes natural family planning; that is, monitoring basal body temperature and mucus to determine when a woman is ovulating. A lifelong celibate, Paula tried to convince me that making love was "sexier" on the natural planning method.

"The couple has to work together," she said. "The man has to correspond to the cycle of the woman. With contraception, she's available any time to him. But with natural family planning she's not. It's a wonderful psychological symbol for the woman. It's like this major sacrifice that they can find other ways to make love. It's a very positive thing for the marriage; he's respecting her sexuality."

Since its founding in 1985, International Life Services has nearly gone under several times. While many workers volunteer their time, Paula pays ten employees at the headquarters. On paper, the organization's administration runs on a $150,000 annual budget. But Paula's frequently late in issuing paychecks, even doling out cash from her own purse to meet employees' needs.

During my visit, just two weeks before Christmas, Paula already was a week late issuing payroll. She estimated the administration's bank account was short twelve hundred dollars. "I'll probably have payroll out in a couple of days," she said, shrugging. Indeed, Christmas donations allowed Paula to issue checks several days later.

"I feel the Lord started this agency," she said. "It's just common that we don't have any money. So I pray: 'You've got to tell me what to do, who to go to.' He's running the agency. I'm not running it. He's the boss here. So He's got to keep it going. It's His responsibility, not mine."

That trust apparently only goes so far. The headquarters, a square metal building hidden behind a white clapboard home, has barred windows and gated doors and is surrounded by an eight-foot-tall iron fence. Inside, the office looks like a small factory with

Sister Paula Vandegaer (center) with
her Volunteers for Life: Marcela
Figueroa (left) and Gloria George (right)

few windows, scattered piles of paper, and bare bulbs hanging from its low ceilings. Spanish-speaking women file paperwork and answer phones. Paula's office has the same décor as her home, early garage sale, with dust-covered plaques adorning the walls. The thump, thump, thump of the small printing press in the next room drones on like a rogue lawnmower about to come crashing through the wall.

Unlike the pro-life organizations I had covered as a journalist whose members routinely chained themselves to abortion clinic buildings, pick-eted clinics carrying placards with enlarged pictures of aborted fetuses, and yelled at women entering the buildings, Paula's seems to have adopted a kinder, gentler approach, a philosophy she said evolved from the Holy Spirit. Clinic workers are not allowed to show pictures of aborted fetuses to clients. Instead, they stress child development, presenting pictures of a growing fetus. Clinics don't picket or endorse candidates. They encour-age chastity, not contraceptives, and they don't push any particular reli-gion. If a woman wants to give up her child after birth, she's referred to a licensed adoption agency, not private adoptions.

At lunchtime, a neatly dressed volunteer passed through Paula's office, a direct path to the "lunchroom"—little more than a table next to the printing press. Paula stopped the woman, who was carrying a pizza box, and asked what was inside. She opened the box to reveal half a pizza, left-overs from the previous night's dinner. Was there enough to share? Paula asked. The stunned volunteer said surely there would be.

I had shared many leftover meals at convents and monasteries. At first I was repulsed by the idea of eating someone else's old food and some-what surprised that sisters would serve it to guests. Gradually I learned that leftovers are a part of their frugal way of life, part of their poverty. Sisters waste nothing. They were among the first environmentalists, refus-ing to throw out anything that could be recycled, reused, donated. Despite my offer to take Paula to lunch, she insisted that we partake of the leftover pizza.

Several workers gathered around the lunch table. One ate soup out of a can. Another offered lunch meat he'd brought in a sandwich bag. Paula dug into the refrigerator and brought out a Tupperware bowl containing pasta salad; she couldn't remember when someone had brought it in. The only other offering for a half dozen people was the pizza, which became like the biblical loaves and fishes, feeding everyone present with some left over.

While we ate, the pressman provided us with entertainment. A hefty Hispanic man with a pockmarked face, a large nose, and slicked-back silver hair, he sang passionately to opera music on the radio, throwing out his hands with their sausage-sized fingers smeared with ink. When "La donnaè mobile" came on the radio, Paula joined him in a duet.

PROFESSIONALISM VERSUS POVERTY

Just because a nun works with the poor doesn't mean she has to live in poverty. Despite the poverty vow and the many sisters who balk at accepting a decent salary, there are sisters who feel that nuns' traditionally low salaries are unprofessional, antifeminist, and the reason so many orders are on the brink of ruin.

Sister Diane Donoghue is definitely one sister who advocates that nuns—and especially Sister Paula—should command salaries that are commensurate with their education and talents. Although Diane works with some of L.A.'s poorest cases, she's probably the best-dressed nun I've ever met. That day she wore a blue wool suit with pearl earrings and trendy turquoise glasses that set off her tanned complexion. As executive director and founder of the Esperanza Community Housing Corporation, Diane demands a salary comparable to those of chief executives of other nonprofits—around seventy thousand dollars—making her one of the highest paid sisters in her order. At seventy years old, Diane knows her organization will have to seek her replacement soon, and her salary would also have to be enough to attract someone who isn't a nun.

Paula and Diane's order needs the money, with 81 percent of its sisters' retirement unfunded. Half of their sisters work below fair market rates, mostly because they take parish jobs or work in ministries that pay them no salary at all, living on a small monthly stipend that the order gives them. Although she firmly believes in supporting sisters' ministries whether they are wage-earning or not, she also feels nuns should be paid market rates, especially because such pay supports retired sisters. For every sister working, there are several more sisters dependent on her salary.

"For so many years, we worked for stipends and less," she said. "And we may have as many as seven sisters living off the salary of one working sister who might be making twenty-three thousand dollars. That's below the government poverty line."

There is always a tension, Diane said, between sisters pursuing ministries for the poor on one hand and getting paid for their work, experience and, education on the other. Most Sisters of Social Service have master's degrees and yet they are consistently paid well below what their counterparts make in other nonprofit and public sector jobs.

"There is an expectation that a sister will try to make a professional salary. But we also have a mission here," she said, adding that ultimately the work is more important than the pay. She certainly is one who is proud of her mission. That day, Diane drove me all around town, showing me formerly dilapidated apartment buildings throughout Los Angeles that her organization had bought, gutted, restored, and rented to low-income families. Esperanza provides housing for more than 1,000 people. Still, 250 families remain on its waiting list.

Diane has encouraged Paula to allot herself a salary befitting her role as executive director of her organization. But Paula always balks. How could she award herself a professional salary when her workers often have to go without pay for weeks, occasionally living off the few dollars she doles out from her wallet?

"Paula is a highly educated person who should be making a higher salary—an executive director's salary," Diane argued. "She stews about it and says: 'It just isn't possible. What would people think if they knew I

Sister Diane Donoghue

was getting that much money?'"

"I'm sorry," Diane added, "but this is the real world. Paula flies all over the place and people pay her expenses and her travel and da-di-da and she gets this dinky little per diem. Ugh! That's just not professional!"

Diane's headquarters occupies a big, terra-cotta–colored stucco building. The modern offices are outfitted with the latest computers. Artwork decorates exposed-brick walls, which also display several prestigious awards, including one from the magazine *Mademoiselle*.

In Diane's office, I spotted a photo of her with former president Bill Clinton, who had visited after the L.A. riots in 1992.

"That will have to come down now," she said, shaking her head. It had been only a few days since George W. Bush had been declared president. Diane had voted for Vice President Al Gore but had really wanted to vote for Ralph Nader. Meanwhile, Paula and Kathy had both been ardent Bush supporters.

A progressive sister, Diane had done her graduate work at Berkeley in the sixties, where she'd demonstrated for farm workers and against the Vietnam War. In recent years, she picketed against the Immigration and Naturalization Service at the federal building in L.A. Even before she entered the order in 1955, she'd traveled to India and worked for the American Red Cross. Strongly pro-choice, she said she favored contraception, as did many sisters in her order.

"There is a very wide continuum of political and religious philosophies here," she said. "I don't know why Paula is so conservative, but she is. She has been in the pro-life movement for a very long time."

Paula had suggested I ask Diane how Paula and her mission are perceived within their order. So I put the question to her. At first Diane seemed hesitant to answer, but after realizing that Paula had withheld what she viewed as key information, she spoke ardently.

"She wanted to start her own community," Diane said, not hiding her irritation. "We went through hell with the vicar of religious and the cardinal. It was absolutely a zoomer. We had a meeting to tell her this wasn't a good idea. The cardinal told her: 'This is not a good idea. You should stay within your own communal structures.' I'm sure she didn't even tell you about that."

I shook my head.

"That's why she says she doesn't know how she's received because she's got an armor around her that doesn't allow her to really be received," she said. "Our sisters would be more pro-choice. Paula gets her total and absolute affirmation and support from retired sisters and the older sisters. But in terms of anybody fifty-five or younger, it just wouldn't happen."

I wasn't surprised that Diane feels strongly about Paula's pro-life work. Many highly educated sisters who work closely with the poor feel that endless pregnancies are a major roadblock for women striving to emerge from poverty. They are realistic enough to know that keeping husbands and lovers away during the women's fertile times is harder to do than most natural family planning advocates want to admit. And though no one likes abortion, the sisters often take a pragmatic view that it is cruel and inhumane to bring more children to families who can't care for the children they already struggle to support.

MONEY VERSUS TIME

The tension between making money versus relinquishing a salary to serve the poor isn't just an issue among nuns. The volunteers, too, grapple with the irony that they have walked away from monied cultures only to discover how much nonprofit groups depend on the rich. Whereas serving the poor initially seems to be about time and commitment, the volunteers soon realize that an organization's long-term success often relies on attracting wealthy benefactors.

While Marcela, the daughter of a doctor, had been born into wealth, Gloria, the daughter of Indian immigrants, had gained entrée into the get-rich-quick culture of computer scientists. Having worked for a number of big computer companies, including IBM, Gloria gave up her well-paying computer job and was now on her second Catholic volunteer program. She didn't like how working in the computer industry made her competitive, how it pitted one against another, how it made people strive to "get ahead" and become greedy. She also didn't care for the long hours that often kept her from attending daily mass. Most corporations, she feels, are located far from churches, physically and philosophically. But she also didn't know what to do with her skills.

"Sometimes I wonder if I'm really using the best of my ability," she said, as she typed the Spanish-language version of Paula's pregnancy counseling book into the computer. The task wasn't much more than data entry since Gloria didn't know Spanish.

"I mean, I could work in the technical industry, make a lot of money, and donate that money to the pregnancy center. So is it better to make large donations to the poor or is it better to work with the poor?"

Gloria is what nuns call "a searcher," unsatisfied with the path she's on and unsure of her purpose. A quizzical, erudite woman with an elfish figure and engaging eyes, Gloria is plagued by life's big questions. What does she believe? What does God want her to do? Should she try to become the next Bill Gates or work as a missionary?

"I'm trying to see where I fit in with the Church," she said. "I'm following my heart. The work I'm doing now makes sense to me."

Her decision to reject corporate culture had its detractors, though. A few friends told her that she was going against the grain of capitalism. Even a stranger, a computer scientist who attended a pregnancy center fundraiser, told her she shouldn't be working there.

"You're throwing away all your science skills," he told her.

It's not that Gloria wanted to dismiss her computer skills. Initially she tried to combine her love for Church work with her computer knowledge. But after calling up churches in Boston, where she lived at the time, she learned there wasn't much need for a computer wiz.

Besides, Gloria claimed, she doesn't miss her old salary. And she doesn't feel it's beneath her to perform menial office tasks. She lives off a stipend of one hundred dollars a month. Now instead of buying clothes, she borrows what she needs from Kathy, Sister Paula, or Marcela. That day she wore a tawny green trench coat that Kathy had lent her. Several sizes too big, the jacket swallowed Gloria's petite figure.

Though she had grown up in a Catholic family—her parents both came from India and settled in Ontario, Canada, after they were married—Gloria said she practices her faith out of her heart and not her head. She is confused about how she stands on many teachings, such as the infallibility of the Pope, whether women should be ordained, and the meaning of the Vatican II Council. She questions whether nuns and priests should have vows of celibacy and how the Catholic Church handles homosexuality.

"This is part of my spiritual quest now," she said. "When I was a computer scientist, I didn't have time to read all this theology and stuff. I thought, When I do read and look up all these issues, then the Holy Spirit will make it very clear to me what's going on. But when I started reading, I became more confused."

LIVING IN TWO SEPARATE WORLDS

Fearing another night of leftovers, I insisted on taking the group out to dinner. We piled into Sister Paula's ten-year-old Toyota Tercel, including Kathy, who seems like an extension of this modern version of a religious order.

Stocky, with short-cropped brown hair, oversized thick glasses, and a slight underbite, Kathy looks like an aging, nearsighted security guard. As she "patrolled" Wilshire Boulevard, shining her flashlight into the trees to chase away winos and chatting up clerks at the local 7-Eleven, I became convinced that Kathy is somehow involved with the police. She remains elusive about her involvement, saying only that she has been on a neighborhood watch patrol for fourteen years. Eventually, she admitted she had worked "secret operations" under former police chief Daryl Gates. Paula told me Kathy had been an undercover narcotics detective—an account Kathy does not deny. For twenty-two years, she has also been an editor and graphic artist at Paula's pro-life magazine.

The more time I spent with Kathy and Paula, the more I began to understand the quirky relationship between this gun-toting, NRA-loving woman and the soft-spoken gentle nun who is her best friend. Both are conservative and believe in authority, whether it is the Church hierarchy or the LAPD. Both are single women in their sixties who have never married, never had children, and are adamantly opposed to abortion.

Kathy reminded me of a nun, and I wasn't surprised to learn that after she graduated high school she had considered joining several orders, including the Sisters of Social Service. Kathy's mother had been a nurse and Kathy wanted to follow in her footsteps. But the more she delved into the philosophies and rules of religious orders, she concluded they were too limited for her. She thought she could accomplish much more on her own. She also knew she was too much of an individualist to fit in. A few years later, she became engaged to a man who would die flying an F-16 in Vietnam. After that, Kathy never met anyone whom she felt measured up. Eventually she accepted that she has a vocation to the single life.

Nearing an Indian restaurant on Melrose Boulevard, Paula began searching for a parking space. Suddenly she called out to the spirit of a woman named Karen. Though she had never met Karen, Paula has immortalized her as the patron saint of parking spaces. Karen had been a friend of Kathy's who committed suicide after she aborted a fetus, the result of a rape. She was only twenty-three when she died, but in her short life, Karen had amassed numerous tickets by parking anywhere she liked.

Somehow she was never towed but paid her tickets as if they were scheduled payments. Paula swears that whenever she evokes Karen's help, a
great parking space always opens up. And now, just as she called out
Karen's name, a prime space appeared.

After dinner we walked down Melrose Boulevard, poking our heads
into shops vibrating with metallic music and looking in the windows at
mannequins dressed in revealing leather outfits, chains, and spiked collars.
We passed by transvestite shops laden with stiletto heels, blond wigs, and
sequined dresses. I imagined that this must have looked like a modern
version of Sodom and Gomorrah to Sister Paula. But her face revealed no
sign of repulsion. She just walked along with Kathy, laughing and staring
good-naturedly like the rest of us.

During the drive back, Kathy pointed out to Gloria famous land-
marks, like Paramount Studios and the Ambassador Hotel where Robert
Kennedy was shot. At Marcela's urging, Paula drove to Beverly Hills. As
she turned down Rodeo Drive, Paula again called upon Karen's spirit to
find a parking space; just then we spotted one in front of an art gallery.

The street was festive. Storefronts were bedazzled in red and twin-
kling Christmas lights. The street's center median was planted with bright
red poinsettias and the trees had matching red ribbons. Down the hill, the
Beverly Wilshire Hotel was enveloped in ivory lights. We strolled the
sidewalks, admiring the high-priced merchandise in the windows: Ar-
mani, Gucci, Christian Dior, Coco Chanel, Tiffany, Saks Fifth Avenue.

For a few minutes we dreamed aloud about living the kind of life that
could afford such splendor. Having scoured the three blocks of Rodeo
Drive—shocked at how short the famed shopping district is—we walked
up the cobblestone streets off Via Rodeo, which resembles an old European avenue. Reaching an Italian piazza with a bubbling fountain, we
watched men in tuxedos and women in long evening gowns elegantly
sipping from champagne glasses. Marcela stared ahead as if she were seeing a ghost. She explained that she and a former boyfriend had once routinely dined at such lavish restaurants in Beverly Hills and Hollywood.
She then owned a closetful of gowns and fancy dresses.

"It seems so foreign to me now," she said, almost wistfully. "It's like I have lived in two separate worlds."

The next day I saw more clearly how much Marcela had sacrificed to pursue her pro-life ministry. Meticulously decorated, Marcela's office revealed her former passion as a fashion-design student and her privileged upbringing. Marcela had grown up in the wealthy suburb of San Marino but did not fit in at her public high school, populated by mostly upper-crust white kids. Yet, she couldn't connect with Los Angeles's Chicano culture, whose political agenda centers around Hispanic poverty. Her parents are Mexican, but their extravagant lifestyle separates her from many American Hispanics. Marcela feels most at home in Mexico with her mother's relatives. Her extended family is warm and has strong values; she can relate to her cousins.

"I didn't know how to fit into the American side of me," she said of her teenage years. "I always felt like a painting with a lot of abstract colors splattered on the canvas. That was what being an American meant to me."

The more she tried to fit in, the more materialistic she became.

"I fell into following the American way of life. The culture feeds you this story about sexual freedom: Do whatever you want and no consequences to pay for your actions. I think that kind of thinking influenced my decisions," she said, coyly. "I was very hard on myself in my twenties. I had a lot of depression."

At thirty-three years old, Marcela has the exotic look of an actress—short black hair, dark eyes, bushy eyebrows, pouty raspberry lips—and the mannerisms of a nun. She speaks softly and with the calm infused by habitual meditation and daily mass. She carries herself with a simple sophistication. Regardless of her outfit, she always wears a long silver medallion of St. Benedict, like those worn by Benedictine nuns. (The Sisters of Social Service follow the Benedictine Rule.) On that day, Marcela was dressed in a long black skirt with a black and gray sweater. She also wore a tiny gold lapel pin the size and shape of an unborn baby's feet at ten weeks after conception: It is the international pro-life symbol.

Marcela met Sister Paula while attending a charismatic prayer meeting. The chance encounter would change her life. "I felt there was something—a connection—between us," she said, nervously tapping her fingers on her desk.

When she learned Sister Paula was looking for "guardian angels" to donate money and time at her pregnancy centers, Marcela started helping out a few hours a week at the headquarters. She wanted to connect herself with an organization that had a pro-life mission. She'd considered joining the Sisters of Life, the new religious order in New York whose ministry is counseling women who have had abortions and assisting pregnant women. But New York was a long way away from her family. And even though she was in her late twenties, Marcela had never moved out of her parents' home. Then Sister Paula started Volunteers for Life, her new pro-life volunteer corps. It was exactly what Marcela was looking for. She moved out of her parents' posh house and into the Rampart apartment building, where she has lived ever since.

"I don't think my parents understand the real reason why I'm so involved in pro-life," she said. "I know a lot of people personally who've been through abortions and I know the consequences of it, how it affects them spiritually and psychologically and physically. I think it's the most horrible thing that could happen to a woman."

The Los Angeles pregnancy center, which opened in May 2000, was actually Marcela's idea. She had noticed that the phone book didn't list any pregnancy centers in the area but had a long list of abortion clinics.

"I think they definitely target minorities and Hispanics," she said. "They even put coupons for abortions written in Spanish in the telephone booths and on cars. They hire Hispanics to pass out flyers. They have abortion commercials on Spanish TV and on Spanish radio. They don't have the same stuff in English."

Whenever I spoke with Marcela I sensed her passion for pro-life was more than being devoted to a cause, that she was trying to work out something from her past. Her woundedness is evident in her personality, her mysterious beauty, in her soft yet zealous devotion. She compares her dedication to pro-life as akin to someone who has recovered from an addiction to drugs and alcohol and is spending her life trying to help others recover.

"I think it helps me feel better about not having done good things in the past," Marcela said, refusing to be more specific. "It helps me to heal."

A SPIRITUALITY OF POVERTY

In L.A., the tension between living frugally to serve the poor while trying to lure wealth for a cause is especially trying in the shadows of Hollywood and Beverly Hills. Conspicuous displays of wealth—sprawling mansions, pricey clothes, showy cars—are revered. The only people who seem to matter in Southern California are celebrities and the megarich. Everyone else is disposable, especially poor Hispanics and their unborn children.

While struggling to keep their pro-life ministry afloat, Paula, Kathy, and Marcela dream of landing a wealthy patron who could donate an apartment complex for their cause. Then they could consolidate their ministry in one building. Meanwhile, the Sisters of Social Service order is practically homeless. After losing its mother house in a recent earthquake, the sisters launched a multimillion-dollar fundraising campaign to build a new home and assisted-living quarters for retired sisters, who account for about 20 percent of its U.S membership. With the large majority of sisters' retirement unfunded, the order's financial security remains tenuous.

The struggle between pursuing a ministry and making money isn't just limited to sisters. During her year as a Volunteer for Life, Gloria felt the strain of living like her clients while knowing she had the skills to command a good salary. She questioned whether she could do more by making money and giving to good causes. Toward the end of her year in Los Angeles several of her quandaries became clear.

After attending church two and three times a day, pleading with God for answers, Gloria decided she was no longer able to integrate her beliefs with official Church teachings and decided to leave the Catholic Church altogether when her time with Sister Paula ended. Among the issues she couldn't accept were the infallibility of the Pope and the need for a celibate male priesthood.

"I've learned that you don't do something just because people have been doing it for centuries," she explained shortly after leaving Los Angeles. "In India, there's a terrible Hindu tradition. When a man dies, his wife is thrown on top of the [funeral] pyre because she is considered useless. I am concerned whether it is really God's will to have only men ordained. It looks like it could be a human mistake. Yet, Pope John Paul says his teaching on women's ordination is infallible, and if you don't agree with what he says, then you are not really Catholic. Under that definition, I am not Catholic."

Her decision about making money versus continuing full-time ministry also became apparent: She needed to follow God through action, regardless of what religious institution she was connected to. One aspect was essential: She had to minister to the neediest cases. So, six weeks after leaving Los Angeles, Gloria joined a group of non-Catholic missionaries headed for Sierra Leone in Africa, long torn apart by civil war. She would live and work in an orphanage.

I envied Gloria's clarity and her courage to go off to a dangerous country, shielded only by her faith and determination. Her chosen ministry was simple and unambiguous, yet it also seemed glamorous. I had often fantasized about joining the Peace Corps and working in Africa. Sometimes I'd come back from my stays with the nuns, after weeks of experiencing their various missions, and feel vaguely discontented. So much of "real life" is consumed with making money and paying the bills, a facet that became painfully obvious after living so purposefully with the sisters. I often questioned whether it was selfish to care for a single family, my husband and two children, when I could be out there, like the nuns, caring for many. But the alternative—uprooting my family and dragging them to some foreign country because of my personal commitments—also seemed selfish.

When I shared my quandary with a sister, she simply smiled and said, "It's because of our vow of poverty that we can do what we do. We are unencumbered. We have no responsibilities. We go where God sends us."

Poverty, she went on to explain, isn't about deprivation. It's about traveling light in life. It's about taking only what is needed. Indeed, many sisters say that the vow of poverty is vastly misunderstood. Poverty, they say, isn't about being poor. Poverty is about trusting that God will provide, somehow, someway. It's more about having faith than security, believing in prayers more than a big bank account. It's truly putting into practice what Jesus said: If God can care for the lilies of the field then we shouldn't worry about what we will wear or what we will eat.

Modern women, though, have been raised to always have a security plan—the twenty dollars stuck in a side pocket in case the car doesn't start, the secret savings account in case the relationship or the job goes sour, the stock and 401(K) retirement plans for when the paychecks stop. We've learned from earlier generations and the message is clear: don't count on a man; have a backup plan.

But religious life asks professional women to relinquish that hard-earned security. Trust that—while nothing else in the world is secure, not even the safety of the country—God will be there. The sisters contend that He is their backup plan. He will send the right people at the right time. Ultimately, the poverty vow, they say, is about depending on the mysteries of life: the loaves and the fishes, the leftover pizza, the freed-up parking spaces, the daily coincidences. It's about believing, in the middle of a recession, days before Christmas, that dozens of ten dollar checks written primarily by little old ladies will show up in the mail so that pay-roll can go out.

PART FIVE

SPIRITUALITY

MATURING AS A NUN MEANS TRANSCENDING THE VOWS. IT requires a sister to explore her spirituality beyond the confines of religious rules. The vows serve as the initial steps to a deeper, more personal relationship with God and the community. But their meaning isn't fixed or immovable. In order for the vows to be relevant to contemporary times, their significance must be adaptable. If a sister doesn't keep evaluating what the vows mean, her commitment becomes stagnant and her spiritual life rooted in the past.

Often the vows transform into a commitment completely different from when a sister initially made them. Whereas obedience in the 1950s

connoted a deep dependence on authority and seeking the permission of superiors, today's definition can be described as a sister following her conscience, seeking consensus with her sisters, pursuing ministries and lifestyles that are reflective of the order's charism or spiritual gifts, or simply listening to her inner voice. That is certainly the case with several of the Sisters of St. Joseph in Minneapolis, who risk arrest every time they protest. For these sisters, the true meaning of their vows surpasses any traditional definition. Ultimately, their commitment exceeds following the hierarchy of the Catholic Church and, in some cases, the authority of the United States government. They remain sisters because religious life supports their larger mission of peace.

In other cases, a sister accepts the vows as part of the entrance cost of becoming a sister. She doesn't dwell on these formal promises but allows them to lead her to a closer, more intimate spirituality. Such is the case for Prioress Dawn Mills at the Benedictine Sisters of Perpetual Adoration in Tucson, Arizona, who accepts that chastity and poverty—along with her specific Benedictine vows of stability, conversion of life, and obedience— allow her to live in community. But she still made a deal with God on just how much she was willing to give up. Religious life, she said, is no different from any other kind of life: There are always trade-offs and negotiations. Sister Dawn, a former Protestant and a modern mystic, helped me overcome my doubts about the value of the vows and the relevance of religious life.

Sometimes an entire community's spirituality can mature to such a point that they find the vows unnecessary and working within the confines of the Catholic Church too restricting. This is what happened with the Sisters of the Immaculate Heart in Los Angeles, who, as a community, chose to leave the official registry of the Catholic Church because staying would have meant restricting their spirituality. To them, their feminist beliefs and their community were more important than keeping the vows and retaining the approval of the Church.

11

SPIRITUAL PROTESTS

SISTERS OF ST. JOSEPH IN MINNEAPOLIS, MINNESOTA

"I don't think much about the vows. I can't even remember the last time I gave serious thought about what the vows mean in my life."

—SISTER RITA MCDONALD

In the early morning chill, Jane McDonald squatted on the sidewalk in front of Alliant Techsystems, one of the country's largest munitions makers. Setting up her usual display, she lit a candle and affixed a poster next to a small plastic leg, a child's prosthesis. Nearby stood the three-foot-high bombshell casing her sister Brigid hauls around in her car for weekly protests. Two other McDonald sisters, Kate and Rita, also were among the clutch of about thirty people, most of them gray-haired, waving signs and chanting.

"Peace, conversion without loss of jobs!" they shouted in staccato bursts, admonishing the company to stop making land mines and bombs and "convert" to nonlethal products.

Jane greeted the Alliant employees as each passed from the parking lot to the company headquarters. "Good morning," she said, brushing back white hair and fixing a smile on her gently wrinkled face.

Workers usually ignore her, but on this morning a stern-looking man in a business suit kicked the child's prosthesis into the street. Jane chased after the man. "I've never seen such lack of respect," she scolded him. "Don't you know this is a prosthesis a child has to wear because of what you make in that building?"

The man turned to face her. "You're a moron," he hissed and walked on.

Jane stood in the crosswalk staring at the man's back. She wanted to hit or trip him but remembered that she was there to stop violence. "God have mercy on you," she shouted and walked back to the protesters huddled in the snow.

For two decades, Jane McDonald and three of her biological sisters have endured verbal abuse, threats, arrests, and imprisonment. They've demonstrated outside corporate headquarters of weapons makers, blocked the doors to the federal courthouse, rallied opposition to the Gulf War, protested U.S. military action after the attacks on September 11, 2001, participated in "die-ins" in front of the Pentagon, marched into the U.S. Army's School of the Americas in Fort Benning, Georgia, and even held protest sit-ins at the St. Paul cathedral. Their beliefs have publicly pitted them against family members as well as the Catholic Church. Yet, these sisters aren't just biological siblings: They are Sisters of St. Joseph of Carondelet, a four-centuries-old order whose mission has been hospital work, direction of orphanages, visitation of the sick and poor, and instruction of young girls.

During the turbulent sixties, the sisters lived semicloistered in the convent, dressed in habits, and taught at Catholic schools or worked at Catholic hospitals and orphanages. By the time they became protestors, it was the early 1980s. Vietnam was a distant memory. Reagan was president, and the McDonald sisters were four aging nuns who had emerged from the convent only to find the vanguard of protesting had passed them by. Their spiritual conversion from traditional to radical sisters forced them to redefine the meaning of their vows. They made civil disobedience their calling, their mission in life to stand up to violence and to prejudice, whether it is speaking out for welfare moms or gay and lesbian Catholics. Nothing—not declining health or even an edict from the Pope—has stopped them.

"We turned around in our souls," explained Jane. "Once you turn, with that conviction and passion, you can't turn back."

The first time I met the McDonalds, Jane was pounding her drum, Kate was reading prayers for a "new world order," Rita was standing over a chalk silhouette of a land mine victim, and Brigid was singing "Oh, My Darling, Alliant Tech," to the tune of "My Clementine."

> *Dear Alliant, we're defiant. We'll be back with many friends!*
> *It's like David and Goliath. And you know how that one ends!*

At first it was hard to tell the women apart, with their short slight frames, bushy gray-white hair, and booming tenor voices. But as I watched their Wednesday morning vigils—even in a fifteen-below-zero wind chill—and their arrests for more than three years, I came to see them as four very different women.

At sixty-seven, Jane is the youngest. She has been known to burst into tears when she hears about a mistreated animal. Her belief system borrows from many religions, including Native American spirituality, Wicca, and Goddess worship. She is a grandmother to neighborhood children and stray cats. She makes no claims to sainthood; on occasion, I've even caught her telling dirty jokes.

Brigid, seventy, is the most spirited, laughing and dancing around tables at the diner where protesters gather after their vigils. Brigid's trademark eyebrows, dramatically drawn in black charcoal, mark an unconventional attitude friends jokingly call "risqué." This friendly, energetic woman idolizes Pavarotti—though she prefers bluegrass to opera. Her favorite holiday is St. Patrick's Day, an event she spends months preparing for. Impetuous, she commits to causes at the spur of the moment.

Kate, seventy-three, is reserved. With oversized glasses, she appears the prim but fashion-conscious Catholic schoolmarm. Intellectual and deeply contemplative, Kate is the most articulate, if not the most diplomatic.

Even after working with homeless and abused women for years, she is continually shocked by their stories.

At age eighty, Rita is the matriarch, although she looks as young as the others. Outspoken and sassy, Rita takes on anyone or any institution she believes is wrong—even chastising a judge in court.

Despite their age, and recent bouts with cancer—all but Jane have been diagnosed in recent years—the sisters routinely protest all over the Twin Cities and the nation. They even plan chemotherapy and radiation treatments to fit around their daily protests.

"They're all like Irish elves," explained Marv Davidov, who, himself, at age seventy, is Minnesota's elder statesman of protesting. Davidov has known the sisters since he instigated their entrée into protesting in 1981. "They're youthful and have an interior life. They're powerful women who went through a great transformation and liberated themselves."

COMMITTED TO AN ACTIVIST COMMUNITY

By 8 A.M. the protest had ended and the sisters and their fellow protestors had reconvened at a restaurant near Alliant headquarters. The diner gathering is almost as vital to the activists as the actual vigil. They pushed together several back tables and ordered breakfast and carafes of coffee. The once-empty diner was suddenly filled with loud voices and infectious laughter. Women and men hugged each other. Some talked about their grandchildren; others discussed upcoming protests. A young man passed around birthday cards to sign. Another man displayed pictures he'd taken at a rally. One woman had nearly covered herself in protest buttons, and others took turns envying her collection, as though examining a steamer trunk plastered with decals from exotic locales.

Jane whispered in my ear, "When I die, I want my casket decorated with stickers of all the causes I've been involved in."

She was still upset about her confrontation. "That's twice that someone has kicked the protest signs or the little prosthesis," she grumbled.

"The first time it happened before this morning, a man kicked it and said, 'Get this shit out of here!' It just goes to your soul."

Jane's soft white hair was pulled back to reveal dangly dream-catcher earrings. Silver rings adorned her short fingers and an assortment of silver bangles clanked together on her arms. An attractive woman, she had a sweet, delicate smile and penitent blue eyes.

"We come here for our sake, too. This community calls me back," Jane said, gazing around the room.

The sisters don't see their political activism as separate from their religious commitment. Indeed, many of their fellow St. Joseph sisters consider their weekly Wednesday morning protest against land mines as sacred as Sunday morning mass.

Their membership in Women Against Military Madness is equally important to them. "It's very parallel to being a CSJ [Sister of St. Joseph of Carondelet]," said Jane. "I don't feel Roman Catholic, but I feel more catholic, or universal, than ever. Catholicism is oppressive. I've become less shackled since I've discovered the gift of the Goddess. I'm much closer to earth and animals. My God was too small, microscopic. I feel I've gotten reeducated about spirituality."

The sisters grew up in the midst of the Depression on a 160-acre dairy farm about thirty-five miles west of Minneapolis. Their parents, Kenneth and Margaret McDonald, were devout Catholics and dedicated Democrats. Family dinners were often dramatic affairs as the family argued politics between mouthfuls of pot roast and potatoes.

Kenneth McDonald fought in France during World War I, and although he was critical of the army's inefficiency, he raised his eleven children to believe in the "just war theory," the notion that war was necessary to defend the nation and maintain a democracy. As the United States prepared to enter World War II, the older McDonald children were eager to get involved. When the eldest girl graduated high school in 1941, she went to work at the Minneapolis aircraft field welding military planes and later joined the navy's WAVES (Women Appointed for Volunteer Emergency Service). Rita, the second oldest daughter, got a job cleaning and vacuuming B-25 bombers. The oldest son served in World War II; the other sons would serve in the Korean War.

In 1946, twenty-two-year-old Rita shocked her family by announcing she was joining a convent. She wanted to pursue nursing; many nurses were religious sisters in those days. The closest convent at the time was the Sisters of St. Joseph of Carondelet in St. Paul, which ran six hospitals, two orphanages, a home for unwed mothers, the College of St. Catherine, and nearly one hundred parochial schools.

Upon taking her first vows, Rita was required to stop using her given name. She asked her superior for the name Sister Kenneth. The consequences of the cloistered life were not lost on her younger sisters, who cried inconsolably when Rita left.

"It was like she was going to Siberia," remembered Jane, who was eleven at the time. "There were so many restrictions. She couldn't come home for five years. It was a real loss."

Once a month, the family piled into the station wagon and drove to the St. Paul convent to visit Rita. To the young McDonald girls, their older sister seemed to have a fascinating and important life. As the years passed, three of them followed Rita into the order.

When their father learned that Jane, the baby daughter, planned to follow three older sisters into the convent after her high school graduation in 1954, he became distraught. "This is worse than the army," he said. "The army took my sons, and the convent is taking my daughters."

When she first entered, Jane didn't really understand what the vows meant. She'd read a book about the virgin martyrs and thought giving her life to God was an honorable pursuit. Interpretation of the vows then was quite rigid. Obedience required that the sisters seek permission for even the most trivial things, including the use of cleaning supplies. The order's "blind obedience" required sisters to accept their superiors' decisions without question and to follow whatever mission they were given. (Rita never got to be a nurse but was sent out to care for children at an orphanage.) In those days, chastity meant denying a woman's sexuality. She was to avoid close friendships with other sisters and, above all, rebuff friendships with men. Their poverty vow required that they owned nothing, exchanging the pronoun "my" to "our."

"We were supposed to say, 'Our pencil, our habit, our toothbrush,'" Rita remembered.

By the late 1960s, the Sisters of St. Joseph, like many orders, shifted from running institutions, such as hospitals and colleges, to providing social services for the poor. Eventually the McDonald sisters worked in the order's newly established shelters, runaway centers, nursing homes, and transitional housing for former drug users. They taught English to Laotian, Vietnamese, Hmong, and, later, Somali immigrants. They began questioning what was going on outside their cloistered world.

Jane's attitude about war and defending democracy started changing during the Vietnam conflict. At the time she was working as a cook in a Catholic elementary school. One day, the school's history teacher invited her to hear a guest speaker, a peace activist. "She just came into that classroom and into my life that day," Jane said. "I remember her talking about the economy and the large piece of the pie that goes to military financing, and that just seared my soul. That was my spiritual, radical awakening."

Privately, Jane came to believe that true poverty should be eradicated, not elevated to a virtue. She decided she could no longer follow authority blindly. But she didn't express her beliefs publicly until 1969 when her nephew, fearing he was about to be drafted, asked Jane what she thought about Vietnam. The eighteen-year-old didn't believe in fighting and wanted to become a conscientious objector.

"I was at such a different place," she recalled. "It was a one-hundred-eighty-degree turn to sit down with him and say, 'Our prayer and hope is that you do not go to war.'"

Not long afterward, Jane attended her first protest, outside the Minneapolis federal building. She was working at a home for unwed mothers at the time. Wearing a modified habit, she was reluctant to call attention to herself by holding a sign or shouting slogans. So she and several young expectant mothers made cupcakes, decorated them with the Stars and Stripes, and handed them out to protestors. She called it "evangelizing for peace." After that, though, she began sporadically marching in street protests denouncing the draft.

Jane's first arrest occurred at a stockholders' meeting of a munitions company after she and others disrupted the meeting and blocked the doors. Though Jane practiced the speeches she planned to make in court, the company dropped the charges.

By this time, other Sisters of St. Joseph were becoming involved in the antiwar movement and encouraged Jane's participation. Quickly Jane adopted the language of a peace activist. Authority, she would come to say, means authoring her own life, not relying on a superior to give her permission. Over time, she would interpret the vow of obedience to mean keeping an open mind and listening to the spirit of her community. Chastity means creating compassion among her sisters. Eventually, she would take the poverty vow as her marching order to protest against the rich and powerful, including the Catholic Church.

"It's revolting to see the rich get richer and the poor get poorer," she said. "The male-dominant, white privileged class is not okay. Even the Church is perpetuating a spiritual class system."

A CHANGE IN THEOLOGY

Brigid's induction into the peace movement came as a result of her theology studies. One summer in the early 1970s, Brigid attended a Catholic college in Wisconsin where she heard teachers emphasizing liberation theology, a new doctrine that focused on the struggles of the poor and encouraged the religious to champion nonviolent resistance.

Clockwise from top: The McDonald sisters dressed in their traditional habits on a home visit to their parents' farm in 1961; Sister Kate McDonald; Sister Rita McDonald encouraging protestors at an anti-landmine demonstration

"I had my theology stretched," she explained. "We were taught that the Church was the living people, not the structure and not the doctrine. And that changed everything for me."

In 1974, Brigid took part in her first antiwar demonstration; she joined a group sitting on railroad tracks trying to stop a munitions train. At first, Brigid felt foolish sitting on the tracks, but after listening to the protestors sing and talk, she realized that this was a way of life for people who had gone "all the way for peace." Her order had just come out of the habit and she was relieved that her clothing no longer exposed her as a nun. She wondered if she would ever make the kind of commitment she admired in those around her. When the train didn't come that day, Brigid was convinced the protestors had stopped it.

And yet, it would be several years before Brigid protested again. "I didn't start out in that radical way," she said. "You just kind of gradually got into it."

Brigid started collecting activist literature. She questioned people involved in the peace movement. She listened to radio interviews with those who had been jailed for peacefully demonstrating. She attended political rallies where speakers forced her to see the world from a different angle: U.S. foreign policies were harming other countries. Leaflets and flyers became her new prayer book; she was studying them for reasons she should get involved.

"They were like my new scripture," she said. "They tell you where the kingdom of God is really happening."

Within a few years, Brigid was protesting regularly outside a Minneapolis munitions factory that made bombs for the Vietnam conflict. During one large demonstration, Brigid allegedly resisted arrest. Police accused her of "screaming and creating a dangerous situation" and said she attempted to pinch and kick an officer while they forcibly restrained her.

Brigid said the police officer punched her in the stomach after she refused to move from the sidewalk, taking a seat at the bus stop and insisting she had a right to be there. Another nun became so enraged that she stomped on the officer's foot and was swiftly arrested. That night, police released the sisters to the care of the order's "mother superior," who by that time, was just one of a team of sisters running the order and who supported the sisters' causes.

The incident sealed Brigid's commitment. She moved away from the traditional spirituality that emphasized prayer as the means to a relationship with the deity. Instead, she came to view relationships with people, especially with the needy, as her way to connect with God. Brigid, like her sisters, came to see chastity as a vow that allowed her to care for children everywhere. Her vow of obedience means following her conscience. Poverty requires her to pursue justice.

"I feel I cannot stop being a protestor and resister of what is evil of humankind. If not I, then who? A lot of people have bigger responsibilities of jobs and children and can't take time out."

Meanwhile, Kate and Rita, the oldest sisters, were almost oblivious to the war in Vietnam. They watched little television and rarely read newspapers. In 1969, Kate moved out of the hospital's convent and into a nearby house with another Sister of St. Joseph. Four years later Rita joined them.

"I lived and worked in that hospital," Kate recalled. "Worked seven days a week. Finally, we had one Sunday off a month. Recollection Sunday, we called it. Of course, what do you think we did most of the day? Sleep.

"I'm almost ashamed to admit we weren't involved in that war," Kate continued. "Such a horrendous, horrible thing. Vietnam didn't touch my soul. I must have had an inside bell turned off or something."

In 1970, Kate gave up her position in hospital administration to work at Catholic Charities, interviewing those seeking services, including homeless people, alcoholics, drug addicts, and abused women.

"I went from an ascetic situation at the hospital to getting shocked every day," Kate remembered. "That was my first education."

At the same time, Rita became a social worker at the Bridge for Runaway Youth, counseling teenagers fleeing domestic violence, incest, and alcoholic parents. The sisters quickly had to connect with another culture, one unlike any they'd ever experienced. All those years of devotions, self-discipline, and piety hadn't prepared them for the true test of their vows.

The sisters converted the basement of the large house they rented into an apartment for the homeless, especially refugees they met through Minneapolis's Center for Victims of Torture. The longest "cellar dweller" was a Vietnamese refugee who lived with the sisters more than seven years. From her, they learned the horrors of the Vietnam War.

By 1981, Kate and Rita were cheering on the sidelines as protestors—including Jane and Brigid—regularly blocking the doors at Honeywell. Peace activists since 1968 had been demonstrating Honeywell's production of metal canisters for the cluster bomb. Later, the company made Trident missile parts and the triggering mechanism for the cluster bomb.

Eager for recruits, Honeywell protestors found the sisters to be ideal demonstrators: single women who didn't have children or husbands to monopolize their time and who couldn't be fired from jobs for standing up for their consciences.

"It seemed natural for people who are religious," explained Marv Davidov, who organized the protests.

Early in 1984, police arrested 577 protestors, Minneapolis's largest mass arrest. That year, Rita joined the protesting ranks; Kate was the lone holdout.

"I was kind of a coward," remembered Kate. "I really didn't think I'd ever get to the point that I would risk civil disobedience."

Then in April that year, Kate attended another Honeywell protest in support of her sisters. She planned to slip away early so she could get to her classroom at a Catholic parochial school. Around 8:20 A.M., Kate was walking to her car when a police officer grabbed her, frisked her, and ushered her to a bus filled with forty-eight other protestors, mostly plucked off the sidewalk and street. Kate's arrest was eventually dismissed; she even received an apology letter from the police chief. But the incident pushed her from the sidelines into a full-fledged protestor.

As peace protestors, the sisters' lives took on a broader dimension. Devotions and personal pieties seemed trivial in light of people who had lost limbs to land mines or who didn't have enough food for their children in countries ravaged by war, often backed by weapons from the United States. The ritual of religion was removed from their lives when they realized it was more important how they treated people than how many prayers they recited or how much time they spent in the chapel.

"Saying prayers was once so important," Kate said. "Acts of Attrition, Acts of Love, Acts of Faith, Nicene Creed, Apostles' Creed, and the rosary—fifteen decades of the rosary—all that put together. They served us well at one time, but I need my own words."

The sisters don't regret their early religious life. But they have grown beyond what they see as an immature spirituality.

"I'm not grateful for the stuff that was dysfunctional and oppressive," Kate said. "Now our lives are so much broader and challenging. Rituals make up only a tiny bit of our lives. We have evolved. The vows have changed."

CIVIL DISOBEDIENCE

While sisters in their order have served county jail time and months in federal penitentiaries, the McDonalds have yet to serve time, despite at least a dozen arrests each. In a few cases, officials dismissed charges, saying that putting hundreds of protestors on trial was a logistical nightmare. In other cases, especially early on, paperwork was lost—they believe deliberately so; nun defendants presented a difficult obstacle for the prosecution. Other times the sisters were forced to go to court and take their chances.

One jury trial lasted several days. Jane delivered a whimsical closing statement, singing and lighting a candle in the courtroom. The jury brought back a guilty verdict—several jurors fought back tears as their decision was read—but still the sisters didn't have to serve time. In one instance the judge gave the sisters a choice of either paying a fine or writing a ten-page article about why they protested against weapons making. They opted for the paper. Another time, the judge sentenced them to community service. "So, we just went to our daily jobs and wrote it up," Jane recounted. "It's already community service."

When their Gulf War protests seemed to have no effect and American nationalism was rising, the sisters began to question what they were doing.

"The Gulf War destroyed a lot of things in me," Brigid remembered, the bitterness evident. "I had to ask myself why I was going to continue to protest. The motivation keeps changing. I think I'm dedicated to life giving, and so I resist what I think is death giving. I said I would be faithful to this. I didn't say I'd be successful."

In 1996, the sisters began to demonstrate at the U.S. Army's School of the Americas at Fort Benning, Georgia. Graduates have been linked to killings, tortures, rapes, and disappearances—including the murders of six Jesuit priests, their housekeeper, and her daughter.

At the 1997 demonstration, thousands lined up in twos and walked silently past the school's gates carrying white crosses, each bearing the name of someone allegedly murdered by paramilitaries the school had trained. Kate was paired with her friend, and fellow Sister of St. Joseph, Rita Steinhagen. Immediately police arrested the demonstrators. Since it was the first federal arrest for the McDonald sisters, they were released with a misdemeanor citation. Because it was Steinhagen's second arrest at the school, she was charged with a felony and later sentenced, on her seventieth birthday, to six months in a federal prison.

Steinhagen's imprisonment inspired the Sisters of St. Joseph order to focus on closing the school. The order campaigned for several bills that would have curbed the school's funding. If anything, Steinhagen's arrest stirred sisters who had not been active in protests to join the cause. Now about twenty sisters routinely get arrested; others support major demonstrations.

The sisters faced a public backlash after the September 11 attacks. On September 12, 2001, the women went to their usual Wednesday 7 A.M. protest at Alliant Tech headquarters and that evening to a downtown Minneapolis bridge where for years they had been protesting U.S. sanctions against Iraq. In the past, drivers occasionally hurled bottles and trash at them, but on this day they threatened to run them over. Some yelled: "You killers! Now are you satisfied?"

"Some drivers give us their silent affirmation," Rita said, showing me the more common feedback—a raised fist with only a middle finger extended. "We see it as half a peace sign."

AGAINST FAMILY AND CHURCH

Their family has been relatively unfazed by their very public and controversial activities.

"They were always rebels and stood up for what they believed in," said Margaret Borer, the eldest McDonald sister at age eighty-one. A grandmother and a mother of eight, Margaret has joined her sisters for years on the protest lines.

While the McDonald sisters are in solidarity protesting for peace, their brothers remain in favor of peace through strength. Differences in their politics flare up at family get-togethers. The sisters argue the most with K.J. McDonald, an Independent-Republican who served in the Minnesota legislature from 1976 to 1990. McDonald is a former district commander of the American Legion and a member of the VFW, the Lion's Club, the Christian Anti-Communists Crusade, and the Rod and Gun Club.

"I'm probably a bigger mouth, a little more articulate than they are, and have a little more braggadocio," explained K.J., who, at sixty-eight years old and retired from politics, runs a photography studio with his son. "There's less and less exchange on these lines over the last few years because it probably appears on both sides to be a fruitless effort to try to change each other's opinions. I do try to encourage them to look at our side and maybe be a little more objective. But we don't allow it to become a bitter argument in any way that would diminish our love and friendship."

K.J. often took pictures of his sisters when they visited the McDonald farm.

"I have a picture of all four of them in their habits aiming shotguns up in the sky, as if they were going duck hunting," he remembered. "They cringe when they look at that one."

There are occasions when their beliefs become more than family discourse, though. When their brother Patrick was killed in a car wreck, the sisters insisted no guns be fired at his military funeral. In 1990, a profile of the sisters in their hometown newspaper provoked a cousin to write a letter to the editor chastising the sisters for campaigning to stop land mines while refusing to protest abortion clinics.

"In a way it hurt, but we kind of understand them by now," Kate said of the letter-writer. "We remember that some of our male relatives are staunch Rush Limbaugh–type men, and we really don't take it personally. Our brothers come from a macho background. They tolerate us. We have good old card games, and our arguments don't last more than twenty-four hours."

Public disagreements with relatives, though, weren't nearly as upsetting to the sisters as getting arrested by their own archbishop. In late September 1990, the sisters were part of a fast and sit-in at the St. Paul cathedral to protest U.S. aid to El Salvador. By this time, many nuns and priests took part in such protests. Jane and Brigid, along with four El Salvadorans, were singing on the cathedral steps when the archbishop had them arrested.

"I'm sure this is some kind of mistake," Jane said as she was being led away.

Days later, church leaders had 104 people arrested at the cathedral, claiming that the hunger strikes disrupted daily church business.

"It's very sad to see that the Church is no longer a refuge," Rita said after her arrest.

The archbishop's antics didn't deter the sisters. Months later the sisters demonstrated at the chancellery office because the church wouldn't give a Catholic lesbian and gay group a place to meet.

"The Church has no business judging these people," Jane said.

The McDonald sisters also have protested in other ways—rejecting the honorary title "Sister" because they feel it is a legacy of "the Church's spiritual caste system." They don't attend mass every morning but instead participate in other religious services, including a "Goddess singing circle," celebrating the feminine face of God.

"Any institution that doesn't change becomes stagnant, irrelevant, and then extinct," Jane explained of the need for change in religious life.

While the McDonald sisters' beliefs may seem heretical, especially to conservative Catholics, the Catholic Church permits merging traditions from various religions, including Native American spirituality, Hinduism, and Buddhism. Burning sage and praying to "the Goddess" is accepted as long as it doesn't conflict with the basic precepts of the Catholic faith.

These days, the sisters don't reflect on their vows of poverty, chastity, and obedience. "I can't even remember the last time I gave serious thought about what the vows mean in my life," Rita said.

Added Kate: "It's uncomfortable, awkward, and embarrassing when you hear those words in a commitment ceremony. The old meaning doesn't fit with our lifestyle now."

Because they have spent most of their lives fighting poverty, they don't believe there is anything virtuous about it. They don't believe they are poor: The order provides them with cars and modest homes.

Yet, their own individual definitions of the vows differ from one another.

"Chastity means being faithful to a commitment and to relationships," Rita said, her chin jutting out in resolve.

"I thought it meant something about the body," Kate said, looking at her sister with a quizzical expression. "Isn't it about celibacy?"

"In my book, chastity means more than celibacy," Rita debated. "Being chaste is so broad it could be interpreted for sisters or married people. To me it means faithfulness."

The prevailing theme in the sisters' lives is their consistent railing against the privileged class, especially within the Church. "Who needs a privileged-class papacy?" Jane said. "Get rid of the Roman collar, clericalism, the Pope. Jesus would be the first one to say so."

She and her sisters feel so strongly about such matters that they sought out a parish that allowed women to give homilies, a practice forbidden by Church policy. "I think that's what saves me from leaving the Church totally," said Kate, a licensed minister who occasionally performs weddings—though never in a Catholic church.

The sisters advertise their beliefs as much as possible. Their rusty cars are covered with bumper stickers that announce a plethora of causes, such as *In the Goddess, we pray.* Their clothes are emblazoned with slogans from Gandhi to Buddha. Their politics aren't just something they trot out for protest days. Even when they answer the phone, they greet callers with maxims. "We pray that peace is possible" is Jane's.

They aren't concerned about the lack of women entering their order. Perhaps, they reason, religious life needs a major overhaul and should be made up of people who don't take vows. Yet, they feel no need to leave their order, especially at their ages.

"Being in a women's community gives me a reasonably good platform from which to speak about injustices," explained Rita. "Otherwise I wouldn't have the freedom and the support to speak out and manage this work."

No subject is taboo. Kate admitted that her biggest challenge is trying not to hate men because so much violence and abuse comes from them. The sisters support lesbian nuns. Brigid sits on a diocese board that is trying to incorporate a program for homosexuals in Catholic schools.

"We're lucky in this diocese," Jane said. "They know that there's a radical dimension of St. Joseph Sisters. The bishop is quite aware that we're alive and kicking."

The Sisters of St. Joseph, a papal order founded in France in 1650, technically answers only to the Pope, who has threatened excommunication for Catholics who disagree with Church doctrine. Several theologians have lost jobs at Catholic universities; books challenging Church laws have been banned. In 1999, the Pope personally ordered two Americans, a Catholic sister and a priest, to stop their decades-long church ministry to homosexuals.

Such papal edicts don't have much clout with the McDonalds.

"The Gospel says to do as Jesus showed us," explained Brigid. "To stand up and speak out for justice and for people who can't speak for themselves—the powerless and the voiceless. I don't see the Pope excommunicating nuns. It's a vague threat to keep people in line."

TRANSCENDING THE VOWS

Although I'd come to suspect that traditional vows mean little to many modern nuns, few sisters dare to confront the foundations of Catholic religious life like the McDonalds. Having lived both traditional and modern interpretations, their opinions carry a great deal of credibility with me. While so many sisters lament the demise of religious life, the McDonalds suggest that sisters shouldn't take vows because they are irrelevant. Indeed, the McDonald sisters' modern definitions of the vows hardly seem exclusive to celibate women. Their message is straightforward: follow your conscience, be faithful to your commitments, and simplify your life.

Modern theologians have also reworked interpretations of the vows. Poverty, they say, is not so much about sacrificing or depriving oneself of wealth and property as it is about caring and being responsible for the earth. Chastity now stresses the basic human need for intimacy and friendship without emphasizing sexuality. Obedience is universally viewed as a need to listen attentively to others and one's inner voice.

Adjusting the vows isn't heresy. It's recognizing that religious life and the vows aren't stagnant and have, in fact, evolved over centuries. Initially, virgins and widows dedicated themselves to prayer, meditation on scriptures, and good works, but didn't take vows. They maintained celibate lives because they understood themselves to be spouses of Christ. When the vows were first adopted by the devout in the fifth century, they were about holy people separating themselves from the world. In the Middle Ages, those who professed the vows were deemed more holy than lay Christians. Religious life was called "the life of perfection" because nuns took a superior path of chastity, obedience, and poverty, while other Christians were bound only to the observance of the commandments. Vatican II's theology viewed the world not as something to be escaped from but rather to be immersed in, living as a sign of God's presence. Religious vows were reinterpreted as a way of life instead of part of a religious caste. Vowed women were deemed as equal to married or single women.

Today, many sisters have transcended those definitions, and they feel the emphasis of the vows doesn't reflect their modern spirituality. The McDonald sisters stress that connecting one's daily work with one's beliefs marks a fully developed theology and the path to true happiness. Finding pleasure in life is about discovering the vocation that feeds the heart and the soul. No amount of money, they insist, can act as a substitute.

There were times when I questioned whether the sisters' protesting lifestyle was as effective as their former prayerful lives or their work with drug addicts and runaways. But the sisters made the point that standing up for one's conscience has little to do with effecting immediate change.

"The [protesting] vigils give me meaning in life," Kate told me. "I can't imagine getting up in the morning and not having some driving force that really fits in with my belief system—gospel values, justice. Everything I do comes out of my faith values."

So, standing on a bridge holding signs against the United States attacking Iraq isn't entirely about changing foreign policy. It is about the sisters being faithful to their beliefs, about following their commitments and consciences, about finding joy in life, and about supporting their community. In other words, it is about following the modern interpretation of their vows.

12

THE MYSTIC MOTHER SUPERIOR

BENEDICTINE SISTERS OF PERPETUAL ADORATION IN
TUCSON, ARIZONA

"If you don't believe there's a Higher Power, then this life is the biggest waste of time you can possibly imagine."

—PRIORESS DAWN MILLS

I arrived at the imposing Spanish-style monastery with its pale-pink walls, baroque façade, and orange-tiled roof expecting an elderly, habited mother superior. But the woman who opened the steel door at the Benedictine monastery in Tucson could have been comedian Louie Anderson's twin sister: portly, with rosy cheeks, an enormous smile, and auburn hair. Her plain black skirt and long black blouse seemed too casual for the prioress of a semicloistered monastery. She didn't even wear a veil.

"Hi. I'm Dawn Mills," she said, extending her hand.

She grabbed my heaviest suitcase, lugged it to the cavernous basement, then sat to catch her breath. "I'll let you unpack and then we'll have that 'what's a woman like you doing in a place like this' conversation."

I liked her already. At forty-seven, she was one of the youngest mother superiors I'd ever met, and her attitude suggested that she didn't take her superior title too seriously. She didn't seem the type to unravel if she discovered wrinkled doilies in the parlor or worry that the only place she had to put the visiting journalist was in the spooky cellar, a room filled with hospital beds, several of which I was certain were last used by dearly departed sisters.

Minutes later I joined Dawn in the front parlor. Propping her legs on a stool and rocking back in her chair, she appeared to be settling in for a long while. She spoke so loudly that at first I thought she might have a hearing problem. But it was merely one aspect of her abundant personality.

Dawn complained that women considering religious life today seem unable to commit. These "monastery groupies" spend years flitting from one order to another, searching for the "perfect community." Such women, she said, miss the point: Entering an order is making a commitment to God and growing with that community, not meeting personal requirements or trying to find a community that fits a woman's lifestyle. Becoming a nun is about transformation.

"There's a lot of comparison shopping going on these days," she said. "I don't think it's particularly productive. It's like the dating life. Do they ever get to know anyone or stay with someone long enough? If they are always waiting for the better offer—the next man or the next monastery or the next woman, for that matter—can they fall in love or are they always going to be shopping? There is no such thing as a perfect man or a perfect monastery."

In some ways, Dawn was summing up my last four years trekking from order to order, monastery to monastery, trying to determine whether religious life was still a viable choice for modern women. And if so, which community offered the most relevant lifestyle.

I felt so perplexed about religious life: Active sisters' ministries fed my social justice aspirations but their lifestyle didn't feed my spirituality; at contemplative monasteries, I felt immensely at peace, but after a few days, idleness set in and I thought my talents and energies could be better used elsewhere. I understood why picking a community was so tedious and why some sisters jumped back and forth from contemplative to active orders. The lifestyles balanced each other. But living one style indefinitely seemed stifling.

The closest I'd come so far to finding a blend of social justice and prayer was the Visitation monastery in Minneapolis—the contemplative sisters who befriend inner-city poor. But even their work seemed unfocused and disparate. I also admired the Benedictines in St. Joseph, Minnesota, who run a college where the sisters are professors and theologians. Sharp intellectuals, they aren't afraid to challenge traditional thinking. But in their rural environment, they seem isolated. Even their students complain that the sisters' lives appear irrelevant.

The McDonald sisters had heightened my awareness of greater world issues and, like them, I began to seriously question whether taking vows or following rituals of religious life were worthy endeavors. Is religious life an ancient concept that should end? What is the point of spending hours kneeling before crackers in an elaborate tabernacle when people are starving and homeless?

I'd shown up at Prioress Dawn's doorstep doubting, questioning even the basic premise of an order whose name stood for the religious practice that I considered the most frivolous—the round-the-clock adoration of the Eucharist. Later, I would come to understand that encountering Sister Dawn and her Perpetual Adoration monastery was no coincidence.

SISTERS OF A DIFFERENT GENRE

When Dawn decided to become a nun at age twenty-two, she longed for an order that allowed women to sleep in. Knowing this desire was impractical, since all orders had morning prayers and usually morning mass, she settled on three criteria.

"I said to God: 'I want a contemplative community, but they can't be cloistered because I do not have the nerve to tell my mother I can't come home, and we have to sit and talk through a grille from now on,'" she said, speaking in an almost theatrical flair. "'Also, none of this getting up at three o'clock in the morning. Three o'clock is a fine way to end a beautiful evening. It is a lousy way to start a day. And no vegetarian communities; I am not giving up meat and men in the same lifetime! If I can't have a man, I get to eat steak.'"

She let the words hang in the air as she tried to read my face for the shock she, no doubt, was accustomed to receiving from women unfamiliar with her progressive attitude. When she was elected in 1995, Dawn was the youngest nun in not only her community but the entire order. A hip superior at forty-two, Dawn was unlike any who had ever ruled at the sixty-five-year-old Tucson monastery. Leading the aging community with a sardonic wit and contemporary philosophies, Dawn quickly developed a reputation among area orders as a woman who said whatever she thought, sometimes startling sisters with her candor. Her Tucson sisters viewed her as a bit quirky, a collector of plastic unicorns and spiders and a *Star Trek* fan.

"I've been a Trekker longer than I've been a Catholic," Dawn proudly told me, spreading her fingers to outline a V. "I mean I didn't become a Catholic until 1972, and I've been watching *Star Trek* since 1964. Never missed a series or a movie."

Dawn is the kind of mother superior I would have wanted had I chosen to become a nun. She makes religious life seem an adventure, a personal journey. There aren't all the hierarchal levels I heard about from other nuns who speak of God in reverential tones as though they fear Him, worship Him, adore Him, but do not consider themselves pals. Dawn talks as though chatting with God is as casual as gossiping with girlfriends. She makes God seem like a friend and not the Darth Vader figure so many religious people portray Him to be. She also isn't afraid of tackling the big questions and seeking out answers that are more realistic than theoretical. She is a friend of gay clergy and a public advocate for married priests and women priests. Dawn hasn't swallowed Catholicism or religious life whole. Her spirituality incorporates the vows in an intellectual, philosophical way that makes sense. She has transcended the institutional culture and makes the vows both personal and relevant. In short, she is the coolest mother superior I've ever met, and in that moment I wanted to become a nun just so I could hang out with her.

The next afternoon, as the sisters lined up in the hallway outside their modern refectory, I noticed a cryptic message scrawled on the sisters' blackboard: *Sister Rose Marcella died at 2:30 a.m. at the St. Louis monastery.* Sisters told me that Sister Rose had lived at the Tucson monastery ten years earlier, before suffering a stroke that put her in the order's nursing care in St. Louis. The sisters were planning a memorial service that afternoon.

As we entered the cafeteria the sisters' somber mood changed. Several were decorating tables and setting out bottles of wine and sparkling cider to mark the feast of St. Hildegard, honoring a twelfth-century German Benedictine abbess. It was also the subprioress's birthday. Sisters were laughing and elbowing each other with stories. As I got closer to the food buffet, I saw the main entrée was filet mignon. I had never eaten steak at any monastery, not even chicken-fried steak or pepper steak or some other less expensive cut. But here the sisters were feasting on filet mignon! Dawn wasn't kidding when she insisted that in giving up men, she got to eat steak.

Many sisters poured themselves glasses of cabernet sauvignon; some stuck to the nonalcoholic bubbly. We sang happy birthday to the subprioress and happy name's day to the sister named after St. Hildegard. Then we ate sugary birthday cake and fell into a jovial mood, with sisters recounting stricter days when they'd had to seek permission for everything from an overbearing mother superior. Now they negotiated what they wanted.

Despite their conservative name, the Benedictine Sisters of Perpetual Adoration had quietly adopted a more modern lifestyle; their spirituality had outgrown their traditional practices. Originating in Switzerland, the order arrived in the United States in 1874. They established several houses in the Midwest but made their foundation in Tucson in 1935 because they needed a warm, dry climate for sisters with tuberculosis. While most orders of Adoration Sisters maintain twenty-four-hour vigils in front of the Blessed Sacrament—at least one sister always kneeling before the blessed communion host—the Benedictine Adoration Sisters gave up that arduous tradition in 1987. Now, in addition to two hours of private prayer, each sister spends half an hour a day of her choosing before the gilded box, sitting, kneeling, or standing. The sisters believe that living out their dedication to the Eucharist means more than saying ritualized prayers in marathon kneeling sessions.

The crowd in the refectory had slimmed down, and someone announced that the memorial for Sister Rose was about to begin. The women gathered in their private prayer room. Sister Rose's picture was placed on a table beside a vase of flowers. Nearby were some of the items she'd often used: knitting needles, yarn balls, and a rose pruner. The sisters sang "Jesus Remember Me," the Twenty-seventh Psalm (God Is My Light and Salvation), and the Twenty-third Psalm (The Lord Is My Shepherd). Several older sisters dabbed their eyes with handkerchiefs as the sisters shared stories about Rose, not all of them complimentary.

They described her as a born musician. One sister told how Rose would be very depressed in the infirmary, but if a workman arrived, she suddenly snapped out of her morose mood. An eighty-two-year-old sister wept as she said Rose had been her companion for many years. Others recalled Rose as having "big fits of anger" and suffering from migraine headaches. Another sister remembered Rose saying she needed to be transferred from the order's various communities every two years because she felt she had worn out her welcome.

"I'm glad she's at peace now," one sister said. Then the sisters filed out silently.

I felt an overwhelming sadness, even though I'd never met this sister. The portrait her sisters gave reminded me of many nuns I had met. It was truly admirable that these sisters depicted her as a human being with faults and not as a saint.

Sister Patricia Vereb, who had entered the order ten years earlier, walked out of the prayer room with me. She didn't know Sister Rose but stifled tears nonetheless. Patricia was young—fifty-four—with long gray-and-white hair and flowing, hand-sewn skirts.

"I honestly believe any one of our sisters who dies goes straight to heaven," she said. "Of course I don't believe in hell. I'm not sure what to do with purgatory. I'm beginning to think we live purgatory."

Patricia admitted that she often feels a tinge of guilt that not everyone can live in a monastery, spending hours alone praying every day, listening to scriptures and the Benedictine Rule read at meals. Yet, even she struggles to get in half the private prayer time required. As one of the youngest sisters—there are only eight sisters under the age of seventy—she often is asked by older sisters to do things they can't do, such as sorting out computer glitches or driving to the store.

It seemed paradoxical that a woman who had initially approached religious life wondering what it would be like to pray all day, now has difficulty finding the time to pray her allotted time. "Being a contemplative nun doesn't mean you pray all day," Patricia explained. "It's being able to go through your day where the majority of the time, everything you

Sister Patricia Vereb holding an incense container in the chapel

do is a prayer, which to me means I don't have to have everything my way but be open to the grace of God."

At dinner, the sisters were still in their feasting mode. We ate deli sandwiches with shrimp cocktail, potato salad, fancy cheese and crackers, ice cream and cookies—and drank Heineken beer in honor of the subprioress, born of Danish immigrant parents and a Heineken lover. The sisters gave her gag birthday presents, including a small Christmas tree laden with internet disks that twirled on a windup microwave tray.

Afterward, they gathered for their last prayer of the day, compline. A revolving disco ball, set in the corner, cast shades of purple, pink, yellow, red, and blue across the sisters' pale faces. The dancing light reminded me of a nightclub, making the statues of Joseph and Mary look overdressed in their flowing tunics. As the sisters sang "beddy-bye tunes," psalms for a good night's sleep, I stared at the disco ball, mesmerized by the light and the murmur of chanting voices.

A HOUSEWIFE FOR GOD

The story of Sister Dawn seemed like a tale of mythic proportions. The more she described her intimate conversations with deities, the coincidental events she portrayed as God intervening in her life, the more I began to see Dawn in the tradition of Saint Teresa of Avila, Saint Catherine of Genoa, Saint Catherine of Siena—nuns who had numerous visions and seemed to converse regularly with God. Occasionally I had met sisters who described mystical experiences, and, certainly, many "calling" stories had mysterious elements to them. But Dawn was the first nun I met who claimed she had felt God's presence throughout her life, directing her, leading her, whispering reassurances, and providing answers. I sensed I had, indeed, discovered a modern mystic.

Dawn grew up in Hobart, Indiana, thirty miles south of the Chicago Loop, the daughter of Buck and Dotty Mills, religious parents who weren't into going to church. Nonpracticing Methodists, her parents decorated their home in religious art: a Madonna hung in the living room, Solomon's Head of Christ appeared above her parents' bed, Christ at Gethsemane graced the hallway. There were Bibles in every room. Her mother frequently read scriptures.

"I have memories of playing with Jesus that go back to being two years old," Dawn said. "Chasing butterflies with Jesus among purple thistle, yellow dandelions, and white Queen Anne's lace. There were yellow imperial swallowtails and monarch butterflies and those little white butterflies. I don't know if I could see Jesus. I could probably hear Him, which has been always pretty much part of my life."

At three years old, Dawn announced she wanted to attend Sunday school—she was not sure where she got the idea. Not thrilled with the prospect of having to get up early on Sunday mornings, her parents allowed her to walk with the children next door to the neighborhood church. So Dawn became "Presbyterian by geography."

A few years later, when Dawn's kindergarten teacher asked her what she wanted to be when she grew up, Dawn replied with conviction, "I'm going to be a housewife in God's house."

"Now, it's not that I knew there were such things," Dawn said. "We are talking about 1957, 1958. I knew I wanted to live in God's house and to live in His presence and to tend His house and be available to entertain when He had company. Later on in my life, after I got to religious life, is when it kind of hit me: Gosh, I did do that."

Her father died of a heart attack when Dawn was ten years old, and her family was beset with financial worries. So Dawn turned to the constant force that had been there for her. She'd always had a sense that God would take care of her. That's when Dawn says she heard God say to her in prayer, "I will be your Father."

At fourteen, Dawn took a part-time job at the public library, where she often read books with titles like *What Is a Methodist?* or *What Is a Baptist?* She began attending friends' churches, visiting twenty-seven churches and studying seventeen denominations in high school. She believed that God had given her a creed, and instead of adopting a church's beliefs, she needed to find one that believed as she did. Despite her seemingly universal search for a church, Dawn stayed away from the Roman Catholics.

"Everybody knew the Roman Catholics were weird," she said, rolling her eyes. "All of my Catholic friends were neurotic. All of this incredible guilt by the time they were seven. And God doesn't talk to them because they had to go to confession before they could go to communion because by the time they were seven they had already committed too many worldly sins. I mean, what garbage! You know! What a horrible thought!"

Meanwhile, her relationship with God intensified. While high school classmates protested Vietnam, Dawn felt the world's problems were too big to have human solutions. "I went into a dark, quiet place, and I would get God in the corner and say, 'Do something!' I would go straight to the top! I would be praying. And I had a sense that that did more than anything else."

At sixteen, she felt God began dropping suggestions at her feet—literally. One night Dawn was trying to straighten the magazine shelves at the library where she worked. Instead of getting a ladder and piling the magazines on the top shelves, she pitched them as high as she could until an avalanche of magazines fell on top of her. At her feet, a *Cosmopolitan* lay opened to a story about religious retreats for lay women. The only retreat house listed in the Chicago area was one run by a group of Cenacle nuns. She thought what she really needed to do was spend eight days in silence at the retreat and then she could really hear what God was telling her.

Dawn had her mother drive her the seventy miles to the monastery, where the nuns assumed she was trying to escape problems at home. But Dawn assured the sisters that she was simply there to listen to God. She didn't know it was the other voices she heard that would strongly affect her.

"I heard them saying the Divine Office [psalms], and I fell in love," she remembered, closing her eyes as though she were hearing them again. "I went to mass. And it made such abundant sense to me. And I had the gift of faith and the real presence of the Eucharist just sort of handed to me right there. And it was the first time I understood there were housewives in God's house."

While she was with the Cenacle nuns, God offered her an invitation.

"God and I are having this conversation," Dawn said and then began whispering as she recounted their dialogue. " 'This place is magnificent,' I said. 'Why aren't there women beating the doors down to do this?' And God said to me, 'Well, would you like to do this?' And I said, 'Excuse me, I'm Presbyterian.' And God said, 'We could fix that.' And I said, 'Don't hurry.' And yet I knew at that encounter that there was a part of me that had come home."

After her retreat, Dawn appeared a changed person to her family and friends. Dawn knew she was on a religious high, but she was mature enough not to make any rash decisions. That year, the library moved to a new building across the street from a Catholic church. Every day after school, Dawn spent two hours in front of the church's tabernacle before heading to the library. After she graduated high school in 1971, Dawn began attending Catholic church services and taking instruction. Eventually she was baptized.

At the time, she and her best friend, "a good Catholic boy," had talked of getting married. The two attended church together, arriving for seven o'clock mass two hours early so they could pray and then staying after for confession.

"I was in love with him and he was in love with me and it was very serious," she said. "He also knew I was hungry for God in a way he couldn't satisfy. I wasn't choosing between God and Jim. I was choosing between God coming with me in my sharing my life with Jim or God and I having a level of intimacy that I would not be able to accomplish as Jim's significant other. I knew that Jim was probably the greatest gift God could give me. But me being greedy, I went for the giver instead of the gift."

After a year of frequents visits to the Benedictine Sisters of Perpetual Adoration near Chicago, Dawn applied to join. She had just turned twenty-two, the youngest age the order would accept. But she needed to raise several thousand dollars before she could enter; postulants paid their own personal travel, phone, and medical expenses until taking their vows.

One day, Dawn went to church, kneeled before the tabernacle, and whispered to God in her informal manner: "I need the money."

Fifteen minutes later, her priest knelt beside her.

"I understand you could use some money," he said.

"Where did you hear that?" Dawn asked, looking around her as if there were a hidden microphone.

"Actually, someone came to the rectory yesterday and left a donation for you, to help with your expenses at the monastery," he answered.

An anonymous woman, the priest explained, had left a modest donation for Dawn. Apparently the woman had considered entering a monastery when she was young but didn't have the required dowry. The priest told Dawn that it wouldn't be enough. He took out a large ledger that listed church donations. He tallied Dawn's contributions and then wrote a check for every dime she had ever given.

"That ought to cover it," he said, handing her the check.

In 1975, Dawn and four other women entered the Benedictine Sisters of Perpetual Adoration. She would be the only one who stayed, though she experienced an intense period of questioning during her novitiate, the stage before taking vows.

Her year-long crisis began in October 1977 after a thirty-day retreat in preparation for taking her temporary vows. She began to have numerous questions about her beliefs and her faith. Like most young nuns, Dawn struggled with the meaning of the vows.

"You may have been doctor, lawyer, Indian chief, and then nine months later, you are Toilet Cleaner First Class who has to ask permission to make a telephone call to her mother. It's relearning our basic value system. What does poverty mean? What does simplicity mean? What does enclosure mean?"

Dawn even questioned her concept of God. She realized she had made God into a father figure, perhaps to replace the father she'd lost. Dawn had pictured God as a separate being. But during her thirty-day retreat that image faded and she began to see God as inseparable and permeable, in persons, places, things, and experiences. Suddenly God became much bigger than Dawn had ever allowed Him to be.

"There is a process in the spiritual life where idols have to fall," she said. "Where the God who is so much bigger than the God we have allowed into our hearts shows up and explodes both our idols and our hearts."

Dawn was speaking about what is known in religious circles as "the dark night of the soul." It is a time when a religious woman loses her innocence. It's an awakening when she realizes that the portrait of God she has carried around in her head her entire life is not accurate. She begins to question who God is and if there even is a single entity who is God. She finds what she thought was a rock solid relationship with God is now slipping like quicksand beneath her. She questions her faith. She reexamines her dedication and her motivations. Sometimes this coming-of-age happens before a woman takes her vows. Sometimes it happens much later in her religious life. And sometimes it never happens. But the sisters say that if a woman is to mature spiritually, she must come face-to-face with the image she has assigned to God.

Prioress Dawn Mills

Dawn's explosion killed off the concept of a great God "out there" overlooking the universe. It was the most important turning point of her spiritual life. For the first time, she began to doubt whether she was really called to religious life.

"I experienced a great absence of God. I did not doubt the existence of God; I doubted the goodness of God. I doubted that God loved me. I doubted that God was loving. I was fighting with the question of whether I had created a loving God out of my need for a loving God. I questioned whether any of the spiritual and mystical experiences that I'd had to that time were real or was it all some kind of fantasy that I'd convinced myself of."

Dawn was so confused by her experience that she wrote her former boss and asked if she could have her old job back. She contacted a friend to see if there was a place she could live if she decided to leave. She also called her mother, who had always told her she could come home any-time she wanted. But this time her mother informed her she couldn't come home. Dawn was shocked by her mother's reaction and believed God had inspired her mother to act contrary to her nature, to tell her to stay.

"I figured a God who could convert my mother about this was not a guy to be handled lightly. So I was like, All right, I'll sit tight and see how this works out—and ride it out."

So Dawn stayed. Just before taking her vows, Dawn went on another retreat where she began to see through her confusion. A new kind of God appeared to her.

"The joy returned. God was bigger than I had ever imagined. No magic wands, but a love that won't quit."

Having heard the doubts of a mystic, a woman who had maintained an intimate connection with God her entire life, I thought this might be the best opportunity to confront my own misgivings about God and religious life. If there was anyone who could help me make sense out of what I'd experienced over the past four years, it was this oracle sitting before me. For all I knew, God had led me to this irreverent superior. So I began setting out my doubts.

How could she believe that shutting herself inside a monastery helped humanity?

"If you don't believe there's a Higher Power, then this life is the biggest waste of time you can possibly imagine," Dawn said. "If there is a Divine Energy that runs through the universe, then it seems that somehow making contact, plugging into it, channeling, connecting with that energy and bringing it in contact with humans has value."

She cited studies that have shown patients who are prayed for, whether they know it or not, heal faster, have less complications.

"I think that's an indication that prayer does affect the real world. It's not just this thing that people do in a corner. There is an effect. It seems that a monastery like this, as a center of peace, radiates peace to the neighborhood."

But if God is good, then doesn't He already know what we need? Why do we need to ask, beg?

"God is all knowing," she said. "God doesn't need me to ask Him to be nice to anybody. It's not like God needs to be lobbied. What God seems to want is for me to love you. God seems to want me to care what happens to you. I don't know if my caring actually changes the electrical magnetic field or whatever on this planet. One of the things God seems to have done was to give human beings free will. The only thing we can give God is love. And the only love that's really authentic is love that is freely given. God seems to have made some kind of covenant with the universe to keep his paws off human free will. God can knock, God can nudge, God can inspire. But God usually does not stop a speeding bullet. God usually does not create new train tracks because of a computer glitch. God usually does not hold an airplane in the air when the mechanics mess up a job. I believe that God will prick consciences but I don't believe God will disarm all the nuclear weapons in the world without our cooperation."

So what happens if at the end of her time on earth she discovers that those crackers she spent all this time adoring are not Christ's body, but just crackers? I asked, probing even deeper, knowing I was verging on the heretical.

"In the best sense, the sisters are praying before an icon, not an idol," she said. "God knows the intentions of their hearts, that their intention is to love God. God is omnipresent, all knowing, and all loving. Whether we pray before the host of the Eucharist or pray before a cross or whether we pray before the rising sun, God knows. We're the ones who need the image. God sees the heart and it will not be wasted. Personally I happen to believe the cracker is Jesus."

Why do you think it is so hard for us to believe in this ethereal power?

"I think the fear of believing has to do with fear of commitment. I have to commit to a church that is both human and divine, one that has both saints and sinners and very often all wrapped up in the same person and often sitting in my choir stall. My belief is based on experience," she added. "God shows up, sits on the edge of my bed and says, 'Good morning.' And I say, 'I don't want to get up.' My God is more real for me than you are. And I'm willing to pause at your existence. God was here before you showed up. God will be here when you are gone. You have to believe in some of what you see and some of what your heart knows."

But what value do religious rituals have when there are so many real needs in the world? Is it selfish for a nun of her intellect and energy to shut herself up in the monastery, praying? The questions rolled off my tongue one after the other. I had longed for a modern nun young enough to relate to contemporary problems, someone who could understand my doubts and my misgivings about religious life and, at the same time, someone who was well established in her spirituality to answer my questions intelligently.

Dawn didn't take offense at my queries. She had come of age during the radical 1960s and had witnessed much of the revolutions that aspired to change the world.

"We were going to eliminate all racial prejudice. We were going to stop the war and clean up the ecology and give equality to all women in all places," she said. "You will notice that there is still war, still discrimination and hunger and poverty and all those other things. Justice is not necessarily going to come from what we do."

If Dawn had wished, she could have opted for a life of social work without becoming a nun. At the time she entered the monastery, the Catholic Worker house was drawing hundreds of politically active young Catholics who wanted to reach out to the disenfranchised. While Dawn valued that work, she realized it only helped a limited number of people—a sentiment I had heard from so many contemplative nuns. Dawn believed that changing the world required connecting with the Divine.

"I decided to get a job where I could badger the boss. I decided to become a lobbyist of the highest level," she said.

Despite knowing monastic nuns who at times feel guilty that they aren't doing more physically with the poor, Dawn has never felt that way. To her, joining a monastery and taking on the vows is the ultimate self-sacrifice for God. It is a witness to the world that God has enormous power in people's lives, so much so that they will give up everything the world claims is important.

"This is what Christ asked us to do: to lay down our lives for others. We have laid our lives on the line here. We have said: 'Getting ahead in this world is not all it's cracked up to be.'"

While sisters have modified the meaning of their vows over the years, Dawn believes professing such commitments still holds value. Poverty, chastity, and obedience fly in the face of what most humans strive for: sex, power, and money, she said. The vows confront shallow desires. They provide a countercultural witness that says humans can be happy without material attainments.

The wording of the vows, though, isn't so important to Dawn. In fact, the specific vows she took as a Benedictine nun don't even mention chastity or poverty, although they are implicit with her other vows: stability, conversion of life, and obedience.

"No matter what the wording of the vows is, it is much less about the minutiae and more about the total gift of self to God. There is much less childishness about it. Much more maturity. The words on the contract are not really the issue. If you have to go back and read the fine print, you're in trouble."

Even the way sisters profess their vows has changed in recent years. Most orders have stopped using the mythology of a nun marrying Christ; candidates usually do not wear wedding dresses during their profession, but they are given a sign or symbol—usually the order's pin—to connote their new commitment.

"You may not have the bridal dress but it's very clear you're making a covenant and that you're taking a community and being incorporated into that community," she said. "Those things are very important."

But just because the definitions of the vows have changed doesn't mean orders should get rid of them or that the commitment from sisters is different, she said. Dawn drew a corollary between religious vows and wedding vows. While once upon a time, women routinely professed to "love, honor, and obey" their husbands, now the word "obey" is often removed from modern ceremonies and even when it isn't, many women translate the word to mean "negotiate."

"That's not so different than the kind of maturity we've also developed," Dawn said, chuckling.

Ultimately, she said, professing religious vows is about agreeing to a lifestyle that allows women to live together in community. "Community is the basis of religious life. It's people who come together to do what they feel in their hearts most drawn to do but know they can't do it alone."

So it all comes back to community. A woman seeks out a community she feels most comfortable with; she professes vows to help her achieve a deeper commitment to God, which ultimately leads to a richer relationship with the community. It becomes a circular movement, a circular spirituality. One begets the other.

If religious life is truly relevant, then which form is the best? How does a woman know whether she should commit to an active or contemplative community?

"A lot has to do with personality types," Dawn explained. "Those of us who are the intuitive/feelers, we want more rituals, more devotions. People who are more sensate/judges and thinkers, they want less of it."

Dawn compared her religious commitment to the biblical story of Mary of Bethany, who poured out a jar of fragrant oil on Jesus. "Sometimes the most dramatic statement one can make is pouring out everything. It's a wake-up call that cannot be ignored," she said. "My life is that fragrant oil being poured out on Jesus."

DEMYSTIFIED

I had come full circle. While I had initially thought choosing a community was a sister's first step in religious life, I had discovered that ultimately it is her perpetual journey. As a nun matures in her understanding and commitment to the vows, she also develops a deeper relationship with her community and to God. The vows merely provide her with a foundation for that connection. Because the vows are so vague, sisters have been able to modify them according to the era. And since they have existed for nearly fifteen hundred years, perhaps they aren't as irrelevant as I had begun to believe. Just as every married couple works out the specifics of their commitment, religious women work out their relationships with their communities. A mature nun has to come up with her own words, her own definitions. In the end, they collectively mean the same thing: commitment, love, community.

To me, becoming a nun is simply a choice, a lifestyle. Choosing an active ministry is akin to choosing a career. Opting for monastic life is, indeed, similar to being a housewife, a comparison so many nuns had made. Certainly one could argue that sisters have given up sex, riches, and freedom. But Dawn, like many nuns, is quick to point out that theirs is not the true sacrificial life.

"No one makes more sacrifices than a mother," she said. "If you really want to give up your own will, you have children. Sisters can still negotiate."

13

FINDING THE FUTURE, SEEING THE PAST

THE IMMACULATE HEART COMMUNITY AND THE IMMACULATE HEART OF MARY SISTERS IN LOS ANGELES, CALIFORNIA

"If a religious community is going to exist in the future, it's got to be radically different than the past."

—TOM MCGUINESS, IMMACULATE HEART

COMMUNITY CANDIDATE

The high-pitched notes of "Alleluia" floated through the dimly lit chapel, a rustic building of stone blocks and wooden beams. A couple hundred people filled the pews, with several left standing amid the shadows of flickering candles. They'd come to witness the Immaculate Heart Community induct its newest member, Angie Dickson. Like the secular group she was joining, Angie had given up her religious vows thirty years earlier.

Angie appeared at the back of the chapel looking regal in a purple-and-rose gown trimmed in gold under a sinuous cloak. She walked down the aisle carrying a bundle of wheat to the altar, positioned before a glass wall overlooking an old twisted oak tree. Then she sat next to her partner, a tall blond woman. The two held hands throughout the ceremony, occasionally glancing at each other and offering supportive smiles. Two members encircled Angie in sage smoke. Several candidates entered the chapel holding banners representing earth, water, air, and fire. Others beat on drums while a woman sang an Indian song. Someone gave a short lesson on ecology. Then Angie stood up and, before the large gathering, told her story.

She'd spent her first seven years of adulthood living as a nun. In 1970—the same year that most of the Immaculate Heart of Mary Sisters in Los Angeles liberated themselves from the Church's male hierarchy and formed this new secular community—Angie left her teaching order, the Little Servant Sisters of the Immaculate Conception in New Jersey. Over the years, she longed for a community of women. Then five years ago she attended a solstice ceremony in Newport Beach, where she met Lucia Van Ruiten, a former nun and an Immaculate Heart member, who introduced her to the group.

"I have changed," said Angie, now a fifty-five-year-old psychologist. Short and incredibly thin, she keeps her silver hair closely cropped and wears elegant dangling jewelry. She was not the community's first openly lesbian candidate, but she was the first to include her partner and lesbian friends in the ceremony and celebration. "I'm much more conscientious and focused on what's important: ecofeminism and inclusivity. I'm grateful to honor Robin, my life partner. She did all the decorations."

Though most commitment ceremonies include a mass, Angie kept hers secular, honoring the earth and indigenous people. No longer a Catholic, Angie sees herself as a "post-Christian" who strongly connects with Buddhism. She is attracted to Immaculate Heart's feminist spirituality because she feels a need to be part of something larger. Angie believes the community teaches her more about the environment than she can ever learn on her own.

In front of the crowd, Angie promised to be faithful to the Gospel, to uphold the community's decrees, to honor its goals, and to give of her "time, talent, and money." Then board members placed a community ring on her finger, handed her a Bible and the group's decrees, and swore her in as a full member. Angie turned to the audience and yelled, "Yahoo!"

Immaculate Heart Community members look decidedly different from their nun counterparts who still wear habits and veils and who have chosen to remain under the Church's auspices in a separate, vowed order called the Immaculate Heart of Mary. The lay community has expanded to include former nuns, several families with children, a priest, and a former cop—the kind of diverse community envisioned three decades earlier when 440 Immaculate Heart sisters, tired of fighting with the L.A. Archdiocese and the Vatican over control of their order, chose permanently to sever ties with the Catholic Church and dispensed with their vows. They felt their spiritual development was more important than their Church-approved status.

Although it seemed doubtful that a lay community not bound by religious vows would survive, it now has 165 members, twenty-two candidates—including families and men—and another half dozen others asking to join. Meanwhile, the fifty-three sisters who remained habited have dwindled to fewer than twenty; no one has joined in over thirteen years.

At least twice a year the secular branch meets here at their retreat center nestled in the foothills of the Santa Ynez Mountains in Santa Barbara. The center, which once served as the order's novitiate house, is a collection of lodges, a large stone and timber church, tennis courts, a swimming pool, a hermitage, a massage room, and a meditation chapel. The retreats give members a chance to get together apart from their volunteer work in Los Angeles.

Members support themselves financially. Each year they make out a contract with the community detailing their financial and time commitments. The community cares for the former nuns who were retired or near retirement when the order split. They also maintain four institutions:

an art gallery, a spirituality center, and two community centers in impoverished Los Angeles neighborhoods.

Immaculate Heart candidates go through a standard application process involving interviews and complete medical and psychological evaluations. Once accepted, they begin a two-year orientation. Finally, they enter the community in a commitment ceremony like Angie's.

Amid a loud clamor of excited voices, well-dressed men and women milled around hugging each other and laughing after Angie's ceremony. Young couples with infant children circulated among gray-haired women, many former nuns now wearing stunning jewelry and bright scarves. A few hip, urbane women in jeans and boots quickly introduced themselves to me, expecting that, like them, I was considering joining.

While I had come to check out the community, my intent was to compare how the two sides of the order were faring three decades after their historic and bitter split. After spending several days with the non-vowed community, I planned to return to Los Angeles where I was scheduled to stay with their counterparts at their Hollywood mother house. I had no idea of the disparity I would discover between the two groups.

THE REVEREND MOTHER WHO TOOK ON THE VATICAN

Among old and young members, Anita Caspary is viewed as the secular community's respected matriarch. Yet, it was difficult to associate the hobbling, thin-haired eighty-five-year-old as the former Rev. Mother Mary Humiliate, the radical superior who led her order—formerly the California Institute of the Sisters of the Most Holy and Immaculate Heart of the Blessed Virgin Mary—against the Los Angeles Archdiocese and the Vatican. In 1967, at the order's Ninth General Chapter, held at this very retreat center, Anita and her sisters decided they would discard the habit, simplify their names, suspend a fixed time for rising and retiring, and discontinue set hours for prescribed prayers. Though such changes eventually became the norm at orders across the United States, they were considered revolutionary at the time.

I had imagined Anita as a tall, blustery woman, much like some of the more forceful superiors I had faced in my travels. Instead, Anita is short and soft-spoken, with thick glasses and faltering speech. From childhood, Anita has struggled with an intense shyness and an unwillingness to face conflict. In pictures from that tumultuous period she looked like a grandmother, not a woman taking on the Catholic Church's male hierarchy.

But even before the Vatican II changes, the Immaculate Heart Sisters, and especially Anita as their leader, had been subjected to "small kinds of persecution" by Cardinal James Francis McIntyre of Los Angeles. Although the sisters owned their college, the cardinal insisted on approving lecturers and even speakers for their retreats.

"They were just annoying kinds of reprimands and threats, really," Anita remembered. "We were constantly annoyed and made sad by his constant critique of us, his constant worrying about us. It became a very hard thing to tolerate."

The scoldings intensified after Vatican II. Every time the sisters tried new habits or suits, Anita would be admonished. "He really pounced on the habit," she said. "For the cardinal it meant you were really religious or not. To him that meant you still belonged to the Church."

The sisters' battles with Cardinal McIntyre spawned coverage in the *Los Angeles Times* and other newspapers, which portrayed them as radicals in miniskirts, "stepsisters of the Church." Headlines branded them "rebel nuns."

The cardinal's criticisms and demands intensified until his ultimatum in 1968: Immaculate Heart teachers must return to wearing traditional habits or be kicked out of the archdiocese's schools. More than two hundred Immaculate Heart teachers refused. It became a showdown between the domineering cardinal and the feminist nuns. Vatican officials, summoned to investigate, suggested splitting the 540-member order. A conservative sister would lead "the Loyalists," who would revert to the order's "old" rules, the ones they had been following before they voted to update their lifestyle. Meanwhile, Anita would lead "the New Breeders," still a religious order but one in which sisters would continue to modernize.

In June 1968, members were polled as to which camp they wanted to join. About 440 sisters chose Anita's group and 53 sisters, mostly older women, chose to remain in the conservative group. But the battles with Cardinal McIntyre and the Vatican didn't stop for the modern sisters. A year after their split, the Vatican still insisted that the sisters return to the habit and follow a set schedule.

At that point, the modern sisters had had enough and threatened to become a secular society if the Vatican didn't accept their new lifestyle. Six months later, in January 1970—the same month that McIntyre stepped down as cardinal—the Vatican refused to recognize the new Immaculate Heart Community's lifestyle, and the sisters decided to become a lay community. More than 350 sisters asked to have their vows dispensed, marking the first time a religious order left the Church en masse. It remains the largest Catholic order ever in the United States to sever ties with the Vatican.

Anita Caspary

The lay Immaculate Heart Community still considered themselves Catholic in mission, at least at first. They had merely gotten rid of what they saw as the male tyranny trying to rule their lives and interfering with what they saw as Vatican II's mandate to modernize. Amazingly enough, a year after they left the Church's auspices, Los Angeles's new cardinal asked the former nuns to return to teach in the archdiocese schools. By then, most were already employed in the public schools.

When Anita and her sisters were dispensed from their vows, she was fifty-four years old. Although some of her former sisters married, Anita never did. Her lifestyle as a single woman, in many ways, mirrored the life she'd lived as a nun for thirty-three years; she lived simply and continued teaching. When she retired, she moved into Kenmore House, the residence the community had established for their former nuns who hadn't worked in the public sector long enough to have retirement funds.

Because it was never the sisters' intention to split from Church rule and the changes that Anita ushered in became routine at most religious orders, I asked if she ever regretted being dispensed from her vows.

"No! Not at all! No! This seemed like the only way we could remain a community," said Anita, who lost personal friends because of the move. "This was a late decision and one that came very, very painfully because when we made our vows as young people we said it was forever. And to change that, in the eyes of the Catholic world, is like to condemn us. The Catholic public, who was so educated in one point of view, saw us as heretics. There were lots of people critical of us who said, 'Five to ten years, you're going to be gone.'"

There were some former sisters, though, who wanted to keep their vows. For them, the vows represented the essence of their lives. They had lived by the tenets of poverty, chastity, and obedience so long that they didn't want to give them up. Anita told these women they could make private vows. But she doesn't believe many did. The greater problem for the new community was making the older women feel secure, to know that they would be taken care of as they aged and couldn't work.

Eventually, half of those who opted for the new secular society left. While Anita and other leaders believed the Holy Spirit led them, Anita often lay awake at night worrying: Why were people leaving? Would there be anybody left? Didn't they think the idea was workable? Many former sisters felt disenfranchised. They struggled to define who they were without the vows and the title "Sister." Some felt fatigued at having to explain their position to Catholics who blamed them for the thirty-six Catholic schools that had closed during the standoff with the cardinal.

No longer living in convents, the lay community was spread out in apartments and rented houses throughout Los Angeles. The sisters thought other progressive orders would follow them in breaking off from Rome, but only one other order did.

Once the Immaculate Heart Community became noncanonical, they had to redraw their boundaries again and again. First they let in non-Catholic Christians. Although they feared men would try to rule them, they opened membership to males. The few men who joined didn't stay long. Only in the last decade did the community admit openly acknowledged lesbians. Now they had their first family candidates, and there had been heated debate about opening membership to non-Christians.

"It's taken a lot of thinking and praying to think: Is this where we were meant to go?" Anita reflected. "Several years back now we admitted the first lesbian and that was a *big* decision. We had to ask ourselves: 'Are we now going to allow in people we used to condemn?' That was like a *real* turnaround. Now with families coming in, that's a whole different problem."

DISSENTION IN THE RANKS

Standing in line for dinner that night, a few "young" members complained about the amount of volunteer time board members expected them to contribute. Some were put off at the overtly lesbian influence of the commitment ceremony. Several said they would have preferred a mass.

"I'm not entirely at ease with all the lesbianism," admitted Maureen Manning, who had recently been elected to the board as the first member who was not part of the "old guard," meaning she wasn't a former Immaculate Heart nun.

"I don't know if this is an old thing stuck in my head. But you can't have inclusivity of lesbians without having inclusivity of men. And frankly I find men so much more refreshing," she said, tossing back her head and laughing. "I know tonight is a challenge for a lot of people."

When the celebratory dinner ended, we walked to the lodge, now set up like a dance hall. Chairs rimmed the floor. Tables were piled with cake and wine. A band played lively Latin music and older dance tunes. The dance floor filled with members, candidates, and Angie's lesbian friends.

One sixtyish member saw me standing on the edge of the dance floor watching what would have been typical in any gay bar: women embracing women.

"This is really strange," the member said, smoothing her coifed black hair and fingering her pearl necklace. "We've never had anything like this before. But if you say that you are inclusive, you have to live it."

Among the observers staring at the sweating, gyrating dancers were elderly women holding canes and middle-aged members reeling from the display of sexuality. A handsome middle-aged man—a candidate named John Mutz—was a popular dance partner, at first clutching the community's president and then erupting into frenzied moves with Maureen, who wasn't shy about twisting and shimmying with him.

With the average member age at sixty-nine years old, Maureen is two decades younger than most. Short and voluptuous with strawberry blond hair, she wears acrylic nails and thick mascara, hardly the stereotype of a nun. Yet, Maureen had been a nun for nearly ten years with the Sisters of the Holy Names of Jesus and Mary in Los Angeles, also a teaching order. Seven years after leaving that order, she joined the secular Immaculate Heart community.

"I was coming around when I was only thirty-five," she said. "That was a really big deal then. They thought, 'Yikes! We've got a young one! Let's get her!' At that time I had no intention of joining. I mean, I was sick of women and women's communities and women's rules and women's gigs and psycho-problems. Oh, man! I wanted no more of that!"

Maureen befriended an Immaculate Heart member in her school system and soon tagged along on retreats, resisting the attractions that were stirring within her. Then one day at mass she watched several original members receive communion and realized that most had been in their fifties when they left the security of their Church-sanctioned order. Their courage inspired her to join them. Now at forty-nine, Maureen had been a member for fifteen years.

Maureen has a hip, cocky attitude and isn't afraid to assert her opinion, a trait that often gets her into trouble. Because she wears trendy clothes and makeup, she feels she's held in lower esteem than women who dress matronly.

"They feel that I'm not in the same rhythm with the IHM tradition because I haven't been around as long as they have," she said of fellow board members. "I'm not a big in-tellectual type. The fact that I just teach grammar school is kind of looked down upon. Clearly we have a hierarchy of intellectuals."

She believes the former nuns' disapproval stems from their inabil-ity to deal with sexuality. Even though the nuns were dispensed from their vow of chastity when they formed the secular commu-nity, Maureen believes they had cut that part of themselves off for so long that they didn't know how to explore their sexuality when they were free to do so. Although some

Maureen Manning

married after the order became secularized, many did not. Of those who did marry, several quickly divorced.

"Lots of things surface when sexuality is not expressed," Maureen added. "You get people who are controlling. Other personality quirks come forward. Holding back a natural thing like sexual passion, a person becomes angry, frustrated. Some religious orders are very controlling."

Maureen's theory made sense to me. I often felt that the excruciating efforts some sisters invested in maintaining order and decorum, the em-phasis placed on neatness and completing tasks, derived from a deep-seated need to control their own and others' lives. In my view, many women chose to become nuns to dominate their environment and their temptations.

During the party, I met Lucia Van Ruiten, a former Immaculate Heart sister who had been responsible for introducing many new recruits to the community, including Angie. An artistic-looking woman, Lucia caught my attention the first time I saw her. With long black-and-silver hair pulled back into a loose bun, stunning blue eyes, and a softly weathered face, she reminded me of Georgia O'Keeffe. She always appeared in a classic black outfit, often accented by silver jewelry. That night she had draped a purple scarf around her neck. Though her family had immigrated from Holland before she was a year old, Lucia still retained a European elegancy. So it was hard to believe that after the split Lucia had spent twenty-four years teaching "tall galoots with knives" in inner-city high schools. "I loved it. I was never afraid," she claimed.

At the time of the split, Lucia was ready to divest herself of her outward nun role. "We saw so many nunny people. That's why I didn't want to be called 'Sister,' because when I looked at them in the garb, they just seemed out of it to me."

Once she was rid of the religious "baggage"—the rules and regulations that had controlled her for twenty years—Lucia was free to experiment with her spirituality. She started Jungian analysis; she studied other religions, particularly Zen Buddhism and Hinduism; and she began meditating. For her, loosening the Church's grip on her daily life allowed her to spend more time exploring her own inner convictions. "I try to give a considerable amount of my time daily to what I call the 'great inner work,' " she said.

She begins each day with silent meditation at 5 A.M. then she attends the 6:15 A.M. mass at her conservative parish, where she is an active member. She attends frequent religious retreats, including a recent silent retreat where participants meditated together eleven hours a day. She also makes time for sunrises and sunsets. It was at a recent summer solstice ceremony that Lucia met Angie. "I'm very eclectic," she said. "I hunger for where God is calling me. And that's the mystery of what it means to belong to the Catholic Church."

Still, mass remains a holy time for Lucia. Even Sundays are treated with reverence. On that day, Lucia refuses to cook or shop. "I'm very disciplined about it. Saturday night I light the candles and I call Sophia into my weekend. I'm almost like a Jewish lady."

Like many of her former sisters, Lucia often encounters stereotypes about her lay community, but she simply doesn't exert energy trying to explain that leaving Church rule doesn't mean her former sisters left the Church. "People look at you suspect," she said. "That's been the hard walk. We've been judged so severely."

Lucia Van Ruiten

Unlike some of her former sister friends who desperately wanted to marry once they were relieved of their vows, Lucia wasn't convinced that was her calling. Thirty-eight years old at the time of the split, she knew she was still young enough to marry and raise a family, but her spirituality remained her driving force.

"I didn't want to sell out," she said. "If I met a person—a man—who was on the same path I am and he had the same kind of intensity, then I'd be very open to it. But I didn't want to get involved with family life. It was just a clarity I had that I didn't want to spin my wheels."

After she was dispensed from her religious vows, Lucia developed her own definitions to replace the traditional tenets that had ruled her life since she was eighteen. For her, the vow of obedience was replaced with a commitment to listen to others. Her old vow of chastity was replaced with a call to deeply love and not be afraid of judgments. The poverty vow became a pursuit to deal with her own emptiness and to give more fully.

"The three vows took on such rich dimensions for me," she said. "And they still do. I don't think of them as the traditional vows. I mean, I want to barf when I think of 'poverty, chastity, and obedience' because I feel that in some ways they crippled a lot of people."

She remains friends with the sisters who left religious life and decided not to join their lay community. Often they ask her why she stays in the Immaculate Heart Community. "You're not any different from us," they assert. Lucia tells them, "Every meeting I go to, I'm always nudged a few inches to go further."

Despite connections with former sisters, Lucia isn't close to the nuns who remain in the conservative order, calling them "little, old warped ladies."

Lucia believes that her community is a healthy model for the future of religious orders. Traditional religious life is simply not relevant today, she said. "The mere fact that there are so few who are knocking at the doors of religious communities and there are ten here tonight and at least twenty who want to come is telling me that something is afoot."

Listening to Lucia speak of her spiritual journey, her disdain for rigid religious rules, and her aversion for the traditional role of wife and mother, I began to better understand that she and her former sisters left the Church's auspices not because they wanted sexual freedom and individual liberties—but because they wanted to live the ultimate feminist religious lives, totally devoid of any male interference. Lucia, Angie, and many others I met that weekend are deeply religious and feminist women. Even without the vows to constrain them, they didn't seek to marry or have children, but continued to pursue their religious vocations without the constant encumbrances of the Church hierarchy.

THE OLD GUARD

The next morning I ate breakfast with the community president, Mary Kirchen, and board member Lenore Navarro Dowling, both former Immaculate Heart nuns. Lenore entered in 1950 when she was nineteen, Mary at age twenty in 1966, just four years before the split. Mary had been the community's president since 1996 and worked out of their Hollywood headquarters, where walls display silkscreen art by their most famous sister, Corita Kent, best known for her "Love" postage stamp.

As a volunteer, nonprofit organization, the community answers to the state of California now, instead of the Catholic Church, Mary explained. They don't have any age or gender requirements. Their main criteria are that members "identify" with the Christian faith, are healthy, and support themselves financially. Members get together for at least two retreat weekends, one during Lent, the other at Advent. A summer assembly lasts for several days. They also offer day-long workshops, prayer group meetings, and fundraisers. Members determine how little or how much they want to be involved, she said.

Though Mary never married after the community was dispensed from its vows, Lenore married two years later. She and her husband adopted two children but later divorced. At sixty-nine, Lenore has lived a full life: a vowed nun for twenty years, then a wife, mother, and now grandmother.

The two women believe the community has only recently begun to live the diversity its leaders outlined thirty years ago. That openness was why the community was attracting new people, including families, men, and lesbians.

Lenore and Mary felt older members were having a harder time accepting families than lesbians. Five years ago, a member announced she was a lesbian at a community meeting and asked whether the others would accept her. The group assured her they did. Later, one member said she couldn't accept having lesbian members and left the community.

Despite the pains of trying to be inclusive, many members agreed that their community was evolving into what a diverse community should look like.

"Members of other religious communities, of course, have said, 'You know, we look to you. You're the model for the future,'" Mary said. "I hope we are a little tiny microcosm of what the future should look like."

The community's future membership is diverse. New candidates include families and men. One young couple, Kim and John Kelan, have two children. A middle-aged couple, Tom and Jayne McGuiness, came with their adult daughter, Megan Kerr, and son-in-law, Andy Kerr, who brought their three young children. The two generations had asked to enter as an extended family. Another candidate is an Augustinian priest, the Rev. Gary Rye, who often presides at mass at the members' retirement home. The fifth male candidate is John Mutz, now a retired Los Angeles police captain.

John met the community shortly after the Rodney King incident while he was working in the Van Nuys police division, where Immaculate Heart members run a resource center called Blythe Street.

"I was in awe of them," John remembered. "I realized how little I knew about the community that I served. They taught me skills that I hadn't ever known. They taught me a way to have a relationship that was so different. They taught me the importance of just being in living rooms and meeting places with people."

Retired for more than a year, John still looks like a cop, with his angular tanned face, slicked-back gray hair, and square shoulders. At fifty-one, he's ruggedly handsome, a gently aging Michael Douglas. Despite his newly grown goatee and soft demeanor, I could still imagine him in uniform.

"I was very macho, very control-oriented," John said. "I was very much a perfectionist, very much accustomed to getting things done quickly, decisively, and really had no empathy for others. I was very arrogant. And that fit very well with the LAPD. So I was promoted very quickly."

Through the Blythe Street group, John became involved with at-risk

youth and joined a board for a boys and girls club. He attended neighborhood meetings and found himself trying to connect with people who
mistrusted him as a cop, including an ex-con.

"I had a whole different perspective. I got a glimpse at this part of humanity that I had always been oppressing by arresting and writing tickets.
I saw how insidious these problems we face in the community are. Sometimes good men and good families just don't make it."

He seemed to speak from personal experience. John's own children
had become strangers to him. His marriage fell apart; he and his wife
were currently separated and going through a divorce. Four years ago he
began attending workshops at the community's retreat center.

"There would be like sixty women here and there'd be like one
guy—me. I would say to myself, 'What am I doing here?' But the work
that I did here—for almost four years—really made me a different person," he said. "It deepened my spirituality, my sense of God."

John felt more and more disconnected from his fellow cops. He began to see police work more as a community service. Instead of measur-
ing competence by the number of tickets his officers wrote and the
number of arrests they made, John felt the real test should be whether officers were respectful and helpful and used arrests as a last resort.

"I would have these conversations with other police and my bosses
and they would say: 'You know, you're not one of us anymore.' I kept
thinking if I could work harder or be more creative, I could find a way to
get them to wake up."

Finally John realized he didn't think like "a good cop" anymore. And
he was glad. He'd been in the department for twenty-five years, risen to
the top echelons, and wasn't happy. So he replaced his quasimilitary institution with a new community run by former nuns.

For the first time, John is living by his conscience—not his loyalties.
He has a different group of friends, and he spends his time reading diverse
philosophies that he never would have read as a cop. Old friends and his
extended family no longer understand him or his association with the Immaculate Hearts.

"I feel I've broken out of prison and I'm a free man," he said. "This is my home. I'm very comfortable here. When I'm with them, I'm a different person. I get strength, I get love, I get nurturing, I get validation, I get courage."

That morning, a candidate family was having their infant daughter baptized. Her mother, Megan Kerr, had been baptized in the home of Immaculate Heart members twenty-seven years earlier. Her parents, Tom and Jayne McGuiness, felt they were coming full circle by having their granddaughter baptized in the company of some of the same Immaculate Heart members. The baby, who had been adored and passed around all weekend among the former nuns, was dressed in a long Italian lace dress, a gift from two of her three godmothers, all of whom were connected to the community. Father Gary Rye, another candidate, conducted the baptism.

The priest for eight years at the community's retirement home, Gary now works at a treatment center for clergy with addictions. He is drawn by the ecology issues members have adopted and because they are more progressive than his own religious order.

After the baby was sprinkled with holy water and adorned with an oil cross on her chest, one of her godmothers, a twenty-three-year-old candidate, gathered the baby in her arms and danced around the chapel singing along to a country-western ballad called "I Hope You Dance." Many, including the men, dabbed at tears running uncontrollably down their cheeks.

Afterward, Tom McGuiness introduced his twenty-nine-year-old son, Chris, and asked if everyone present would lay their hands on him: Chris had been diagnosed with lymphoma. The tall sandy-haired man stood in the center of the chapel with his eyes closed while members placed their hands on him and prayed silently for his recovery.

Standing among them as a group was intense. I expected electrical energy to surge up my arm, which rested against the man's back. I felt a powerful awe that these people believed so fervently in prayer, that they hoped their collective energy might unleash this man's strength to fight his disease. Though they had lengthy academic degrees and had distanced themselves from the traditional Church, these men and women weren't embarrassed to be part of something mystical. I was experiencing the community's core faith: They were spiritual people trying to live their spirituality not in a convent but in common, everyday ways. Eventually the prayer ended and everyone released their touch.

"That felt great," Chris said as members hugged him.

His father, Tom, a doughy, Irish-looking man with a soft voice and an energetic personality, wiped his eyes as he embraced members and his family.

"Where else could you get this kind of community?" Tom asked. "You couldn't get this energy in a parish. We've done prayer groups and marriage groups and charismatic prayer groups. We keep coming back to the IHMs. There's so much acceptance here. There's so much diversity. My son-in-law and I are very attracted to the feminine spirituality. It hurts me having to live in a male-dominated world. Here it's not about power and control."

Tom and Jayne became involved with the Immaculate Heart Community in 1972 when they joined a prayer group in the home of two members. Tom started thinking about joining the group then, but it was still "reeling in transition," he said. After the prayer group dispersed, the couple searched for more dynamic ways they could live their faith. They joined the youth ministry at their parish and cared for the homeless. They formed a ministry with four other couples who have prayed and volunteered together for years. Still, it wasn't enough.

"We were looking for that experience of trying to live the Gospel more radically than we were hearing it preached or advocated in our parish," he said. "We were looking for something deeper, as a way of life, not just as rituals or activities. As the hunger in us grew for doing more, we matured in our faith. We love our parish, we love our Catholic community, but it just wasn't enough."

In recent years, Tom took up Tibetan meditation. Then in 1995, he filled out the Immaculate Heart application and carried it in his briefcase until his wife said she was ready to join with him in 2000.

Daughter Megan and her husband, Andy, were drawn to the group for different reasons. As the mother of three young children, Megan wanted a community that would allow her and her husband to contribute along with their children. The young couple wanted their children to know they were part of something bigger than their family or parish. The McGuinesses and the Kerrs were the community's first extended family. Other families have since asked to join, too.

"There are thousands of couples who are deeply spiritual and long for this way of life that involves peace and justice, affection for the earth, and walking with the poor," explained Megan, twenty-seven years old with cascading black hair. "There's such alienation in the world, we wanted to belong."

Her father, Tom, agreed. "If a religious community is going to exist in the future, it's got to be radically different than the past."

With the baptism over, the retreat officially ended. Everyone was packing and leaving. I lingered at the lodge listening to members make plans for the coming weeks. I felt like I was leaving summer camp having befriended strangers whom I knew I probably would never see again. I drove the long way out of the center, passing the former novitiate house—a Spanish-style dormitory—the sculpture garden with its marble Indian statue, then past the orange groves. Once I pulled out onto the main road and back into the "real world," I felt sorrowful. I had experienced something exceptional that weekend. There was an intensity among members, a phenomenal sense of community and family. The beauty was that members are allowed to be so different. The former nuns are like a room full of sages, women who are so accomplished, so intelligent, and yet, they don't seem set on controlling their members' lives.

THE HOLLYWOOD NUNS

I was curious as to what kind of community I would find among the other Immaculate Heart nuns. Did retaining the vows provide a closer-knit community, a deeper spirituality? Before traveling to Hollywood, I had spoken several times with Sister Mary Rita Stuckey, superior of the Immaculate Heart of Mary order, who was excited about my visit. Sister Mary Rita said she remained friends with women in the modern group and even offered to introduce me to her former sisters.

By the time I drove to Hollywood from the Santa Barbara retreat, it was dark and I got lost meandering through the hilly streets. Finally I found the sisters' driveway, which wound along a steep hill and opened into an Italian-style piazza. I thought I had taken a wrong turn, but a sign indicated that these were the grounds of the Immaculate Heart of Mary Sisters. I pulled up to what looked like a medieval castle on a hill over-looking the skyline of Hollywood and Los Angeles. After the order split, a faithful millionaire had donated the mansion to serve as the convent—albeit one with a stone tower, stained-glass windows, a large fountain pool out front, and gargoyles guarding the entrance's steep stone staircase.

A woman wearing a flowery apron over her habit came down the stairs and introduced herself as Sister Jean Marie. I dragged my suitcase up two flights of stairs and, with Sister Jean following, made my way through a dark, narrow passageway mirroring those in castles. I felt a surge of déjà vu as I remembered one of my nun nightmares in which I am running from a medieval nun through a similar hallway. Suddenly, I felt panicky. The air was hot and I was sweating from the climb. That's when Sister Jean Marie told me that no one knew I was coming; I would not be al-lowed to stay beyond that night. When I questioned her, Sister Jean Marie informed me, "Hon, I just do what I am told."

The passageway opened into a more expansive hallway that wound up to an elevator. Sister Jean Marie deposited me in a small room. A few minutes later, she returned with a woman who said she was Sister Margaret Rose. She wore a short pink bathrobe that revealed crisscrosses of varicose veins shimmering up her red and scaly legs. Her straight gray hair hung in limp clumps.

"Sister Mary Rita is sick and she won't be able to see you," Margaret Rose informed me coldly. "We just found out about your visit this morning, and we tried calling you."

She showed me a torn piece of paper with a phone number written in shaky handwriting. Several numbers were transposed and the area code was wrong. I told her that I'd been in California for the past week and was scheduled to stay with them for three days.

Sister Margaret Rose shook her head. "Sister Rita has hurt the entire community. We're in the middle of turmoil here," she said without explanation. "It's Christmas and our sisters don't want to be eating with a stranger."

I stared at her in disbelief.

Sister Margaret Rose led me to a guest bedroom and told me I'd have to leave in the morning. I was ordered to stay in my room and not roam the halls because sisters were sleeping and would be startled if they saw me in the hallway. Then she turned and closed the door with a thud.

A few minutes later I heard a soft rapping at the door. It was Sister Jean Marie. She handed me a scrap of paper with the name and number of an Immaculate Heart lay member.

"You could go stay there," she whispered. "They're really nice."

As I lay in bed, I gazed out the window at the flickering lights of L.A. I felt like a prisoner. I had never felt so alone at a convent before.

Early the next morning, clattering dishes in the refectory down the hall woke me. I packed quickly and carried my bags into the hallway, hoping for directions to an exit. Several elderly sisters and a couple of priests were eating. The Church runs a retreat house for priests on the sisters' grounds. No one said anything to me. Feeling unwanted, I scooted my suitcase down the hall. Margaret Rose, primly dressed in a pressed dark habit and veil, popped her head out of the dining room.

"Would you like some breakfast?" she asked in a pleasant voice I had not heard the night before.

"No, thank you," I said.

"Well, where will you go?" she asked, more curious than caring. She'd come around several times the night before, asking the same thing, and I had told her I knew no one in Los Angeles.

I wrestled my luggage past her and walked down the long hallway until I found a door that deposited me in front of the convent. I threw my bags into the car and looked back at Sister Margaret staring. She stood at the door watching as I drove down the long driveway. It was like the scene out of *In Search of Van Gogh* when the author was thrown out of the French convent and former asylum where Van Gogh once lived. Like that author, I felt like I was escaping an asylum.

Feeling my liberty, I waved happily as I drove past the Hispanic gardeners tending the extensive flowerbeds. The order had long since donated their property to the Church, which maintained the monastery and grounds. The men gawked at me, seemingly surprised to see such a young woman leaving the convent. The order hadn't had a woman enter since 1987. Since most of the sisters were elderly and frail, I wondered if they ever left their hilltop compound.

CONNECTING TO A MODERN WORLD

I had experienced an incredible dichotomy that week: sisters holed up in a Hollywood sanctuary turning away a woman without a place to go while their former sisters welcomed homosexuals, families, men, and strangers. I had seen the past and the future of religious life. One is a model of inclusivity and is growing, evolving. In contrast, the Immaculate Heart of Mary nuns are simply waiting to die—and apparently want few witnesses.

This isn't to suggest that the secular Immaculate Heart Community doesn't have its own challenges. Older members grumble about the community's lesbian persona and worry that such a reputation will dissuade straight women and men from joining. Some feel an open membership dilutes their mission, their vision. They grouse about the lessening of Christian traditions and fear men taking over. They complain about distractions caused by new members' children. Members who weren't part of the old order criticize its hierarchical structure that seems to elevate former nuns above newer members. Yet, even the sternest critics are quick to defend their community's growth. Thirty years is but an echo in time, they say, compared with the fifteen hundred years of religious tradition that they are trying to change—a system created by men set within an even more masculine church structure. Added to this friction is an evolving community philosophy that offers membership to a cross section of people that the Catholic Church traditionally has excluded from women's orders: homosexuals, married women, children, and men.

Despite the conflicts and power struggles, Immaculate Heart members are trying to modernize and make their community relevant. They insist that vowed religious women haven't cornered the market on communal spirituality, and they believe such a community and ministries should be available to anyone. Their clashes are no different from when younger nuns urged their orders to modernize after Vatican II and were met with opposition by traditionalists who refused to budge.

What's striking about the Immaculate Heart Community is that their deeply profound religious beliefs—often rooted in Catholicism—haven't alienated them from their equally profound feminist values. They contend that the two are not mutually exclusive. To me, these women are the ultimate religious feminists. They bucked the system because they believed in their hearts that what they were doing was guided both by Church leaders and by the Holy Spirit and not because they sought to have more freedom to marry and make money. Most of them continued to live the principles behind the vows even after they were relieved from their religious obligations. They wanted religious life; they just didn't believe that men should run that life. And despite the fact that most modern orders have adopted the ideas that these women first advocated and still retain their "Sister" title, these former nuns are not bitter about leaving their reverential titles behind. For them staying would have compromised their religious and feminist convictions.

Though I lament the demise of an all-women community because of the intense friendships it offers, the secular group's diversity provides a fuller community. There's such a need for a community that cultivates women's spirituality and allows them to share its social justice mission with others. While I appreciate the grounding a women's religious order can provide, it often offers an isolated experience that excludes some of the most important aspects of a modern woman's life: men and children. I wish such a community existed near me. Yet, I know the secular group has created something that isn't easily replicated and franchised. In some ways, the lay group has become its own inclusive church instead of an exclusive community. Had there been men in leadership positions, I might feel differently. But creating a community open to families, spouses, and children feels more responsive to the realities of modern women who want a spirituality that embraces the totality of their lives. After all, feminism is about giving women more choices.

I had traveled from coast to coast, interviewed hundreds of nuns from radically liberal to fundamentally conservative, but I felt I had learned more in that week than in virtually any other. The future of religious life is not dependent on whether sisters are cloistered, whether they wear habits, or whether they pray most of the day or work. It is contingent on whether an order extends itself to women outside convent walls, whether sisters' spirituality and lifestyles are relevant. It is about understanding the modern woman and appealing to her complexities, her needs. It is about treating women as mature adults. The more controlling the order and its superiors, the less mature are the women those orders attract, the less stable their community's future. The task ahead for modern orders is redefining what a religious sister is.

LIFE AFTER THE NUNS

Leaving the complex world of nuns was difficult. I had entered with childhood stereotypes and was exiting with a modern woman's inimitable spiritual experiences. I felt fortunate to have spent more than four years surrounded by some of the most amazing women I had ever met. But just as the nuns had convinced me of the power of prayer and shown me their mysterious methods of connecting with the Divine, a darkness descended.

After the September 11, 2001, attacks, I, like many, began to question where the nuns' God was. Didn't He hear all those prayers begging for peace? I began to doubt God's presence in the world and whether such a "good" God existed. Why were some spared and not others? Not long after that tragedy, a series of crises beset my own family. After suffering some professional setbacks, I began having health problems and finally had to undergo serious back surgery in which part of a rib was removed and used to fuse my spine. The day after my surgery and while I was still in a tenuous state, my husband told me he'd lost his job that morning. Within weeks he had to take a job in another state, and soon I was left alone to recover in a back brace for months, often dependent on our teenage children.

I felt like Job and imagined that God had wagered as to how much I could endure before losing all faith. The sisters call such turmoil the "dark night of the soul," when God tests the faithful, forcing them to strengthen their belief or desert Him. In essence, it's God's hazing. Sisters view such trials as that which seals their transformation in religious life. Almost all the nuns I'd met talked about their passage of dark nights when they doubted God's existence. Such an experience was a prerequisite for truly appreciating a life in pursuit of the Divine, they said. Perhaps I should have felt flattered to be included among the spiritual elite. But I didn't.

Friends suggested I seek a priest's spiritual advice. But having reported on the pedophile priest crisis, I was distrustful of the male clergy. Instead, I sought out the only spiritual people I trusted: the nuns. I told them I had lost my faith, my religion. They didn't judge me. They understood and validated my anger. They prayed for my family and me when I no longer could. They carried my faith when I couldn't fathom trusting in a God so far removed, if such a being existed. Indeed, on my most difficult days, the only thing that seemed to offer any comfort was remembering how the nuns themselves have struggled, some for decades, under medieval rules, power-hungry mother superiors, and abusive clergy. They surpassed such injustices by believing and trusting in what they couldn't see. And, ultimately, their faith continues to carry them.

For months I lived with immense doubt, questioning whether prayer was a waste of time. After all, I had prayed intently for the very things that had been taken from me. I considered that the nuns were deluding themselves. I begged God for some small sign of His existence, for the meaning of my current crisis. There was nothing. As I continued to question, my nun friends maintained their vigils for me. I often thought of such nuns as Prioress Dawn Mills in Tucson, whose own dark night of the soul had caused her to wrestle with many of the same issues that plagued me: If there was a God, why wasn't He there when we really needed Him? Why did He allow senseless violence? And worst of all, what if there was no God? What was the point of life? Where was the hope?

Gradually my inner turmoil receded as my physical health improved. Surprisingly, it wasn't through my Christian beliefs that I found relief but through Eastern philosophies. I often thought of Sister Maureen Boyd, the Chicago nun who had turned to Buddhism to help her heal from her twin sister's suicide. I realized that I had to let go of my attachments and look at my circumstances differently. Eventually I came to see that the negatives in my life were actually positives, my losses were actually opportunities.

I also realized that my vision of the Divine had to change. I began to see God much as Sister Dawn does, as a much more complex entity. Like her, I had to bury the fairy-tale God, the superpower, the father figure, and get rid of the human characteristics I'd assigned to it. There is no quid pro quo with God. There are no assurances, no guarantees. Just because a person prays and attends church, it doesn't mean she will be spared disaster. With God, there are no definite rationalizations. I'm not sure, even as I write this, whether I've even begun to figure it out. But I'm comforted knowing that the nuns have spent most of their lives trying, and they admit they can offer few absolutes.

What they tell me—and what I sense in my own life—is that God is simply a presence, a being, a knowing, and a trusting. Perhaps it's a trusting in ourselves or in the universe or in other people that somehow circumstances will work out, that we'll come through it all and maybe even be better people as a result. Maybe it's developing patience in a fast-food world where the answers aren't always convenient or emminent. What I know is that there is real value in the sisters' contemplation, in the way they meditate—sometimes for days or weeks or even years—before making decisions or expecting answers. Life isn't about finding God, it's about searching for God. The nuns had been telling me that for years. I just had to find out for myself.

I wanted to thank the sisters who had helped me through those dark days. So, in the summer of 2003, shortly before I moved to Chicago to resume my work as a newspaper journalist, I returned to St. Benedict's to say good-bye to the first group of nuns I ever met. These are the women I have known the longest and whose nearby monastery in St. Joseph, Minnesota, I returned to most often.

For five years I had observed as some, like Sister Arlene Hines, the mother nun, suffered in failing health and had to move from the main monastery to the sisters' retirement home. Others, like Pat Reuther, the sister who adores red dresses, have stayed the course, while some, like Sister Denese Rigby, decided to leave the monastery. In true Benedictine fashion, though, the sisters helped Denese furnish an apartment in town and allowed her to keep teaching at the college as they welcomed her at prayers. Despite her failing health, Sister Jeremy Hall remains a hermit in her trailer, though she now reports in once a day so that the sisters know she is well. Sister Linda Kulzer, the writer and historian, has retired and reduced her publishing schedule yet remains an inspiration to the women writers who rotate through the monastery's writing studios. Over the years, Sister Linda and I formed a unique friendship. She was the sister who had encouraged me the most during the down times, advising me not to stifle any unholy sentiments but to inform God of my anger and disappointment.

One night during my stay as we sat around the guesthouse drinking Milwaukee's Best, Sister Linda asked me to detail how I'd gotten through those troubling times and what conclusions I'd reached. As I began unraveling my complex feelings, Linda nodded and often finished my sentences.

"I was in my early thirties," she said. "And none of this made sense. I didn't understand what I was doing. But I just kept going to prayers. Sometimes all you can do is sit there. There are no words. And sometimes all you can say is, 'Help me believe.' It lasted for about a year. You're never the same after that."

In recent years, Linda began exploring God's feminine side. It had especially helped during the recent priest pedophilia crisis when it seemed the Catholic Church's masculine authority had become so dogmatic and controlling that their power had corrupted them and victimized many. Though they lived in an all-women community, the pedophilia scandals had touched Linda and her sisters; several of the priests who came from the neighboring men's monastery to preside at the sisters' masses were accused pedophiles. When the media reported their pasts, the priests were banned from leaving their confines. Nearly every day, newspapers and televised reports carried details of the molestations. The sisters at St. Benedict's reeled from the controversy. Some were glad the sordid affair was out in the open; several confided that priests had inappropriately touched them, too. Other sisters refused to believe the priests were capable of the accusations and instead accused the victims and the media of making up horrific stories.

Linda wondered if this wasn't the beginning of the end for the forced-celibate priesthood, if finally the Vatican would have to open up its leadership to married men and women. It was a point of view I'd come to expect from sisters: seeing something positive arising out of a sickening situation.

"In truth, we're still trying to work through how we feel," Linda said. I could see the pain in her eyes. The past few months had not been easy for her. Her disgust for the institutional Church had only hardened. After all, the world sees her and her sisters as part of the church that shielded child molesters. Their image has been tainted by association. And even though she doesn't care if she's Catholic or not, she remains because what matters are her relationships to her sisters and to God.

Sister Linda Kulzer

I wasn't sure whether my affinity for Linda was simply one-sided, but as we hugged that night, Linda—nearly forty years my senior—told me she'd always felt a special kinship with me.

"It was there from the beginning," she said. "And it's been there ever since. It's like we're soul sisters."

I beamed. Soul Sisters. If I wasn't going to become a nun, wasn't be-

ing a soul sister with a nun the next best thing? It was then that I fully realized how much these women had become my spiritual godmothers. I
had learned more about spirituality in the years hanging out with them
than I had in decades of attending church and religious schools. Suddenly
I felt comforted in the thought that no matter where I traveled in the
world, there would most likely be a community of sisters nearby upon
whom I could call.

I had discovered the Catholic Church's biggest—and littlest known—
asset. While many have lost faith in the Church and certainly in its clergy,
there exists a hidden society of religious women who can provide us a
chance at discovering true religion without the male hierarchy and the le-
galistic rules. For many women, like myself, who have grown distrustful
of a male-led Church, the nuns offer us a church outside that hierarchy,
whether it is through their secular oblate memberships, meditative retreats, spiritual direction, or simply friendship. It's a network that Rome
seems to know little about and quickly dismisses. Yet, if there is any hope
in the Catholic Church for women, it is through the nuns. They provide
a connection with the Divine that isn't tainted by politics and dogma.

I suppose if there's one consolation in all of this for those of us "on
the outside," it's that there is no perfect community. There's no panacea
to our messy lives. Joining a religious order doesn't necessarily mean that
a woman will find balance. Even nuns have to strive for down time and
meaningful work.

During my years researching and writing this book, many people—
including sisters and priests—have sought out my impressions. Surely,
they say, after experiencing so many orders, talking with so many sisters, I
must have come to some overarching conclusions about religious life and
its future.

I had set off on my exploration to understand whether becoming a
nun is a viable option for contemporary women. Is living in a monastery
simply an attempt to run away from the real world's chaos or is it a means
for a woman to concentrate on spirituality, to build a community with
other women? Do women really need to take on religious vows in order

to help the poor or are obedience, chastity, and poverty simply religious relics, irrelevant to a modern era?

While I still question whether I, and most spiritual women I know, could live religious life as it's currently interpreted, I am glad that such communities exist and that there are nuns whom I can consult about my own spirituality. These women are mentors and guides for younger generations who long for a spirituality separate from a male hierarchy. Yet, few women know about these orders and the fascinating characters they have cultivated or the resources they offer.

The one prevailing sadness in my journey is how inaccessible and out of touch many sisters and orders are. I believe there is little value in sisters cutting themselves off from the world. Not only does it prevent them from attracting new members, but, from my experience, it keeps their spirituality stagnant and irrelevant.

It seems that religious orders still cling to an ideal of what a sister should look like. Though orders have few incoming women, most are overwhelmed with oblates—women in their lay programs. Yet, they continue to lament the demise of religious life, blind to the possibility of more fully incorporating these women into the life of their orders. Orders would greatly benefit if they eliminated this elitist approach and integrated "secular" women instead of treating them like a separate fan club.

I believe religious orders should be more approachable; sisters need to connect with real people and address real spiritual needs. Monasteries need to return to St. Benedict's open-door philosophy that called on monks to welcome guests of all kinds and to treat them as if they were Christ in disguise. Indeed, monasteries today are opening up and offering various retreats to women, though I suspect much of the impetus is financial rather than philosophical. Still, monastic retreats shouldn't become religious resorts for the well-to-do who can afford to pay the forty- to one-hundred-dollar-a-day donations, but rather sisters should consider inviting welfare moms and homeless women. Perhaps they could offer massages and meditation for the unemployed or victims of domestic violence and rape. They could provide new mother retreats for women who are overwhelmed and isolated with young children. In essence, they should respond to the needs of the times and not keep operating as if they were living in a medieval culture. It's not enough to just pray for people; sisters need to know the faces of those they pray for.

At the same time, active orders should relinquish their immigrant work ethic. While I applaud the sisters who work with the needy, whether it is teaching on reservations or running homeless shelters, most modern women are seeking spirituality and labor that feeds their souls. Most eligible women today weren't raised on farms with large immigrant families who rose before dawn to milk cows. They don't want to join orders that retain arduous work schedules. Most women seeking religious life today have given up successful careers and obsessive agendas. They want balance between work and prayer, between action and contemplation.

I believe that eventually religious communities will have to offer women more than one way to commit. Currently, there are a handful of women's orders that are allowing women to join for limited terms, three to five years. These communities have been attracting young, talented women who want to belong to a religious order but realize that making an eternal commitment is unrealistic these days, especially in a world where people change careers several times during their lifetime. Of course, these communities have experienced intense pressure from the Catholic Church to maintain the traditional lifelong commitments.

Most young women will probably never commit their lives to the Church in the numbers and ways the sisters in this book have. This is the story of an end of an epoch, a time when women had few choices other than servitude through marriage or devotion through the Church. Yet, there will always be a trickle of deeply religious women clamoring for structure and community, sacrificing their freedoms in exchange for living an ideal, an absolute commitment to God. Appealing to the larger populace will require vows and lifestyles that reflect contemporary values. As I see it, modern women today are searching for a balance of life, not an abstinence of life.

While I haven't found the order that offers the kind of balance between prayer, devotion, work, and justice that I crave, I also recognize that finding such a balance in a secular life is difficult, too. Could I ever give up my freedom, my lifestyle, in exchange for the sisterhood should I find myself divorced or widowed? Not for the rest of my life. If I found such a group as the lay Immaculate Heart Community near my hometown, I would rush to join. And I would definitely consider entering a religious order that had limited terms, perhaps making a three- to five-year commitment, much like joining a religious Peace Corps. But these kinds of experimental commitments are just beginning to evolve. Of course, if I joined such an order, like Sister Dawn in Tucson I would have my own list of demands: no rising before 8 A.M., no perpetual leftovers, weekends off, and no sisters whose first name starts with "Mother."

ADDITIONAL CAPTIONS

Photograph on page iii: A sister professing her permanent vows

Photograph on page 1: Franciscan sisters kneeling during their final profession of vows ceremony in Alton, Illinois

Photograph on page 49: The Sisters of St. Benedict's chapel and monastery in Ferdinand, Illinois

Photograph on page 129: Sister Kay Kettenhofen meandering the grassy paths of her Trappistine monastery in Crozet, Virginia

Photograph on page 181: The back of the San Xavier Mission Church on the Tohono O'odham Nation Reservation, where the Franciscan Sisters of Christian Charity run an elementary school

Photograph on page 257: Blessed rosaries to be given during the profession of permanent vows